TELL IT TO
THE DEAD

An East Gate Book

TELL IT TO THE DEAD

THE DEAD

STORIES OF A WAR

New Edition

Foreword by Arthur J. Dommen

Photographs by Donald Kirk

DONALD KIRK

M.E. Sharpe
Armonk, New York
London, England

An East Gate Book

Copyright 1975, 1996, Donald Kirk

All photographs by Donald Kirk

Some of the material in this book appeared in different form in the following newspapers and magazines, whose support and cooperation is gratefully acknowledged:
The Washington Star (© 1967, 1968, 1969, 1970); *Chicago Tribune* (© 1971, 1972, 1973); "The Old Guard," September 23, 1991, and "Hearts and Minds," December 2, 1991, *The National Review* (© 1991); "The ICCS's Impossible Mission," June 11, 1973, "A Visit to Kompong Cham," October 1, 1973, and "Vietnam Looks to the West," July 25, 1988, *The New Leader* (© The American Labor Conference on International Affairs, Inc.); "Why They Call Lon Nol the Mayor of Phnom Penh," June 27, 1971, "Who Wants to Be the Last GI to Die in Vietnam?" September 19, 1971, "Banging Holes in the Land," June 4, 1972, and "How Major Buu Fights His War," August 20, 1972, *The New York Times Magazine* (The New York Times © 1971, 1972); "Searing Memories of Napalm Attack," *Newsday*, April 28, 1995 (© 1995); "Pol Pot Specter," February 1986, and "Tale of Two Cities," August 1986, *Soldier of Fortune* (© 1986); "The Legend of Tony Poe, CIA," January 1972, *True* (©1972); "Letter from Vietnam: The GIs Speak," *Tuesday* (© 1965); "Perspectives," October 1989, *Vietnam* (© 1989).

Published in the United States by M.E. Sharpe Inc.
80 Business Park Drive, Armonk, New York, 10504

Library of Congress Cataloging-in-Publication Data

Kirk, Donald, 1938–
Tell it to the dead : stories of a war / Donald Kirk. — New ed.
p.   cm.
Originally published : Chicago : Nelson-Hall, 1975, with subtitle : Memories of a war.
Includes Index.
ISBN 1-56324-717-8 (hardcover : alk. paper).—ISBN 1-56324-718-6 (pbk. : alk. paper)
1. Vietnamese Conflict, 1961–1975—Personal narratives, American. I. Title.
DS559.5.K57   1996
959.704'38—dc20   95-53180
CIP

First printing, 1975, Nelson-Hall, Chicago
Second edition, revised, enlarged, M.E. Sharpe, 1996

Printed in the United States of America

The paper used in this publication meets the minimum requirements of American National Standard for Information Sciences—Permanence of Paper for Printed Library Materials, ANSI Z 39.48-1984.

∞

EB (c)   10   9   8   7   6   5   4   3   2   1
EB (p)   10   9   8   7   6   5   4   3   2   1

In Memory of Richard Critchfield, 1931–1994

Life is a voyage, not a harbor, and we're a long way from home.

—Richard Critchfield, *Villages*, 1981

Contents

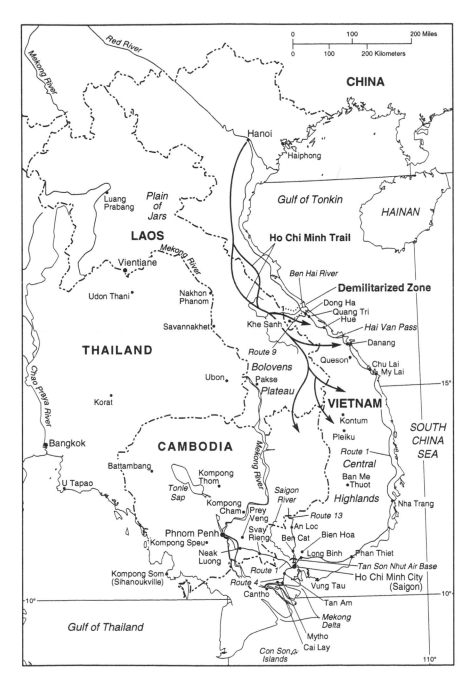

Foreword

by Arthur J. Dommen

In 1975 North Vietnamese tanks rolled into Saigon, and the Vietnam war became a memory for the foreign correspondents who had covered it. In that year Donald Kirk published a book whose title, *Tell It to the Dead*, was the comment a marine had made to him years before at Khe Sanh, one of the bloodiest battlefields of the war. The comment is as evocative as ever of the bitter feelings of those who fought a war the American public has not yet come to grips with. It is fitting that Kirk's book is being reissued today, for it constitutes not only a major contribution to the American literature on the war but also firsthand evidence of that bitterness, collected by one of the best of those correspondents, sometimes under fire.

The first wave of American correspondents who went to South Vietnam in the early 1960s (North Vietnam, under communist rule, was closed to all but a handful of foreigners) found themselves in an Asian country about which their editors knew little and the American reading public couldn't have cared less, although their government was already deeply committed as a result of the 1954 armistice that made the 17th parallel, like the 38th, one of the front lines of the Cold War. Left to their own means by a suspicious and even xenophobic government, they hired taxis to take them to the scene of an atrocity or the occasional clash that testified to a nasty shadow war going on in the countryside.

Given Hanoi's hostility to the South, broadcast over Radio Hanoi every night, the war alarmed them, particularly because of what was at stake for the United States, whose young president had declared the pursuit of freedom worldwide to be his goal. More and more, they crisscrossed the country on the American helicopters and transport planes that ferried South Vietnamese troops and American advisers in search of the elusive communist guerrillas. Wittingly or unwittingly, they made themselves the spokesmen for the Army lieutenants, captains, and majors from whom they drew much of the information in their dispatches. These were men who were not deluded by the easy assurances delivered by official spokesmen at the U.S. embassy in Saigon and in Washington. The war was being lost, by body counts or any other conceivable measure of progress. Instinctively, the newsmen saw the Saigon government as inept, an obstacle to winning the war. If winning the war meant replacing the mandarins in the presidential palace with a team more attuned to military needs, then that was the way to go.

The problem was that the South Vietnamese generals who overthrew the constitutional government of South Vietnam in 1963 had few ideas of their own except to please their American mentors so as to obtain more aid. They relied almost entirely on the American presence in the form of airpower and, eventually, troops. In the eyes of their countrymen their claims to represent anything but themselves were thin in the extreme. No adversary would offer to negotiate a settlement of the war with such people, since they could be overthrown at any moment with impunity by rivals within the military, and any commitments they gave would not be worth the paper they were signed on. Hanoi, in any case, had decided that any negotiations would be with the Americans, not the South Vietnamese "puppets."

By the time Kirk arrived in South Vietnam in 1965 as a 27-year-old correspondent, a succession of generals had flitted across the stage. The transient leaders occupying the presidential palace in Saigon were grappling with demands put forth by students, by Buddhist monks, by wounded veterans, and by other groups who increasingly took to the streets to press their payments, and so on. It was not until 1967 that a new constitutional structure was finally erected to replace the one destroyed in 1963. The fighting was increasingly left to the Americans, and therefore was making headlines and time on the evening TV news shows. The first big-unit battles occurred in 1965. The second wave of American correspondents, of which Kirk was one, were thus thrust into a deadly war that seemed likely to go on forever, barring only the depletion of Hanoi's available manpower to send into the South, a remote prospect. The North Vietnamese had somehow managed to turn the body count syndrome into a weapon against the Americans; as a North Vietnamese officer later remarked to him in Hanoi, the goal was to inflict as heavy casualties as possible on the Americans so that the American public would turn against the war and demand the complete withdrawal of American troops.

Kirk's reporting often led him into great danger. One day he suddenly came face to face with the Khmer Rouge, and unlike 17 foreign journalists in Cambodia who were executed at their hands, lived to tell about it. On another occasion, on an open road, he was bombed by the South Vietnamese air force. Kirk talked to ambassadors and generals, but he also talked to ordinary GIs, and this is one of the strengths of his book. Like Bernard Fall, the famed Vietnam reporter and scholar whom he resembles in many ways, Kirk harbored a natural curiosity about the soldiers' attitudes toward the war. It was from his conversations with GIs that Kirk was able to report their sense of frustration, their perception that the war was futile. "Why me?" was a widely shared feeling. All they wanted to do was to survive this war of attrition, with its booby traps, its sudden ambushes, its attacks by stealth. What was the point of getting killed? And he came across indications of troubled black GIs who vowed to continue the war at home, against the whites. Kirk reported all this in the direct quotes of those he interviewed, sometimes over the objections of information officers who would rather have kept silent on such matters. "Check it out," the black GIs told him, and more often than not, Kirk did.

In Cambodia, too, the generals who ran the show were not inclined to sacrifice their newfound privileges under American tutelage. As Kirk's portrait of General Sosthene Fernandez makes clear, having participated for years in the profitable trade supplying the Viet Cong and North Vietnamese with Cambodian rice and other material was no disqualification for command under General Lon Nol, whose leadership was even more incompetent than that of the South Vietnamese generals. Fernandez and his high-living staff officers claimed to be waging *la guerre populaire*, which would be ludicrous except that those maimed and killed were truly the populace. Ironically, it would take the Khmer Rouge, in a ten-year guerrilla war between 1979 and 1989 in which they inflicted casualties totaling 52,000 dead and 200,000 wounded on some of the best units in the Vietnamese Army, to mobilize the traditional Cambodian hatred of the Vietnamese.

The Vietnam war was also the war in which the media discovered the power of propaganda—propaganda against the war, which meant, in fact (since only one side of the war was being covered by the international press), against the American war effort. The growth of the so-called anti-war movement at home in the late 1960s made this respectable. A new breed of journalist started showing up in Saigon, far different from the traditional foreign correspondent. These were practitioners of advocacy journalism, which tossed aside the traditional objectivity of foreign reporting. Advocacy journalists reported for small news services or publications mostly unknown to us at the time, and were often affiliated with activist groups calling themselves "concerned."

They were quite talented individuals, but their message was clear. The war was immoral if not illegal, the United States was to blame, and the only negotiable issue was the date of the withdrawal of American troops. Accordingly, the newsworthiness of events was judged by new standards. In 1970 I began receiving telephone calls at the *Los Angeles Times* bureau that went like this: "I hear there's been an atrocity in such-and-such a unit. Are you doing anything with it?" The caller was not only putting me on notice that another news organization, a potential competitor, had a story that might make front-page news back home, but also that it was my responsibility to "do something with it," that is, to, say, make it into a full-blown message for those back home, particularly editors, who still supported the American effort. This art form reached its fullest development many years later in the powerful Vietnam war films of Oliver Stone. Like effective propaganda throughout history, these films use a particular factual incident to convey a general impression, in this case that most GIs in Vietnam were the modern equivalent of SS storm troopers whose main occupation was killing innocent villagers and raping civilians.

The war eventually gave way to a sham peace. The last GIs left. The war had cost the United States more than 58,000 dead. As the last American diplomats left Saigon in a hastily improvised evacuation, to be followed shortly by the last foreign correspondents, a deafening silence settled over Vietnam in American newsrooms. People wanted to forget the war, newsmen told one another reassuringly. Thus there was hardly any coverage in the American media of the plight of those sent to reeducation camps, and the exodus of the boat people. Nearer to home, admittedly, there were real problems to contend with. The GIs took their drug habits home with them, where the Southeast Asian heroin merchants found in the streets of American cities a continuing, lucrative market at prices far above those that had prevailed around every sprawling American base in Vietnam. Victory in this war, too, is still not in sight. Fortunately, the threatened all-out race war did not materialize, but many of the same attitudes toward race relations are still with us.

The American correspondents in Vietnam have gone on to other things. Some have become editors themselves, others network news anchors. Many, like Kirk, have been back to Vietnam to report on a country that has fallen 20 years behind Southeast Asia's economic boom, a country where the heavy hand of a corrupt and dictatorial party is still felt by all. Some Vietnamese, like Kirk's "tea leaf reader," Le Viet, whom Kirk helped bring to safety in the United States, predict there will be a new revolution. With its hopes and illusions, Vietnam remains the same. Officially, Hanoi trumpets its victory over the "foreign imperialists" but has toned this down noticeably in its overseas broadcasts in recent years as it angles for the benefits of U.S. recognition. Few American news organizations take the trouble to wade through Hanoi's turgid outpourings, in any case. Vietnam has returned to the marginal news value it held in the early 1960s.

Pham Xuan An, who deceived journalists from *Time* magazine for two decades to become the most famous double agent of the war, lives on quietly in Saigon, enjoying the meager emoluments offered him by the state and receiving foreign visitors. He no doubt has his successor in the trade, who has been keeping the party informed of what goes on within the walls of the American POW/MIA office, then liaison office and now embassy, in Hanoi. Kirk must have shaken hands with him when he visited. There is plenty of bitterness, still, to go around. Tell it to the dead.

Arthur Dommen, Ph.D., author of Conflict in Laos *and numerous studies and articles on Indochina, was a bureau chief and correspondent in the region for the* Los Angeles Times *and United Press International from 1959 to 1971.*

Preface

Return to old Saigon two decades after "the last Americans" were lifted off the roof of the American embassy building, and you feel as if you were reliving a faded past while standing on the brink of a glittery if uncertain future. Tour guides now show you around the one-time presidential palace, calling your wandering attention to the paneled offices, the paintings, the private family rooms, and the underground "secret" passages, as if the whole sprawling structure had once been a medieval castle or the playground of a Turkish sultan.

Somehow it does not seem so long ago that you and Crosby Noyes, a member of the owning family of *The Washington Star*, for which you were working at the time, had sat through an amazingly newsless interview with Nguyen Van Thieu, the last "permanent" master of the palace, in a room that you now learn was specifically reserved for receiving "only foreign visitors." (The *Star*, an unabashed pro-administration voice that died several years after the war, well after the Noyeses had gotten out, ran Thieu's forgettable words on page one the next day.) The president, your guide explains, ensconced himself in a chair that was slightly raised on a wooden platform so he could "look down on foreigners." Your guide points toward the polished underpinning—a prop you hadn't noticed during the only "interview" you ever got with the leader of the *ancien régime*. The next room, the guide goes on, was for receiving Vietnamese "as equals" from a chair flat on the floor, on the same level with his countrymen.

All is at it was except for the name—and the occupants. The "palace" is now "Reunification Hall," symbol of the communist victory in the war for reunification of the land we once called "North" and "South" Vietnam. A Russian-made T54 tank, glistening with a new coat of olive-drab paint, squats on the vast front lawn, a reminder of the first tank, now in Hanoi, that crashed through the palace gates on April 30, 1975.

For those who may have forgotten historical details, the tour concludes with a videotape in black and white, pieced together from TV and film clips. A grating English voice-over recounts the story as Hanoi wants the world to remember, from the palmy days when Ho Chi Minh, at 29, proselytized unsuccessfully for Vietnam's place at the Versailles peace conference in 1919, to the moments of pathos when South Vietnamese troops, hands up, surrendered nearly five years and eight months after Ho died on September 2, 1969.

The video glosses over the fine print of the "peace" that Henry Kissinger persuaded gullible Americans he had wrought in Paris in 1973 but tells proudly how Hanoi's commanders waited to see how Washington would respond to the first round of victorious attacks in the Central Highlands in early 1975. There is no rationalization, other than the righteousness of the century-long struggle against colonialism and imperialism, for violating a treaty that everyone but the Americans, not necessarily including Kissinger, knew was a sham. Triumphantly, the female voice runs through the final offensive. Town by town, the winning army storms on as leaders in Hanoi test the nerve of the weakest president in U.S. history, Gerald Ford. Finally, as the rasping reader tells us, they realize he has no stomach for sending in American airpower to stem the tide—and press on to *giai phong*, "liberation."

It all happened so quickly, the collapse of the American house of cards in Indochina, that we hardly had time to understand what was going on. No sooner had the South Vietnamese fled the highlands than they were evacuating Hue, mobbing Danang—then fleeing for their lives down the coast to Vung Tau and Saigon, already on the verge of defeat.

Most of them, the South Vietnamese whom we had foolishly tried to "Vietnamize," in the arrogant, neocolonial term, would survive. Some would not. Whatever they did, they would do it without the Americans. There was, among certain commentators, the sense that the American "people," that amorphous, indefinable mass, would accept loss of the dream, if dream is the word, and go on to concerns closer to home. Yet too many Americans had served and suffered in Indochina to forget so easily and so soon. One inevitably fell back on frayed memories—bits of history that helped to explain if not exactly justify the past.

It was several wars ago, in September 1965, that I first went to Saigon. I still remember the hostesses on the Air Vietnam plane on which I flew in from Hong Kong. They were wearing turquoise *ao dai*, the graceful national dress that flows over silky white trousers almost to the ground. I was sure they were costumed for the exclusive benefit of the assorted adventurers, grifters, journalists, provocateurs, and soldiers, most of them American, who crowded the flights in and out of Saigon. For all the "color" stories about the lost charm of the Vietnamese capital, I hadn't yet gathered that the *ao dai* was really customary attire.

Beside me on the plane was an Americanized journalist from Taiwan who had a first name something like Jimmy or Eddy and a last name like Lee or Lo. He was wearing a cord suit, had a crewcut, and chatted from time to time with a balding American who, it turned out, was a *Time-Life* correspondent. The *Time-Life* man was an old hand. As we were winging into the sunset near the Vietnamese mainland, he pointed toward some odd islands and explained they were once French—or Chinese, I can't remember which.*

Like a number of other Americans on their first trip to "the war zone," as the news agencies called it, I was not very interested in geography. I was more curious about the possibility that an artillery shell would rip through the underbelly of the plane—or that a grenade or *plastique* would explode the moment we landed. It was dark as the plane swung low on final approach into Tan Son Nhut airport, but little lights, most of them white and yellow, others red and orange neon, twinkled from the capital. The first real menace to our security, as thousands of Americans came to learn, was the throng of taxi drivers waiting to charge exorbitant rates for the ride from the airport to downtown.

---

*Actually, they were the Paracels, acquired by the French in the 1880s, conquered by Japan in World War II, ceded to Nationalist China in 1946, occupied by South Vietnam in 1954, and, finally, recaptured by Chinese communist troops in a weekend of fighting in January 1974. Latter-day Vietnam still claims them—along with the Spratlys, a few degrees south, also contested by the Philippines, Malaysia, and Brunei as well as both China and Taiwan.

A smiling young man from the *Time-Life* bureau was there to meet the senior correspondent. By chance, a French photographer happened to be at the airport and recognized the Chinese journalist in the cord suit. We happily accepted lifts in the backseat of an ancient French Peugeot, a museum-piece car whose distinguished good looks, dating from the 1930s, were a tribute to French artistic taste if not mechanical finesse.

Again I was looking for signs of war as we drove down Cong Ly, a potholed two-lane road, soon to be paved by glistening brown-shouldered Vietnamese coolies, earning the equivalent in fast-depreciating piasters of two or three dollars a day under the supervision of ruddy American contractors, making it on roughly $40,000 a year, courtesy of the U.S. government. All I really remember from the drive downtown was that it was raining when I got off at the corner of Tu Do opposite the Caravelle Hotel. Little beggar boys asked for money outside Brodard's café, and a wizened woman hawked newspapers.

Pimps offered girls with or without hotel rooms, but a friend in Hong Kong had already suggested I stay at the Royale, run by a drug-ravaged old Corsican a block away on the corner of Nguyen Hue, the fabled street of flowers. Burdened with only one small suitcase, I walked down the darkened alley, past the bars from which Vietnamese girls, as pretty then as they were at the end of the war, beckoned from the doorways.

It was a typical introduction to Saigon, but it is etched more clearly in my memory than most of the depressing days spent chasing politicians and diplomats and officials or searching for stories in "the field," as Americans referred to the rest of the country beyond the capital.

Eventually you got to know the Tu Do scene so well that you could recognize almost every beggar and shopkeeper along the street. There was one little girl whom I watched for years. When she was two or three, barely able to toddle beside her slightly older brother, she offered peanuts while holding out her hand for money. By the time she was five or six she was still selling peanuts—but now she could demand payment in advance and, if the customer were drunk, frisk his pockets and run. There were the newsboys, surprisingly honest in handing out change and arranging deliveries. There were the Indian money changers, operating in their shops behind the cover of shelves full of paperbacks—eager to buy your dollars in exchange for piastres at rates agreed on by the Chinese who masterminded the entire black market in currency.

In a sense the Saigon scene never really changed. There were happenings. The Miramar Hotel, with its top-floor bar, a favorite of British journalists, opened late in the war, 1971 or '72. The Szechuan restaurant on one of the side streets began doing a highly profitable business in '69 or '70, purveying hot, spicy dishes to Chinese and Vietnamese as well as Americans and Europeans. But Tu Do Street, Lam Son Square between the Caravelle and Continental hotels, Nguyen Hue—they all retained their carnival-like flavor throughout the war, through rocketings and offensives, coups and crackdowns.

It was the complexion of the countryside, the "field," that underwent transitions as battles surged back and forth and lines of "security" shifted, sometimes rapidly, sometimes slowly. Even during such turmoil, however, journalists grew accustomed to certain verities. You fought for seats on great C130s to go to Danang and Phu Bai, the town where the ever graceful imperial capital of Hue had its airport, and you rushed to jump on helicopters for shorter runs to firebases and district compounds.

If you'd seen one firebase, or district compound, or major division-level base camp, to paraphrase Spiro Agnew, you'd pretty well seen them all. The dirt, the mud, the sun, the monsoon rain drove into the souls of all those who touched the war, except possibly for some of the middle-aged bureaucrats in Saigon, hired for desk jobs and rarely interested in much more than *pro forma* trips to the rest of the country.

It was difficult to tell who was more responsible, the Americans or the Vietnamese, for the peculiar ambience of these bases—different, somehow, from that of bases in the States or Korea or Okinawa. It was as if a firebase absorbed the atmosphere of a country where small boys sold heroin and marijuana, and motorcycle drivers waited on the nearest road to rip off the unwary, and everyone spoke in the strange argot of the war—a mixture of pidgin English, French, and, every now and then, Vietnamese. (*Titi*, pronounced "tee-tee," was a corruption of the French *petit. No biet*, which the GIs pronounced "no bich," meant "no understand," and "same-same" was English, more or less.)

Part of the flavor of the war—the dullness, the drabness, the uniqueness of it—was "the press," that odd mixture of individuals who swirled in and out of Saigon and the field, always changing but always the same. There were conservatives and radicals, intellectuals and sensationalists, those who believed "politics" was the story, those who spent days, weeks, at a time out of Saigon. There was the rabble that showed up every day for the military briefing, and there were some who made a show of dissecting issues—though no one read their work very carefully.

Someone, someday, will probably write a very interesting book analyzing the Saigon press corps—its idiosyncrasies, its triumphs and failings, its ability or inability to interpret what happened. In my memory, however, the reporters merely merge into the milieu of generals and GIs, officials and politicians, shoeshine boys and bargirls.

In my own reporting on the war, I was constantly frustrated by the question of how to follow politics/diplomacy in Saigon—and still keep up with events and moods in the field. In the later years, I decided the field really was more important, no matter what various analysts might deduce from Saigon politics, and I began focusing on GIs more than I had when I first went to Vietnam. In this effort I am indebted to the editors of the old *Washington Star*, the *Chicago Tribune*, *The New York Times Magazine*, *The New Leader*, *Tuesday*, and *True*. On return trips I have also written for *USA Today*, *Newsday*, *The National Review*, *Soldier of Fortune* and *Vietnam*. It was largely because of my experience with these organizations that I have been able to put down some of my impressions of whatever it was that happened to us in Vietnam.

*　　　　*　　　　*

On my way home to Washington from yet another Asian flash point, in Seoul in mid-December 1994, I picked up the *International Herald Tribune* one evening and was stunned by the headline "Richard Critchfield, Writer on Third World, Dies." I had first met Critchfield while a student in India in 1963 and followed him as *The Washington Star*'s Asia correspondent four years later. I had last seen him two years earlier when I drove our former Vietnamese assistant, Duong The Tu, a.k.a. Le Viet, and two of Le Viet's children from San Jose for dinner at Dick's home in Berkeley after calling to tell him about their arrival in the States.

Getting back to Washington a few days later, I was jolted again— this time to find letters that Critchfield had sent me well before his death along with copies of his latest books and an invitation to a book-launching party that was never held. The fact that his notes were full of his usual ebullience and optimism only deepened the sense of loss. Instead of having missed the book party, I discovered I had missed his funeral.

More than any other journalist or scholar of our times, Critchfield dedicated himself to writing with warmth, compassion, humor, and insight about the innermost lives of the people of all the countries he visited. Thus it seems appropriate, in view of old days in Vietnam and our mutual bond with the *Star* and Le Viet, to offer this edition in Dick's memory.

TELL IT TO THE DEAD

1

"We Must Accept"

The suffering never ends for Du Ngoc Anh, who lives with the memory of the napalming of her village as if it had happened yesterday. "My two little sons were killed on the spot," says Du, now 54. "My baby daughter died three months later in a hospital." Almost ritualistically, Du displays the napalm wounds she suffered as she fled the attack that morning of June 8, 1972. "In the cold weather my legs still ache," she says, showing the scarred, twisted flesh on her arms and legs. "It never goes away."

The horror endured by her family that day was never known outside her village. She and her husband have copies of the Associated Press photographs showing her uncle and grandmother screaming as they carried the bodies of the dead boys in their arms, but another photograph of another victim survives as a reminder of the war. That was the picture by the same AP photographer, Nick Ut, of the napalmed girl running naked from this village, her elder brother just ahead of her, also wounded and screaming, her baby brother tagging along behind, crying but barely wounded.

This reporter was on the road that day, too, just behind the AP photographer, and returned to this village, at a bend in the road about 40 miles northwest of Ho Chi Minh City, to talk to villagers about the

3

tragedy—and the war. "The war was between the Americans and the Viet Cong," says Phan Thanh Tung, now 68, sitting in his newly built thatched roof house behind the Cao Dai temple where the napalm scorched the earth long after the VC had pulled out. "We were citizens. We were in the middle."

Phan's wife, Du Ngoc Nu, 63, sits beside him, reliving the terror she felt as the flames engulfed much of the village. "Sometimes I cannot sleep at night," she says. "I have nightmares, and I feel very tense." She and her husband, once farmers, now spend much of their time working in and around the temple, whose adherents follow a unique mélange of Buddhism and Christianity. They say their daughter, Kim Phuoc, now 33 and living in Canada, never fully recovered from the napalming during years of medical treatment in Europe and Cuba but now is married to a Vietnamese whom she met in Cuba and has a year-old baby.

Their son, Phan Thanh Tam, probably suffered more. "He got some napalm in his eye," says the father. "He does the best he can. He works as a farmer and has three daughters, but he feels pain quite often, and he cannot always think clearly." Phan was so terrified during the attack that he can hardly remember all that happened, but he insists the planes that napalmed the village were American jets, A37s, not propeller-driven South Vietnamese A1 Skyraiders, as widely reported. This reporter, seeing black smoke billowing over the village that day, remembers seeing the jets wheeling and diving a few hundred yards away—and also recalls seeing the Skyraiders blamed for the attack. "I saw the American pilots," says Phan, but I forget what happened next."*

The battle was typical of many in the war. South Vietnamese troops had gone through the motions of clearing out civilians, warning them by loudspeaker that the planes were going to bomb. The Viet Cong, dug into a trench, had already left, and the civilians were picking up their belongings and fleeing when the both Skyraiders and A37s swooped over.

Phan avoids politics and name-calling. "I think I was a victim of the war," he says. "I don't know who to blame. We must accept only that

---

*The U.S. air force history office in Washington, D.C., says it has no records of American bombing of the village by A37s. Another eyewitness, Fox Butterfield of *The New York Times*, also on the road that day, reported, as I did in the *Chicago Tribune*, that South Vietnamese A1 Skyraiders had dropped the napalm.

we were unlucky. We blame no one." He won't even speculate about who began the war—or was responsible for the attack. "I don't know who started it. At that time the Vietnamese from the forests come here and fight the Americans. They live here for five days before the attack. They do not talk to us. They only dig a tunnel to hide in."

Phan credits the government in Hanoi, however, with having made life somewhat easier for villagers in recent years. "For the first ten years after the war, they did not let us worship. But they decided that policy was a mistake. Now we are free to pray in the temple. Life is better for us. We talk about religion, though not about anything else."

Du Ngoc Anh, the woman who lost three of her children in the attack, adopts the same outlook. "I have nothing to think about the war," she says. "I try to think about nothing because the war has stopped, and we must accept the result. I was sad very much, but now I pray and try to think about my religion."

Xuan Dai, South Vietnam, November 1967*

Fires were still burning in the ruins of the brick-and-mud-walled homes. The sickening smell of burnt sugarcane hung in the air. Frightened baby chicks chirped frantically in search of their mothers. From the charred entry of one of the buildings, a middle-aged peasant woman, clinging to a plastic bag, tentatively poked her head, then emerged with a puzzled-looking little boy. Quickly another, much older woman followed her and then several more children, rubbing their eyes.

"Hey, you, get over there," a towheaded marine, barely 20, shouted at the women and children, pointing toward a cement floor bordered by crumbling walls, broken dishes, and blackened cooking pots. Slowly, they padded silently where he ordered.

---

*This report provoked outrage from the Pentagon after it appeared in *The Washington Star*. First, a Defense Department flak, Richard Fryklund, the paper's former Pentagon correspondent, called Newbold Noyes, editor and part-owner of the *Star*, at home to complain about "your reporting from Vietnam." Next, the marines conducted an "investigation," in which everyone denied everything. Then, the commander of the marine press center in Danang got two free-lancers, a cameraman and a soundman, who had covered the incident for NBC, to write statements denying the facts as reported. For good measure, the marines claimed I had "endangered" marines by being in the line of fire—exposing them to fire as well—during the operation.

The scene was part of the drama enacted here after American jet bombers demolished this village and its immediate neighbor, An Dong, with tons of bombs and napalm. As is so often the case in such attacks, the communist troops had stolen away before dawn, dragging with them the bodies of some of their comrades killed the day before in a fight with the American marines. Only the women and children were left, huddled in their bomb shelters, ten feet underground and reinforced by steel railway ties, as their ancestral homes crumbled over their heads.

"We should have killed them all," said the young marine, jabbing his M16 rifle in the direction of the crowd of women and children, fast increasing as more of them came out of their shelters. "There's eight marine bodies lying on the landing zone across the rice paddies. We should have killed the whole village."

An old man with a dirty grey beard, clinging to a small boy with large burn blisters on the back of his neck, extended a tin can and pleaded for water. "Don't give him any," the marine shouted to his buddy. "Let them starve, let them die." Wordlessly, another marine extended his canteen and filled the man's cup.

The anger of the first marine reflected the failure and frustration of driving Viet Cong and North Vietnamese forces from a trench and tunnel network surrounding this and the neighboring village, some 25 miles southwest of Danang. The marines, two battalions of them, left the two villages, satisfied they had temporarily driven out the enemy, including one main force Viet Cong and one North Vietnamese battalion, but not certain what else they had accomplished.

Communist troops, from fighting holes on the treeline in front of the village, had killed or wounded an entire marine platoon as it advanced 300 yards across the rice paddies. "My platoon got hit first," said First Lieutenant Wilbur Dishman, 24, of Raleigh, North Carolina. "Our whole company was pinned down for five hours." Marine spokesmen claim at least 30 enemy bodies were counted, but Dishman said this figure was based on individual reports of enemy soldiers seen falling or dragged away. Virtually no bodies were actually found later. It was not until right after the air strikes that marines dared enter the village— and then the only bodies they found were those of marines killed the day before and a woman who apparently had left her bomb shelter before the last strike.

Marines spent most of the day rounding up the women and children and cajoling them to go to a large bombed-out building, where they were questioned. "My husband was a farmer," one of the women told the marine intelligence sergeant in a voice that was calm but barely audible. "No, I don't know where he is. I think he was killed in the rice paddy. I can't find him." She stopped, then asked, "Where is my water buffalo?"

The marine grinned at his interpreter, then let out a hollow laugh. "Her husband's dead, and she's wondering where the hell her buffalo is. Let's talk to someone else." The next woman was equally uninformative. "My husband is a government soldier," she said. "Everybody here hates the Viet Cong." The interpreter found this response even more amusing. "That's what they always say," he said. "There's not a woman here who won't say her husband's in the government army— and chances are every damn one of them's Viet Cong."

Occasionally, in response to persistent questioning, a woman would admit she had seen some Viet Cong, maybe a day or so before. Some of the women pointed vaguely in the direction they claimed to have seen either Viet Cong or North Vietnamese, they didn't know which, either coming or going.

Across the rice paddies, at a temporary headquarters in an abandoned stone building, Colonel Robert Bohn, regimental commander, talked about the operation. "This is real Indian country down here," he said. "The enemy are all over. We wanted to go down because we had heard there were indications of a buildup." The colonel said that American troops occupied the areas to the north, around Danang, and to the south, but seldom entered the territory in between. "We think the enemy has come here either to get some rice or to set up base for rocket attacks. We hope by next year we'll have some men permanently stationed down here."

Several feet away, marines counted the spoils of the day's work—two malaria-ridden men, blindfolded and shaking, held on suspicion of Viet Cong sympathies, and several "captured" weapons, all of them rusted and probably not used for years, certainly not in the past two or three days. As night fell on the hootch where the women and children waited, some of them started crying. The intelligence sergeant asked what was wrong, and the interpreter reported they were "starving." "Won't anyone feed these people?" the sergeant asked.

An officer, assigned to both calling in air strikes and directing civil affairs, said he'd see what he could do. "First I annihilate them and then I rehabilitate them," he said, laughing at his own joke. Another officer, standing beside him, wasn't that amused. "This is the part of the war I hate the most," he said. "I hate to see ten-year-old kids walking around wounded."

Memot Rubber Plantation, Cambodia, May 1970

"Permission denied, damn it." The words crackled out over the radio in the armored personnel carrier, and the young captain bit his lip and shouted, "Don't shoot, damn it, don't shoot!" While he was yelling, the APC thundered down the rows of evenly planted rubber trees on this French-owned plantation 15 miles inside the Cambodia-South Vietnam border.

Running among the trees, skittering across the road in the patterns of sunlight cut through the branches, we could see tiny, dark figures of people carrying bags, suitcases, sticks—anything they could pick up before the Americans could catch up with them in their tanks and armored personnel carriers. We were sure at first we were chasing down some elusive North Vietnamese troops who had chosen to run rather than fight. At any moment we were expecting to hear the twang of bullets whistling through the air, the explosion of B40 rockets fired from the camouflaged bunkers. The troops clutched their M16s and machine guns and were ready to shoot at anything in sight. A couple of reporters—Bill Currie of the *Chicago Tribune* and I—also grabbed rifles.

All that was needed before we could fire was the formality of permission from the squadron commander, a gold-bespectacled, curly-haired lieutenant colonel named Grail Brookshire. The officer on the APC, Captain Sewell Menzel, a lanky 28-year-old who'd gone through airborne and ranger training, radioed, "Request permission to recon by fire, sir." The colonel's immediate, unqualified refusal not only was a rebuke but, in the tension of the chase, seemed to be a senseless mistake by an officer who evidently was not aware of the immediate danger.

Moments later, it became clear the colonel had known what he was doing. As we approached the fleeing figures, some of them began to stop, and we discovered that half of them were women and children. When they saw they could not escape the galloping personnel carriers and tanks, they stood petrified, hands over their heads, expecting immediate death or at least detention and imprisonment. "We are Vietnamese refugees," some of them explained to an interpreter. "We are running away from Cambodian officials. We stayed in the rubber plantation overnight and are returning to our homes in Vietnam."

Not all the fleeing figures, however, could possibly have been refugees. Some of them were too young and healthy. Some were wearing bits and pieces of North Vietnamese and Viet Cong uniforms. They attempted to conceal themselves among the refugees in an effort to shield themselves from the Americans who had pushed across the Cambodian frontier. "I'd rather let a few enemy troopers get by than kill innocent civilians," explained Brookshire, sitting on his personnel carrier and chewing a cigar. "Our mission here is only to shoot at the enemy when we're sure they're the enemy. We fire only when fired upon or when we have some other means of positive identification."

Despite Brookshire's scrupulous adherence to the carefully drawn-up rules of engagement of the American campaign in "neutral" Cambodia, it was almost inevitable that civilians would somehow be caught in the crossfire of the campaign. After we had raced through the rubber plantations for 20 minutes, searching piles of clothing and other belongings, occasionally finding a pistol or rifle but no substantial evidence of enemy presence, we saw a woman and several children weeping uncontrollably beside a mound of earth. Captain Menzel ordered the vehicle to stop and told the interpreter to "interrogate these people."

"She say children under the ground," said the interpreter. "They buried over there when APC roll over them." Two GIs hopped off the personnel carrier and began to dig into the ground with their shovels. Soon a pallid little arm appeared in the dirt and then the rest of a small form hunched over just as a child would have attempted to do in hiding from the roaring monster bearing down on top of it. A GI medic felt the girl's pulse and attempted to apply artificial respiration. The GIs—including the captain—stood around nervously, uncertainly. "Sir, the mother say one more down there, too," said the interpreter. The GIs dug again. In a few minutes they picked up the smaller form of a little boy.

The child's father yanked it from their arms, vehemently recovering it from those who were responsible for its death. The medic felt the boy's pulse, just as he had the girl's, and shook his head. Slowly, Captain Menzel pulled himself—and the troops—together. After all, a war was on. "Okay, you guys, get back on the APC," Menzel shouted. "We gotta get moving. We gotta finish reconning this place. Get three cases of C-rations and give them to the family." The interpreter was left to offer formal apologies and regrets. "We are very sorry," he said in Vietnamese. "We did not see them. We did not come here to kill you. We only come here to kill VC. We are sorry. We are sorry."

The adventure of the chase through the plantation was over. Everything else was anti-climax, operations as usual. "Cambodia, Vietnam, who gives a damn where the hell we are," said one of the GIs manning a .50-caliber machine gun, not at all impressed by the importance of the American operation in Cambodia. "It's all the same wherever we are," he went on, slouching down behind his gun. "You get shot at by gooks in Vietnam. You come to Cambodia, and you get shot at by more gooks. Hell, no, I don't like being in Cambodia. I don't like being in Vietnam either."

The philosophy behind the GIs' outlook was based not on politics but on survival. "I don't like getting shot at, that's all," he offered when asked why he objected to the war. "This business is strictly for lifers." Among the "lifers" was Captain Menzel. As far as he was concerned, the Cambodian campaign was "the best thing since we went to the Yalu River in Korea." The only difficulty, he noted, was that it may have been a case of too little, too late. "We should have done this thing three years ago," he said, echoing the opinion perhaps most often heard from American officers and sergeants. "We should have invaded North Vietnam. If we'd done that, we could have wrapped this thing all up by now."

Menzel ventured this opinion in a brief stop before our entry into the rubber plantation. We were in a village where North Vietnamese troops had been holing up for years as a base for operations in South Vietnam. The stench of death still hung over the village—a cluster of closed doors and darkened windows, of overturned and burned-up motorcycles, of twisted bicycle hulks. "There's still some bodies laying around in there," said one of the GIs. "The ARVN had a helluva fight in there two days ago." ARVN—Army of the Republic of (South) Vietnam—troops were still patrolling, sticking their rifles into doors, peering around the vegetable gardens where the VC had grown what they needed to live.

As we rolled through the jungle toward the plantation, we saw countless trails and tracks, large enough for small trucks, motor scoot-ers, and bicycles—all of which the communists had used in Vietnam. The trails were barely large enough for our tanks and APCs, which often had to stop or slow down while GIs cleared away the under-growth. Eventually we hit a smooth dirt road on which we rolled toward the plantation.

The smell of death also rose from the vacant buildings of the planta-tion headquarters, surrounded by manicured green lawns, flower gar-dens, and soaring trees. Most of the buildings were vacant. South Vietnamese plantation workers—on whom the communists had relied for food and labor—were scurrying among them, picking up their be-longings, preparing to run away in the face of the American armored Goliaths. "The communists were here last night," our interpreter re-ported to Captain Menzel after talking to some of the Vietnamese. "A hundred of them were in here and then left. Some of them walked down the main road."

The Americans had tried to cut off the communists with this cross-country dash through jungles and rubber plantation, by gardens of banana trees, past lowing cows frightened for the first time by the hollow growl of the enormous vehicles on which we were riding. "I still think most of them are in there, behind us," said Colonel Brook-shire. "That's why we're cutting off this road. Some of them will get away, but we will get a lot of them."

American airplanes and gunships had gotten to the plantation before the tanks. The plantation warehouse was a mass of charred rubble, twisted glass, still-burning papers, and heaps of tiles. Beside the warehouse was a green soccer field, newly pitted by machine gun fire. Then, incongruously, a dazzling row of bright red and yellow flowers streamed down from a fence. Behind the fence was the home of the manager. It had been deserted for four weeks, since the Vietnamese communists began harassing Cambodian authorities in the region.

We did not linger long at plantation headquarters. The mission was to move up route seven toward the town of Snuol, near the vital junc-tion of routes seven and thirteen, the main road leading to the frontier. We pulled onto route seven, a narrow but well-tended macadam distin-guished by the presence of a telephone line linking Snuol and Memot with the Cambodian capital of Phnom Penh. The last time I had driven the road was in the fall of 1967 while in Cambodia during the visit of

Mrs. Jacqueline Kennedy, guest at the time of the "neutral" chief of state, Prince Norodom Sihanouk, deposed on March 18, six weeks before U.S. troops crossed the frontier.

Route seven was now deserted except for the speeding tanks and APCs. We saw an occasional bicycle frame and a jeep with the windshield shot out. We paused briefly at a blown-up bridge before the soldiers put in place an enormous strip of steel designed to carry a tank. We passed by the same villages I had seen three years ago, but the houses were all deserted. Sometimes we saw refugees—not only Vietnamese but Cambodian, too—who smiled and accepted GI handouts of chewing gum, cigarettes, and candy. We saw no sign of Cambodian civilian or military officials.

At the end of the day we stopped short of another blown-up bridge. The tanks and APCs pulled into what the GIs call the "night logger position" off the road. The captain got off his APC and walked over to Colonel Brookshire. "We killed one enemy soldier," reported the captain. "He fired two shots at one of our APCs, and my men opened up at him and shredded him. We got his rifle also. And here's some identification papers showing he got medals from the North Vietnamese for killing American soldiers in Vietnam."

I had not heard the shots fired, but I had seen the body as we left the rubber plantation. I was sure, after looking at the papers, that he had indeed been an enemy soldier who had not been alert enough to merge quietly with the refugees and hide his weapon. Our "body count" for the day was one enemy KIA. No one mentioned the little boy and girl we had run down in the middle of the plantation.

Ho Chi Minh City, April 1995

A capitalist explosion reverberates here 20 years after North Vietnamese troops stormed into the capital proclaiming *giai phong*, for liberation—and the worst humiliation ever suffered by U.S. forces overseas. The shock troops this time are not American GIs or contractors but legions of businessmen from Japan to Taiwan, Hong Kong, and Singapore in often uneasy alliance with corrupt Vietnamese bureaucrats eyeing enormous profits from everything from hotels and coffee shops to electronics and textile factories.

"Nothing gets done without payoffs," complains a foreign businessman one morning in the coffee shop of the Far East Hotel, one of scores of relatively luxurious lodgings sprouting up on a street of shops and restaurants near the center of the city. "It's fifty dollars here, and a hundred dollars there," says the businessman, attempting to carve a niche as an importer in a joint venture with local Vietnamese. "The locals have the contacts and show you how it's done."

A foreigner coming back a generation after having covered the war for American newspapers sees the system at work when applying for a visa in the Vietnamese embassy in the Thai capital of Bangkok. Come back in a week, says a consular officer, but a travel agency above the Vietnam Air office around the corner obtains the visa in a day—at four times the normal fee. Try to find out who gets all the extra loot for the visa, and the answer is both simple and obscure. "We have our special contact," says the travel agent. "It goes back to Saigon," as this city, renamed for the legendary national leader who led his people against the French and then the Americans, is still widely known. "It is the way things are done."

On a much larger scale, it is also the way things are done in groping through a labyrinth of rules and regulations ostensibly designed to jumpstart an economy mired for the first decade after the war by hard-line communist ideology. "You can see we now have changed our approach entirely," says Nguyen Xuan Oanh, an aging economic consultant who served as finance minister and, briefly, as prime minister under the old U.S.-supported regime and opted to stay here after the communist victory. "I have long suggested programs to open the economy and bring us into step with the rest of the region."

On a superficial level, the program appears to have been so successful that Saigon now appears as a cornucopia of capitalist goods and pleasures. Modern offices bloom on the sites of old American government office blocks. Hotels have redecorated and spruced up. Late-model cars, from small taxis to limousines, now clog streets still packed with motor scooters, bicycles, and three-wheeled pedicabs. Shops burst with VCRs, television sets, cameras, stereo equipment— and traditional lacquerware and silks.

The display of rampant capitalism provides a setting for another kind of show as authorities stage carefully rehearsed parades here and in Hanoi, wellspring of Vietnamese communism and center of old-style national power, for the 20th anniversary of *giai phong* on April 30. The anniversary begins with a rally in the park in front of

"Reunification Hall," the palace from which American-backed South Vietnamese leaders ruled until fleeing as the North Vietnamese barreled toward the city in the final offensive. The celebration comes complete with all the trimmings—from roaring tanks and jets to goose-stepping troops to colorful floats to bands to old-fashioned lion and dragon dances.

In the French-built opera house, a landmark where the old South Vietnamese assembly once engaged in futile debate, dancers flaunting multicolored banners prance and pirouette through what an energetic young director believes is "a revolutionary performance in a modern style." Down Le Duan Street, named for the late secretary of the Workers' Party, the broad boulevard running by the onetime American embassy to the zoo, craftsmen hammer, paint, drill, and saw at exhibits displaying every landmark of the final offensive that won the war.

"Everything must be perfect," says Pham Van Phao, a young man from Hanoi with a name card that identifies him as "technical manager" of a company named "VietSoft," described on the card as "solution, software, computer & network." Right inside the doorway is a montage of grainy photographs of American presidents from Eisenhower to Ford—the men in the White House from first days to final defeat of U.S.-backed forces. Inscribed over the pictures are the words "Three Hundred Billion dollars"—rough estimate of the sum total the Americans poured into Vietnam before *giai phong*.

In a large park the other way from the old palace, workmen hammer away at still more displays showing off the fruits of the revolution—and the benefits reaped by Vietnam's 70 million people. A chart painted on billboards in the center of the park boasts of the gains for the city's 4.7 million people—including a gross domestic product that has gone up nearly three times and "capital joint ventures" that have increased 1,000 times from 1976 through 1994.

The figures may reflect some wishful thinking, but there is no doubt the government has yielded both to economic reality and popular sentiment by providing a level of freedom unimaginable here in the first decade after the communist victory. In effect, central authorities have agreed on a form of compromise. "Find new economic space for yourselves," is the message, as interpreted by an Australian scholar, David Marr, "and leave us in control of politics"—that is, in charge of government and party.

It is a message the government has carried to the rest of the world, forming relations with the United States while cooperating in the search for the remains of U.S. troops, improving frayed ties with China, the Vietnam war ally with which it broke in 1978, and disporting itself as a "good neighbor" with Southeast Asian business partners. Vietnam has done so well that it is joining the capitalist alliance known as the Association of Southeast Asian Nations or ASEAN—and promises to slash much of the red tape involved in business around the region.

The numbers seem to bear out the burgeoning success story. The gross domestic product is rising at about 8 percent a year, reports the Asian Development Bank, while inflation has sunk to about 10 percent, from many times that amount ten years ago. At the same time, foreign interests have invested a total of more than $10 billion—on the way to more than $100 billion a decade from now.

Wander into one of dozens of newsstands on downtown streets, and a plethora of glossy magazines and newspapers report on the success of capitalism to come. The cover of one features the flag of capitalist South Korea over a report on South Korean business here—and not a mention of Stalinist North Korea. The cover of another shows off "potential and development" in an outlying province. A third magazine, appealing to the tour groups and trekkers now visible everywhere, reminds visitors, "Vietnam is not a war, but a country," above a photograph of women in traditional conical hats harvesting rice.

Foreigners are often impressed by what they see—despite frustrations. "These people are smart," says Michael Bidwell, a consultant from Santa Barbara, working on contracts for oil drilling between American and Vietnamese companies. "They're getting smarter all the time."

Big-time business interests are not the only ones who see a capitalist bonanza here. "We think it's a good long-term investment," says Alvin Ho, opening an upscale clothing store with the unlikely name "Uncle Sam" down the street from the old Majestic Hotel near the Saigon River. Ho maintains a home and office in Maryland but sees Vietnam as "a place to do business even though it may be tough for a while."

Not everyone, though, shares in the success. On the same street, in a store laden with bolts of silk, a middle-aged woman mourns the husband, a former South Vietnamese army officer, who died in a "reeducation camp." The bureaucrats, she says, "make all the money for themselves" while "we stay the same." Few ordinary people are getting the new jobs offered by expanding companies. "They only want educated people. Most people get nothing."

Everywhere, old suspicions seep through. The ruling structure remains secretive, unapproachable—even while intermediaries pass on bribes to mysterious contacts. The secrecy, it is widely believed, reflects the fear that diehards among the populace may not be so happy as the bureaucrats want the world to believe. In a small tourist agency, a man smiles politely when asked what he thinks of the anniversary of *giai phong*, liberation. "I think nothing," he says. "I can say nothing. No one cares. We only try to survive as always." Please, he asks a visitor, "do not use my name or it will be trouble for me."

2

"Too Dangerous to Talk"

Saigon, August 1991

The dateline is not inappropriate. The name endures in more ways than one. The abbreviation SGN still denotes Tan Son Nhut airport on baggage labels, even those used by Vietnam Airlines with its fleet of decrepit Tupolevs and Antonovs. And Saigon is still proper usage for the sprawling downtown of the much larger metropolitan district named "Ho Chi Minh City" right after the communist forces roared to victory one April day 16 years ago.

One cannot say the mystique of Ho Chi Minh, like the name of the city, is dying hard. There never was much of a Ho mystique in Ho City, as some of the foreign entrepreneurs call it, in the first place. Most of the city's 4 million people, those who could not get away at American expense before "the fall," those who have not made it out since then as "boat people" or legally under the "Orderly Departure Program," still yearn to live somewhere else—somewhere, preferably, an ocean or continent or two removed from Vietnam and the inheritors of the legacy of Uncle Ho.

It is the realization that most people here view them with cynicism and bitterness, if not the fanatic hatred of those who suffered through "reeducation," that most alarms the leaders in Hanoi. And it was clearly with a certain disbelieving relief that they listened to the news of Soviet leader Mikhail Gorbachev's ouster. Nguyen Xuan Oanh, "Jack Owen" in his Harvard days in the early 1950s, summarizes the regime's feelings toward the Gorbachev era: "It could not be worse."

The setting for the remark is the bar of the Floating Hotel, an opulent new luxury lodging right on the Saigon River. The occasion: a reception for a German company opening up an office here. Oanh, who became prime minister of the old Saigon regime for a few months in the mid-1960s, wears his Harvard tie while dispensing advice to would-be foreign investors. He doubles as a key adviser to leaders in Hanoi on "free enterprise" and a "market economy"—the very terms that come to mind in discussions of *glasnost* and *perestroika*. (It is, of course, in response to dissent that Hanoi has approved sweeping reforms that may bring about capitalism on a scale unseen here since the French.)

It is hard enough keeping restive Saigonese under control. Dance halls, discos, free enterprise—"the government has to say okay," says a producer of "cultural" performances, "but if there is criticism of top leaders, they will arrest us." Better to entertain with western rock than western ideas. The reasons are obvious. "The government is more corrupt than before," observes an aging intellectual, chatting over lunch in a living room decorated with old lacquer figures and photographs of ancestors. "I hoped it would be better, but it was worse. Everywhere you go you have to pay. Anything you want to do, you have to pay the clerk, the guard, the chief. And if you don't, then nothing's done."

Symbols abound of a desperate realization that something was terribly wrong with the economic philosophy absorbed from readings of Marx and Engels. The markets are brimming with motorcycles and spare parts, radios and VCRs, cans of beer and bottles of mineral water. The streets are jammed, as much as they were at the height of the Vietnam war, with small cars and trucks and darting scooters. "You hear things are tough," says an American bureaucrat in a crowded office processing the flood of applications of would-be immigrants to the United States under the Orderly Departure Program. "What you see is things are doing pretty well. This is an entrepreneurial people. They work like hell."

Gleaming new name plates all over town reflect the national drive both to increase exports and draw foreign investment. Acronyms are in vogue—with state trading firms now flaunting names like

"Getronimex" for "General Electronics Import Export Company" and "Transimex" for "Transport-Delivery Import-Export Enterprise." Always, though, one picks up more than an undercurrent of discontent— a feeling that all may be for show, that nothing much is new. Black Soviet-made cars pull in and out of the driveway of the old American embassy building, now home of VietSovpetro, a joint oil venture. Across the street, at the gate of the district cultural center, below anachronistic banners showing Vietnamese and Soviet flags, an old man repeats local wisdom. "Life in Vietnam is always the same," he says. "If this government is not changed, the people are never better. All Vietnam people hope for change."

A few blocks away, hundreds of Vietnamese wait to meet one of several harried Americans for interviews that may or may not win them visas to the United States. The Americans interview about 10,000 people a month—almost entirely Amerasian or Vietnamese with relatives in the United States or records of imprisonment in "reeducation camps." A young man named "James Coleman" explains realities. "Living here is too hard for Amerasians," he says, breaking into a genial, broad American grin. "I cannot go to school. We cannot get a job. We don't stand a chance." He gives a GI-style thumbs-up when asked if he sees any hope. "I go to America"—a land to which he can bring no education or skills. "It must be better."

The incredible irony now is that Vietnamese, those in and out of power, for or against the small clique of old men who somehow remain at the top through party congresses and "reforms," again expect the United States to pour in the dollars and advice needed to rescue them. The betting is the United States will gradually lift the embargo that bans all U.S. trade and investment here as Vietnam lives up to the two conditions stipulated by the White House—full cooperation in the search for the dead and missing from the war, and noninterference in Cambodia.

An exuberant crowd of Australians and Europeans around a newly opened bar in Saigon called "Shake's"—on the top floor of a building near the Saigon River that once housed the local branch of the Bank of America—reflects the trend. "You blokes are going to lose out on all the business," says one of the partners, a veteran of the small military force that Australia sent to Vietnam in the late 1960s. "You're cutting off your nose to spite your face. Everybody else is getting in here."

The locals heartily concur. "Every Vietnamese people hope they lift the embargo," says Nguyen Van Nghiem, who learned his English while going through nearly two years of training as a South Vietnamese navy petty officer at the Great Lakes Naval Training Center on Lake Michigan during the war. Nghiem chats with me in the "Top Ten Restaurant," which he manages for a Singaporean company on the ground floor of the venerable Eden building on a square opposite the Rex Hotel in downtown Saigon. The restaurant is nearly empty—Nghiem says "we open a year ago for foreigners" with an inviting sign, "24-Hour Fast Food Restaurant" and a promise of Japanese-style karaoke and dancing, but few are interested. "Life here will be better," he predicts, when the Americans are back.

Nghiem places his hopes in large part on the influence of a man who once ran the city from a mysterious warren of musty offices in a delightfully rococo building at the end of the square just a few feet from the "Top Ten." The man is Vo Van Kiet, a top leader of the Viet Cong in the south during the war and then, for four years after the communist victory in 1975, secretary of the Ho Chi Minh City Central Committee—in other words, mayor of Saigon. Neither Vo Van Kiet nor anyone else on the Ho Chi Minh committee has been known to venture from the old city hall, a prize inheritance from the 19th-century French, and stroll among the shops in the Eden building, much less enter an establishment such as Top Ten.

If the members of the national central committee in Hanoi did not consult Nghiem for his sentiments, they still were aware of the respect that Vo Van Kiet commands in the south. It was partly for that reason that Kiet in August was named prime minister—that and, yes, for almost a decade he had been responsible for state planning and economic reform. "I have no chance to see any officials," says Nghiem. Still, "People in the south like Vo Van Kiet."

Saigon, April 1985

It had been more than a decade since I'd been to old Saigon, but it seemed like the old days. Almost every street, every house remained unchanged since the deceptively tranquil summer of 1974, three seasons before the end of the war, when I had last passed through. Things were different now. The tensions of life under the conquerors from the north were visible in the faces of passersby.

As our government car eased its way back into town from a day in the countryside, familiar sights, sounds, and smells flooded over me: little cafés purveying thick black coffee, tiny garages where self-taught mechanics glued together motorcycles, cars, and trucks, steaming restaurants reeking of beer, meat, and vegetables—more legacies from old Vietnam. Still, there was no doubt this was a different world from the one I had seen during the war. Take my guide, for instance.

A former guerrilla soldier from Hanoi, he now had a desk job in the foreign ministry. For some reason he had been assigned to show me around the new, improved Ho Chi Minh City—at my expense. I was supposed to stay with him at all times, especially when talking to Vietnamese, but to get a sense of the suffering of Ho Chi Minh City under communist control I had to get rid of him. We had just returned from a visit to Tan An, a town south of Ho City on the main road to the Mekong River delta. After spending an afternoon at a monument surrounded by the gravestones of about 3,000 NLF fighters who'd "contributed their lives to the fatherland," anybody would need a respite—even a diehard communist. I told my guide I knew the neighborhood and wanted to look around for old times' sake.

Yes, I could get back to the hotel downtown on my own. No, no, I wouldn't interview anybody, I promised. Yes, I knew the guide had to be with me whenever I opened my mouth. No problem, no sweat, as the GIs used to say. I left him sitting in the back seat of the car with a strange look on his lean, weathered face—half skeptical, half glad to be rid of his American charge—and strolled down the street. Actually, I was looking for someone, a Vietnamese who'd interpreted for me years before when I'd covered the war, first for *The Washington Star*, then for the *Chicago Tribune*. I had no idea if he was still around or not, but he'd lived somewhere in this area with a wife and four kids. Hopefully he hadn't changed much since I'd last seen him in July 1974.

I'd been on this same street in February 1968 when U.S. soldiers were fighting block by block to drive out North Vietnamese and Viet Cong troops who'd turned the racetrack a few blocks away into their headquarters for the Tet offensive. The street had been a battleground four months later during the May 1968 offensive but otherwise had been peaceful—even during Saigon's "final days" in April 1975, when the North Vietnamese swept into town for keeps.

A grinning cyclo driver picked me up at a corner and energetically pedalled me wherever I pointed. Kids began to follow, chattering, banging the cyclo, reaching to touch my arm. I asked the driver to stop, retreated into a coffee shop, and reemerged on foot. No luck. I'd just about given up the search when I stared across the street toward a thin, silver-haired man. He was staring back. I decided to ask him for help and strolled over.

"Hi, Don," he said. A nervous smile played across his face. I stopped, stared hard, and stuck out my hand.

"Le Viet!" That was his pen name, meaning "Vietnamese Le," not the French *le* for "the," but the name of the legendary Le dynasty that had ruled five centuries earlier—the only name by which I ever called him. I had to look carefully again. Could this be that inveterate, slightly overweight rumormonger with sleek black hair and a crafty grin revealing gleaming white teeth? Was this the same person who'd regaled me with tales of coups, corruption, and political derring-do over endless cups of *café français* at Givral's and Brodard's on Tu Do Street?

Le Viet had called me after I'd signed on with *The Washington Star* in September 1967. He'd worked for my predecessor, Richard Critchfield, who'd left Saigon to write a book on Vietnam. Dick had wondered about Le Viet's background as a northern Buddhist and one-time member of the Viet Nam Quoc Dan Dang, VNQDD, the Vietnam National People's Party, an old-line nationalist grouping that had fought both the communists and the French. Those credentials, however, seemed better to me than those of other assistants with much more sharply defined political leanings one way or another, or little or no background in the ideological wars that had roiled their country. Over the years I found considerably more truth than hearsay in much of what Le Viet told me.

Le Viet looked like a scarecrow now. His teeth—the ones that were left—were crooked. His face was deeply lined with age and fear. "Le Viet, let's talk," I insisted. He turned and waved me into his house. Quickly, smiling uneasily, he asked me how I was, what I was doing, said he'd written, but the letter hadn't gotten through. How were some of the other journalists he'd known? Then he stopped suddenly.

"It's very dangerous here," he said. "We cannot talk." He began barking at a couple of young men shooting pool on a decrepit pool table set in the center of the cement floor and gave them chalk for the sticks. "Le Viet, what are you doing?" I asked, knowing life had not been easy since the fall of Saigon. "I run a pool hall. I have not been downtown in more than ten years. But you must go. It is too dangerous to talk." His wife smiled politely, and two of his children scampered happily in the dusty, poorly lit rear of the room. A rather tall young woman—taller than either Le Viet or his wife—hung back in the shadows. She was Bac, his eldest, his daughter, now 17, a child of six when I'd last seen her.

"Le Viet, I thought you might be in the States."

With the sadness of fatalistic inevitability he gave me his excuse. "My kids were sick in 1975. I didn't want to leave them. Now I must take care of them. It is very tough." A crowd of curious kids gathered outside the door. Le Viet suggested we meet the next night downtown, outside the Palace Hotel where I was staying on old Nguyen Hue, the Street of Flowers, where women still hawked huge bouquets from stalls on the center island as they had since the French colonial days. He wanted to give me a pack of documents—not political information but letters and U.S. refugee visa applications for me to take to the American embassy in Bangkok.

We met the next night on a prearranged street corner near my hotel and drove around downtown on a motor scooter, just like old times, Le Viet commenting on the return of bargirls to the streets, the general dislike of the government, the weakness of the economy. It was his first trip to the center since the month after the fall during which he had parlayed his background into a final news gig as an assistant in the CBS bureau. The American honchos had gone, but the CBS bureau, run by a wandering British journalist named Eric Cavaliero, had lingered on for a month in the Caravelle Hotel.*

Le Viet was uneasy as we neared Nguyen Hue, insisting on getting off the motor scooter half a block away from the Palace, then slipped me the pack of papers and waved good-bye. We were to meet downtown the next day, same time, same place.

Le Viet had been right the first time. It was too dangerous to be

_____

*Cavaliero had previously hung out in the office as an assistant while filing for a paper in Honolulu. He stayed on for another year and a half, teaching English until the authorities told him to leave. Then, with his Vietnamese wife, he moved to Hong Kong, where he has worked ever since as an editorialist for the *Hong Kong Standard.*

seen, to talk, certainly to pass papers. When he didn't show up, I made my way by cyclo back to the sordid pool hall. Le Viet's wife, Nguyen Thi Mai, was in the doorway. "Have you seen Le Viet?" she asked as I entered the house. "I am scared. He has not been home in two nights." A small crowd gathered; something was amiss. Policemen walked up to the taxi waiting outside.

Mai implored me to leave before the cops questioned me—and her—but it was too late for a clean getaway. The police ordered me to stop as soon as I got to the taxi. They gestured to the driver to wait and escorted me to a small open-fronted office building across the street— "People's Administrative Committee," said the red-lettered sign in Vietnamese. The police were polite. So were the local civilian officials who showed up later. They just wanted to know whom I was seeing and why. "The people," said one of them, had informed them of my first visit.

When could I return to my hotel? Soon, they said. "Soon" stretched into two hours. Through a former South Vietnamese air force officer, who'd been trained in the States and seemed pleased to talk to an American again, they asked about my visit to Vietnam, my background in the country, my relationship to Le Viet. From far off came the thud and crackle of repeated explosions, followed by flickering lights over the distant river—not grenades or shells but fireworks going off in a giant display the night before the big tenth anniversary victory parade. Someone shoved a statement at me, in Vietnamese, dutifully translated by the ex-officer, stating that I "did not have permission to go to this place" and had done so "in violation of the laws of the Socialist Republic of Vietnam."

That was it. Shaking hands, they told the taxi driver to return me to the Palace. Nearly a year was to pass before I learned what had become of Le Viet, who did not come home that night or the next or the next—not until, months later, he had fully "confessed" his error and promised to deviate no more. For me, however, it had been a light brush with a tough system. As an American journalist, I was a privileged character. The authorities, eager to open diplomatic relations with the United States in a bid for trade and aid to bolster the hard-hit economy, did not want an incident.

Life for Le Viet and the 5 million or so other residents of Ho Chi Minh City might not change soon—with or without U.S. aid. It's a desperate struggle just to survive. Shopkeepers showing off souvenirs, street vendors selling cigarettes and candy smuggled in from Thailand, clerks toiling for a pittance in airline offices—they grinned and shrugged when asked how they were doing. As many as half the potential workers are underemployed if not jobless, and the city seethes with tension that confounds the tough types sent down from Hanoi to keep the lid on.

Wherever you go, there is a sense of being watched. Contacts are made surreptitiously, hastily, with elaborate ruses for avoiding the legions of plainclothed informants who keep the city from erupting into open revolt. Wherever you turn, though, you're likely to meet someone anxious to tell his plight, to ask for a favor—money, advice on how to get out of the country.

The sense of revolt is most obvious in the back alleys, in dark, dingy rooms away from prying eyes. A former South Vietnamese army lieutenant colonel spoke in angry defiance of the possibilities of arrest and lengthy imprisonment—or worse. "We don't do anything, just stay home," he said in the pidgin English he'd learned from his American advisers with the South Vietnamese army airborne. "We never ask for jobs. The communists don't like us. We want to kick them out." He was stocky, muscular, in his 40s—ready, it seemed, for another war. At his side was his wife, who begged me not to use his name. He rambled on, naming the American adviser whom he'd known so I could check out his story, talking about those long, ultimately useless operations in the mountains, then describing the eight and a half years he'd spent in prison—"reeducation"—near Hanoi after the war.

Sharing the room with him now was a former South Vietnamese army captain who'd been captured by the North Vietnamese in the central highlands town of Ban Me Thuot a month before the communists' final victory, released shortly afterward, and then imprisoned for seven years after he tried to organize a revolt. "If they know I talk to you now, they will kill me right away," he said, sneering in defiance.

I heard other stories, too. One morning in Givral's, the coffee shop on the main square known to a generation of correspondents and political gossips, a youngish man told an improbable tale about keeping the bodies of GIs buried near his house. The next day he returned with the imprints of three dogtags: Strouse, Howard D.; Clements, Richard L.; and Rangeloff, Roger A., with serial numbers, blood types, and religions. A day later he pressed into my hand a small envelope that he said contained bits of teeth and bones—"evidence" for me to take to the U.S. Joint Casualty Resolution Center. Furtively, looking around for signs of someone watching us, he promised he could lead investigators to the grave of a dozen GIs who'd gone down in a helicopter while fighting north of Saigon during the North Vietnamese attack in the spring of 1972.

Considering the statistics, I could almost believe the guy's story. I'd covered the "Easter Offensive," going up route 13 north of Saigon past the U.S. bases at Ben Cat and Lai Khe to a town named Chon Thanh, on the way to An Loc, surrounded at the time by several divisions of North Vietnamese troops. It was one of the toughest battles of the war, with perhaps 50,000 dead and wounded on both sides.*

A stroll through downtown Ho Chi Minh City reveals how communism has replaced the brief glimpse of life in the United States, as refracted in the war years, with a realistic fatalism. Those who see no refurbished version of the American dream coming soon to Vietnam would gladly leap on the next flight from Tan Son Nhut airport to Bangkok to the United States if given the chance. Some try to make their own chance. "Can you help, please?" asked a woman selling cigarettes at the traffic circle at the end of Nguyen Hue. She smiled, just as she would to a GI in one of the Tu Do street bars, long since converted into souvenir shops.

Beside her, dressed like her mother in Vietnamese-style pajamas, was a girl about 17—brown-haired, light-skinned, and chubby, with a wide-open American-style smile. "I live with her father long time," said the woman. "He don't write to me. I want to go to the United States and look for him. Can you help, please?" She looked around carefully, eyes narrowing. "Police," she said. "They see me, they get me later. Don't talk too long."

Sometimes the faces—lined, resigned, impassive—flicker in recognition. The gap-toothed old man who cleared tables at Brodard's, on

---

*The fate of these three MIAs remains a mystery to this day. I gave the dogtag imprints and bone fragments to a State Department official who later acknowledged turning them over to an army officer at the Joint Casualty Resolution Center's office in the U.S. embassy in Bangkok. When I asked the Pentagon what had happened to my little contribution, I was promised a reply from the JCRC office in Hawaii. I heard nothing.

Tu Do opposite the Air France office in the Caravelle Hotel (the names of the hotels and many of the streets have been changed, but I forget the new ones), said he remembered me.

Down the street at the Majestic Hotel, overlooking the river, I sought out the room where I'd stayed for two years writing a book and scores of articles and discovered it was now an office.* Upstairs, five floors up on a rickety French-built cage of an elevator now encased in tacky fiberglass, the *maître d'* and a couple of aged waiters remembered me, too. They shook their heads derisively when asked how they liked their new Soviet and East European guests. No way to get out, said the *maître d'*—no money for the boats that had already carried hundreds of thousands away through treacherous waters to Thailand or Malaysia, no way to get on the list under which a select few now left by plane on the Orderly Departure Program. "Life is bad," he said, turning his palm up in the French gesture of submissive acceptance.

For an American back in Saigon, though, the sense persists that Saigon will always be Saigon. Hanoi may pretend to rule it but will never really subdue it. Black market stalls laden with goodies smuggled in from Thailand, Hong Kong, and Singapore attest to that. Old Saigon will never quite outlive its boomtown past before the communist takeover.

I went by Saigon taxi to the edge of town, on an American-built highway leading to the air base, checking out the coffee shops where Le Viet had said people might talk freely—or more freely than downtown. Here was where GIs had once hung out, among faded tailor shops and massage parlors and bars, and here, in the first café I saw, sat a couple of Vietnamese, probably intellectuals, judging from their glasses, the pens in their pockets, the pursed, thin lips. I sat down in a tiny chair, ordered a small *café den*, and asked one of them if it was OK to ask questions.

"We talk here," he said. "There are very few police." His narrowed eyes belied his confidence, darting toward the windows and door as we chatted. "More than half the people have no jobs. We hate the North Vietnamese. We hate the communists. Some day we will overthrow them. You will see."

---

*The book, *Wider War: The Struggle for Cambodia, Thailand and Laos,* was published in 1971 by Praeger, New York, and Pall Mall, London.

I laughed. The conversation reminded me of all those coffee-shop interviews of bygone times when political rebels talked darkly of over-throwing the U.S.-backed regime. "No, we will," he insisted. "You wait. We can." Hastily he swilled down his coffee. "We do not like communists. We do not like corrupt people. We want our own govern-ment." I had heard it all before, often. The man looked outside. "Po-lice, no more talk." I belted down my cup and left.

Back at their temporary office in the Majestic, my guide and his supervisor wanted to know more about my meeting with Le Viet. I assured them I had initiated it. I told them the truth—that the papers he had given me were letters and visa applications for me to deliver to the American embassy in Bangkok. The supervisor admonished me mildly for having seen a Vietnamese "without permission" but was full of assurances to allay any concerns about what was happening to Le Viet. "Do not worry, Mr. Kirk," he told me, not once but several times. "He is fine. Nothing is going to happen to him. We understand."

In fact, he said repeatedly, "He is already home."

San Jose, California, June 1995

The travail of Le Viet was just beginning on the night I said good-bye to him for the last time during that visit before the tenth anniversary celebrations of April 1985. Half a year later I received a letter from him, laboriously typed on the same old machine he had used when he worked for foreign journalists in the old days, relayed through his wife's cousin, Nguyen Hung, who had escaped by boat with his family and was now a student at San Jose State University. Enclosed was a statement in Vietnamese headed, "Release from Detention." Le Viet had been held, without the formality of a trial or hearing before a judge, for five months for the crime of "meeting a foreigner."*

"Every day they questioned me about relations with American jour-nalists," Le Viet is telling me as we sip coffee in the small but cheerful

---

*Richard Critchfield, writing his sister on March 15, 1992, was unaware of Le Viet's experience but talked about the dangers. "Visitors who engaged in activities deemed suspicious may be detained along with their Vietnamese contacts," he wrote. Explaining his decision not to go back, he observed that "foreign visitors to Vietnam have been arbitrarily arrested" and "some of those detained have been held incommunicado for months"—with release "contingent on the payment of a large fine."

apartment shared by his wife, two sons, and a daughter near downtown San Jose. "They said almost all American journalists worked for the CIA. They want to know about the package I give you. They said I am American spy and you are CIA. I told them I worked for foreigners a long time ago but in the war, not in politics"—the reverse of reality, since Le Viet hated to visit units in the field while analyzing politics.

Life was harsh in jail. "They had 60 people in a room in the prison"—a slapdash brick structure romantically named Cau Tre, meaning "bamboo bridge," about three miles from his home. "My wife visited once a week with food and medicine. They did not have any."

Still, Le Viet's agony could have been worse. He got a break when the police chief asked Pham Xuan An, a Viet Cong colonel who had attained that rank in secret for his services as a spy while laboring diligently as a political expert for proverbially gullible *Time-Life* correspondents in their bureau in the Continental, to question him. "The police chief wants to let him investigate me to know exactly what is my policy," Le Viet is telling me. "I explain to him." An, by now a deputy secretary of the Ho Chi Minh People's Committee, a position equivalent to a vice mayor, apparently relayed word, "It's not necessary to make bad for me."

Le Viet, once free, dedicated his life to getting out of Vietnam—not by the boat route that had cost the lives of thousands of his countrymen but legally, by plane from Tan Son Nhut, as a political refugee under the Orderly Departure Program. Now I could try to help—not just to express my gratitude for the help he had given me years ago as analyst, interpreter, and translator but also to make amends for the tremendous hardship I had caused him by seeing him.

The job was not as easy as it might sound. Certainly I could and did write a letter stating that he had worked full-time for *The Washington Star*, and I could and did telephone the Vietnam refugee office in the State Department to make sure they had on file the papers from him. In the computer age, all they needed to know was Le Viet's formal name and file number, IV 81440. The Americans said they could do nothing, however, until Vietnamese authorities had approved him and his family for departure and issued them passports—a process that seemed less likely to work when Vietnam slowed departures in a hassle with Americans over MIA searches and recognition.

Not to worry. Once out of prison, Le Viet reverted to the comfortable system that had enabled him to survive since CBS had finally had to shut down its office in the Caravelle for good. There was only one way to get the Vietnamese documents, and that was to buy them. "First I bribe a policeman in my area. Then I bribe the district policemen on three levels, then the Saigon police chief through intermediaries."

The minuet went on for two years. All told, Le Viet had to pay the black-market equivalent in Vietnamese currency of about $200—"a lot of money for me," he tells me—before getting the six passports for his family. When I got to Bangkok with copies of Le Viet's papers, passports, and one more letter in mid-1991, however, I discovered he was far from home free. Thousands of Vietnamese, the bureaucrats at the ODP told me, had similar passports. Le Viet still did not fit the U.S. definition of political refugee—an entirely different category from close relative of an American passport holder, which meant automatic admission, or former member of the South Vietnamese armed forces who had suffered in a reeducation camp—a death sentence for many who went there.

More discouraging, a young woman working for a nongovernmental Catholic organization that reviewed ODP applications told me Le Viet was in a category distinctly below that of civilians who had worked full-time for the U.S. government or American companies in Vietnam. The wife of a banker, ensconced in Bangkok on living allowance and double salary, she was not impressed by the letter I had written affirming Le Viet's previous employment with *The Washington Star*. As for the five months he had spent in prison in Saigon for having seen me, she dismissed that experience as "not the same as reeducation camp."

The woman's patronizing attitude turned to cold anger when I reminded her she had never been to Vietnam, knew nothing about the place or the suffering of its people—and demanded to speak to her supervisor. First she told me to mind my manners, then disappeared for what seemed like a long time before returning with her superior, a kindly, middle-aged woman who patiently heard my plea for Le Viet and his family. At the end of the conversation, as I was thanking her boss for listening, the young woman interrupted and again admonished me for my manners. I told her, "I view that remark as an attempt at intimidation," that I was there to plead Le Viet's case, not my own, and didn't care what she thought of me.

Her boss, to my amazement, did not appear upset—and smiled and shook hands politely as the "interview" came to an uncertain ending. Months later I again got word from Le Viet. He and his entire family were soon to have their ODP interview—an appointment with one of a team of U.S. foreign service officers who came to Saigon once a week to screen applicants—and he wanted a real "certificate of employment" from me, not just a letter.

Getting the appointment was difficult but no guarantee of final approval. I wrote the "certificate," grinning inwardly as I pompously titled it "CERTIFICATE OF EMPLOYMENT," had it notarized as a rhetorical flourish, addressed it to the ODP in Bangkok, copy to Le Viet's wife with a different name over my return address, as I always wrote Le Viet to avoid arousing the suspicions of Vietnamese authorities. Still, I was not optimistic. It all seemed so impossible after my conversation with the ODP people in Bangkok. How could anyone accept a "certificate of employment" with a company that had gone out of business nearly a decade earlier, written by one who had left the company years before that?

I was considering these realities when Le Viet wrote in February 1992 that he and his wife had had their interview, that he would be leaving for the States in six months. Le Viet, his wife, and three of their four children flew out of Tan Son Nhut aboard a Cathay Pacific plane for Hong Kong on September 17, 1992, changed the same day to a Northwest flight to San Francisco, arrived in San Jose that evening, thanks to the international date line, and moved at once into their apartment, rented in advance by cousin Nguyen Hung, now an engineer with an American company.*

"I had to pay one more bribe," Le Viet is telling me at the kitchen table as his wife and two of his children watch American TV in the living room. "I wrote a four-page letter for the ODP, and I gave one of the Vietnamese assistants about the same as $20 to make sure to pass

---

*Two months after they got to San Jose, I drove Le Viet, his daughter, and one of his sons to Berkeley for a reunion dinner with Critchfield, who hadn't seen Le Viet since leaving Vietnam in the fall of 1967. Critchfield, whose first book, *The Long Charade: Political Subversion in the Vietnam War* (New York: Harcourt, Brace & World), reflected his suspicions about South Vietnam's leaders, appeared to have forgotten his old qualms about Le Viet's VNQDD/Buddhist connections and was glad to see him in America. It was to be Critchfield's only contact with Le Viet since the old days in Saigon. Dick died two years later, on December 10, 1994, a week after suffering a stroke in his room in the Cosmos Club in Washington, where he had gone for a party that his publisher, Doubleday, had planned for December 7 to celebrate publication of his latest book, *The Villagers: Changed Values, Altered Lives: The Closing of the Urban-Rural Gap.*

on the letter." Le Viet said the foreign service interviewer appeared stern at first as she asked him why he wanted to go to the United States and what his family intended to do there. He had coached all of them on what to say—and studied the interviewer's expression nervously as a Vietnamese interpreter relayed the replies of his wife and children.

Ever the diplomatic tea-leaf reader, Le Viet was sure approval was imminent when the interviewer turned to his daughter, said, "Well, young lady," and asked what she would do in America. Le Viet grins as he describes the sense of relief that the worst was over. "'Young lady' sounds kind," he says. "She was smiling when she said it. I knew we would get the visas"—all formally approved minutes later as the foreign service officer's smile broadened and she shook hands with all six family members.

Le Viet found one bonus awaiting him when he got here. CBS, which had never paid him for the month's work he did in the abandoned Saigon bureau after April 30, 1975, had no problem with his bill. Indeed, the network's accounting chief was well aware of the debt from a letter Le Viet had written to CBS—and a conversation he had had with Morley Safer, one-time CBS bureau chief who revisited his old haunts at the beginning of 1989. Safer, at the behest of CBS, had asked to see Le Viet and a former CBS cameraman, Pham Duc Suu, already tipped about the CBS team's arrival from a taxi driver at Tan Son Nhut. The pair, escorted by the ubiquitous Pham Xuan An, called on Safer at the Majestic Hotel.

Safer didn't know it, but clever Pham Xuan An before the interview had suggested Le Viet might work for the local party paper, *Saigon Giai Phong*—an idea Le Viet saw as an attempt "to trap me" and avoided by saying he was "too old." An, identified in Safer's account not by name but as "Mr. External Relations," was duplicitous as ever with Safer. "You don't have to talk to them if you don't want to," Safer quotes "Mr. External Relations" as saying. "If you want, I will get rid of them." Le Viet showed Safer a copy of the letter he had written CBS in New York in which he wrote how he and Suu had "complicatedly and haplessly" missed out on payments. The meeting lasted 20 minutes, says Le Viet, with nary a whisper about An's role as prison interrogator.

The real flaw in Safer's account—aside from his omission of Pham Xuan An's name—was a footnote in which he said a CBS vice president had assured him in October 1989 that "the debt was paid in full." In fact, CBS had no idea where to transmit the money and held on to Le Viet's share until I wrote the CBS vice president more than three years later informing him Le Viet was in San Jose, told where to reach him, and suggested he add interest covering the years in which CBS had been holding on to the funds. (Suu, who remains in Saigon, also got paid, somehow, Le Viet tells me.)*

The sum was not a lot by TV standards—Safer calls it "pitifully small," though what's "small" to a network luminary may not be that small to most of us. Small or not, it was enough to pay off mounting debts in America. Then, better yet, Le Viet found another unexpected bonus. As a political refugee, more than 65 years old, he discovered he was eligible for a U.S. Social Security pension—and now gets a monthly check about equal to the rent he pays for his family's apartment, truly small by any standard.

There were other perks, too, including a set of false teeth that returned Le Viet to some semblance of his appearance when I first knew him, and educational allowances for his kids. Le Viet, daughter Bac, and sons Tuyen and Vinh are all at San Jose City College, studying mathematics and computer science, hoping to transfer to four-year institutions after getting their associate's degrees. Le Viet smiles still more as he shows me another "certificate." This one, unlike my "certificate of employment," is real. Titled, "Dean's Honor List," it attests to the "achievement" of youngest son, Tuyen, 22.

Le Viet, at 69 by far the oldest student in his class, goes there by two city buses four days a week "to set an example for my kids." He is serious about wanting an associate's degree—and then maybe going for a bachelor's at nearby San Jose State University. "I spent three years at Hanoi University but never graduated," he says. "The Viet Minh jailed me in their war with the VNQDD for nearly four years, and then I dropped out and went to the south in 1954 when they took over the government in Hanoi."

Even now, as I visit Le Viet and his family, certain habits die hard.

---

*Morley Safer, *Flashbacks: On Returning to Vietnam* (New York: Random House, 1990), pp. 160–63. Safer, who referred to Le Viet by his real name, Duong The Tu, suggests that Le Viet and Suu requested the meeting. Le Viet, however, tells me he would never have approached anyone for such a rendezvous for fear of landing in jail again. (A caption in a photograph of Le Viet and Suu reverses their identification.)

It still seems natural to go on calling him by his old pen name, Le Viet. In real life, however, Le Viet remains Duong The Tu, and his family members, surnamed Duong, never imagine going by any other name. Now Le Viet and his family appear well on their way to achieving an American dream that eludes millions of Vietnamese caught in a country perched on a divide between old-style capitalism and new-wave communism. Or is it new-wave capitalism and old-style communism?

Le Viet is safe now. He doesn't have to make up any stories for his jailers or for the cops who periodically checked up on him in his house near the racetrack. He, his wife, and the two sons and daughter who accompanied him to San Jose under the ODP all have U.S. passports and Social Security cards. The daughter, who learned dressmaking in Saigon, works for an American clothes manufacturer while studying nights. The two brothers think about what universities they'll attend after finishing up at San Jose City.

All the while, the whole family worries about Minh, the eldest son and brother who decided to stay on in the family house on the crowded street of shops and garages near the racetrack. The choice reflected the daily agonies of an upturned society. He wanted to be with his fiancée, hysterical at the thought of his vanishing to an unknown country. With the renaissance of Saigon, however, he may have as bright a future as the brothers and sisters who immigrated to America. After graduating from a local technical college, he is now a civil engineer in a city that is rapidly rebuilding. For him, there is no shortage of work.

Le Viet's wife, Mai, the most worried of all about the son they left behind, returned for six weeks last summer. Armed with her new American passport, she had no concerns, no hassles as she entered and departed through Tan Son Nhut. Le Viet, however, does not quite share her confidence. "I will never go back," he says. "When they find who I am, they can still arrest me even if I have an American passport. They can do anything."

Le Viet doubts if Vietnam has really changed. He believes the old anti-communist nationalist groupings, including the VNQDD, to whose memory he remains loyal, are still alive. "There will be revolution," he predicts. "The more foreign companies invest in Vietnam, the more corruption. The people will rise up led by the underground cadre of all nationalist parties. There will be big change in Vietnam by the year 2000. Wait."

Le Viet often predicted coups in the fleeting days of the American era in old Saigon. I learned never to ignore what he said—just as I didn't report it as fact without checking. Often, as when he told me two weeks before Tet 1968 of VC plans to "capture every city and town in the country," he turned out to have been correct.* This time, though, he can contemplate the future in the safety of a new home, far from the suffering of his people and a nation that remains a battleground in a perpetual struggle between ideologies and realities.

---

*My story on the upcoming Tet offensive—also backed by captured document reports and other intelligence material—was never published. The editor in charge of foreign and national news at the *Star* said he did not believe such reports.

3

Seat of Revolution

Hanoi, August 1991

The suite of makeshift offices and bedrooms on the second floor of the Boss Hotel, across a leafy street from one of those sparkling little lakes that decorate the downtown of the Vietnamese capital, could hardly be mistaken for a diplomatic mission. The five or six Americans who live and work in them prefer sport shirts to coats and ties and are sometimes seen wearing baseball caps at lunch in the dining room downstairs. There is no gauntlet of security guards and secretaries barricading the halls—only smiling Vietnamese hotel clerks glad to wave a visitor up to see "the Americans" with or without appointment.

They are all military people, some of them still on active duty, others retired from the service but working for the Pentagon as civilians. Most of them have spent years in or near Vietnam, beginning with tours in the south more than 20 years ago or on bases in Thailand from which planes flew on bombing sorties over this very city. Now they are here for quite a different purpose—one that evokes sad, bitter memories for all sides but also holds a distinct glimmer of hope. They are here to look for the dead and missing and, in so doing, to form the first quasi-permanent American presence in Vietnam since the heliborne flight from the roof of the American embassy in Saigon in 1975.

"The ministry of defense, ministry of interior, foreign affairs—

they're cooperating," says Garnett "Bill" Bell, who studied Vietnamese in the army and did four tours as an enlisted man in Vietnam. "The people we work with—they've been given more authority." Bell, chief of what is formally known as the "U.S. Office of POW-MIA affairs," says "the number one priority here is to investigate reports of live sightings." Without admitting as much, he leaves the impression the "POW" part of the name is a sop to the diehard clique of politicians, veterans, and family members who persist in believing a few of the missing are still held captive somewhere in the jungles. "I don't know of Americans who are alive. People come up to me, people say they are sure Americans are held, but I don't see any proof."

What Bell does see is evidence of the anxiety of Vietnamese officials to demonstrate conclusively to a stream of visiting congressmen and representatives of veterans' groups that they are doing just about anything he asks to get to crash sites, review data in Vietnamese archives, and interview witnesses. In fact, the United States could declare that Vietnam has lived up to conditions for lifting the embargo any time it seemed politically expedient to do so. A casuist could argue that Hanoi had already honored the first condition by admitting the U.S. team on a quasi-permanent basis and showing them some sites. The point in the end may be to find a face-saving way of certifying the search as successful and giving Hanoi a clean bill of health in the interests of joining the crowd already doing business here.

Thus Bell is recommending that the mission, set up on a "temporary" basis in June, become permanent—a move that could make it the precursor to the opening of a much larger American office if not a full-fledged embassy. Team member Robert Destatte, a Vietnamese linguist who spent five years in the south during the war, shows how much the Vietnamese have impressed their American guests. "For the first time there's a prospect for getting a full accounting. I believe the government has formally decided to help."

As for Cambodia, the conclusion of a deal demanded by the five permanent members of the United Nations Security Council—with the indestructible Norodom Sihanouk returning to Phnom Penh this month as chairman of a Supreme National Council, including former members of the Khmer Rouge—may just be enough. At least the Vietnamese will theoretically be able to pull out the last of their "advisers," hoping the regime they have propped up since driving out the Khmer

Rouge at the end of 1978 will survive the tricky electoral process called for by the agreement.

Vietnam's other longtime foe, its erstwhile Vietnam war ally, its historic conqueror, China, may benefit as well from Hanoi's realization of the urgent need to patch up differences and look for new trade and aid. It was to reopen the vast China market that Vietnam sent an emissary to Beijing to talk about ending the war in Cambodia with the Chinese-backed Khmer Rouge.

The transformation in attitudes may appear downright revolutionary, but several trips back here reveal the desperation of a society that has come to know far more about waging war than peace. The real revolution in Southeast Asia has gone on elsewhere—in Bangkok, Singapore, Hong Kong. While soaring new office towers rise in all these cities, architectural relics of the French colonial era provide the dominant motif here and in old Saigon, the heart of the district formally named "Ho Chi Minh" by its conquerors. A Hollywood director could not find better backdrops for location shooting than the streets of major Vietnamese population centers, almost unchanged except for an occasional boxy concrete building put up since the end of the war.

The timing of a reshuffle in Hanoi, weeks before the stunning sequence of coup, countercoup, and dissolution of the Communist Party of the Soviet Union, could not have been more fortuitous. The shake-up here, however, was far from revolutionary. The regime did not change colors more than a shade. The more the people take the Soviet example seriously, it is clear, the more the leaders have to fear. "There wouldn't be much change here," was Nguyen Xuan Oanh's comfortable view. "If anything it might be just the other way around—knowing that Russia has failed." Thus Vietnam's leaders go on, viewing the reports from Moscow as reason to cling to old, outmoded ideals and ideology.

There is a difference, though, between the Vietnamese and the Soviet experiences. Vietnam wanted *perestroika*—restructuring—without much *glasnost* or openness. The specter of Vietnam's benefactor turning into "a free country" and then fragmenting politically has been a frightening one. Economic breakdown in the Soviet Union had been disillusioning enough; when the Kremlin this year cut off near-worthless ruble payments for arms, oil, and other vital commodities, demanding "hard currency" dollars, Vietnamese leaders began turning elsewhere with real desperation.

Do Muoi, elevated from prime minister to general secretary of the Workers' Party in June, is an old conservative who may be tougher than his predecessor, Nguyen Van Linh. No matter what, the post of general secretary is the one that really counts, just as it did when Uncle Ho himself was in charge here before his death in 1969.

At 74, Do Muoi talks reform and reconciliation, but his record speaks otherwise—including a decade of imprisonment by the French in the same compound dubbed the "Hanoi Hilton" by the captured American pilots tortured there in the war. And Vo Van Kiet, the southerner named prime minister in his place, has often appeared to mold economic change while going along with tough political policies. At 68, Kiet looks back on a career as a hard-core cadre dating from his days in the Viet Minh fighting the French.

While shuffling the deck at home, Hanoi was ready when the first reports came in from Moscow over Tass. The initial news was carefully squeezed onto page four of the papers—worth reporting but less than momentous. The fact that it appeared quickly was enough to show where Hanoi's leaders stood: they would have been delighted if "hard-liners" had replaced Gorbachev, if the CPSU could again set a stirring example of the power of the party—and, above all, if their Soviet "friends" would again pour in the arms and oil payable in rubles, not dollars. In such straight reporting, without commentary, however, was a hint of caution. Reversion to the old days of central Soviet authority in the Kremlin might be too good to be true.

In the restaurants and "cafés"—signs for "café" are everywhere— the subsequent unraveling of the Soviet structure was a topic of small talk reminiscent of the constant gossip about "coups" in Saigon during the war. "It will make no difference to us," said the guide I was compelled to hire by the rules dictating foreign travel here. "Nothing will change. It has nothing to do with us." Press reports on the downfall of the coupmakers were markedly briefer than the ones on the coup. My guide, like most educated Vietnamese, preferred to get his news from the BBC. The guide worked for a "private" travel agency, but his remarks were the "safe" kind the leaders in Hanoi would love.

One wanders among restaurants and shops looking for clues—to the past, the present, the future. Always you wonder if Hanoi and Saigon are prospering or falling into decline, if they are waiting for the proverbial "takeoff"—a favorite phrase of American aid-givers of the 1960s—or barely surviving until the next set of revolutionaries comes along with another panacea. One evening I stop in a restaurant with no name, a small room up a narrow flight of stairs, a few blocks down a narrow street from rows of shops awash in silks and linens. I had dinner there in April of 1985, around the time of the tenth anniversary of the American flight from Saigon, and ask if the same young man who had talked so volubly to me before is still around.

He isn't—but the news isn't as ominous as I am first led to believe by his worried parents, the owners of the restaurant. It turns out, as I question them about his disappearance, that he fled in July 1988 after the police had briefly held him and a friend for watching a banned videotape. They were not heard from again until they wrote their parents from a refugee camp in Hong Kong weeks later. They are still in the camp, unable to work in Hong Kong, unwilling to go home, and unacceptable by any other country. The restaurant, in the meantime, has had its ups and downs. The police closed it several times but have left it alone for nearly two years—a small sign of the freedom that economic necessity has driven leaders to give to free enterprise.

Hanoi, March 1988

Drive a few miles east of here on the road leading to the port city of Haiphong and you begin to see why Vietnam's leaders really mean it when they say they must get out of Cambodia. "We have just enough to eat," says Hoang Thi Lam, mother of six children, talking to me in the office of a village named Yen Phu through the young Vietnamese guide supplied—required—by the Foreign Press Center in Hanoi.

Nearby, at the end of a long day in a surrounding rice paddy, Nguyen Quang Bang complains about rising prices. "Everything is expensive nowadays." True, "there's more free enterprise" and "not so many intermediaries" as before the pivotal Sixth Party Congress of 1986, but the bureaucracy still stands in the way. "For example, the government can investigate requests for insecticides, but often it comes late and is useless."

Go almost anywhere in Vietnam and you're likely to hear a litany of criticism, much of it in private, some of it open, in the presence of minders from the press center. Such criticism, to be sure, almost never focuses on Cambodia. Few people dare question the wisdom of keeping more than 100,000 troops in jungles hundreds of miles from home. In a country inured to war, Cambodia, on the rice-paddy level, appears somehow irrelevant—a distant phenomenon of concern only to bureaucrats and soldiers.

Ask people in the small crowd gathering around you in the middle of Yen Phu about Cambodia, for instance, and they tend to shrug. The relationship between the investment there and shortages at home seems almost too abstruse to contemplate. Anyway, by the standards of modern Vietnam, Yen Phu is relatively prosperous. It's smack in the Red River plain, the rice-rich delta heartland of the north, not so large and fertile as the Mekong River delta in the south but far from desperate.

Stroll through the central marketplace of Hanoi, though, and merchants more attuned to supply and demand suggest the widespread danger of a hunger that prolonged war will hardly satisfy. "We have enough," says Le Quang Liem, selling rice shipped up from the Mekong River delta on a stopgap basis to supplement the shortfalls in the north, but "people elsewhere do not." The state "does not have a good system of buying rice and does not encourage people to produce rice." Analysis of cause and effect revolves around drought—two bad harvests in a row—but the inference is clear. Life would be easier if authorities invested more in food for the people, less in feeding an expeditionary force in another country.

Behind a desk heaped with papers and poetry books, David Smith, an Englishman in charge of the United Nations Development Program here, warns visitors of impending disaster. "There is a real famine situation. Food production is not adequate for the population," rising by 2.5 percent a year. Smith accuses the United States of making matters worse by pressuring other Western nations not to provide aid or engage in trade as long as Vietnam keeps troops in Cambodia. "The United States is shirking its responsibility."

With about 4 million people facing starvation, Vietnamese officials acknowledge the need for "emergency" shipments of food and fertilizer. They say they don't want to appear "like beggars" and make public appeals, but they openly spread the word among Western embassies and journalistic visitors. In the worst food crisis since 1945, when 2 million people starved in the aftermath of harsh Japanese rule before the end of World War II, the official press and radio carry little news about Cambodia.

Or, more precisely, when one does hear about Cambodia, it's not about the ebb and flow of a conflict that has simmered on for more than nine years, ever since Vietnamese troops swarmed across the border at the end of 1978 and drove the bloodied Pol Pot regime into the *maquis*. Rather, it's to reassure the world that the troops will be home by 1990—beginning with the return of 50,000 of them this year. "We fully believe we can do that," insists Major General Tran Dong Man, editor in chief of *Quan Doi Nhan Dan*, People's Army, the daily paper of the armed forces.

The fact that western visitors have quick access to General Man reflects Vietnam's desire to get across a message. It is that Vietnam is willing at least to go halfway toward meeting the American demand for withdrawal from Cambodia—though it's not about to drop its support for the regime that it's propped up in Phnom Penh since Pol Pot's hasty departure. Hanoi-watchers at the American embassy in Bangkok scoff at such reassurances, arguing instead for the "legitimacy" of a Cambodian coalition that includes the once-hated Khmer Rouge along with factions loyal to Prince Norodom Sihanouk, driven out with U.S. connivance in 1970, and Son Sann, a weak middle-of-the-roader with few guerrillas of his own.

General Man's confidence about Cambodia, expressed over cups of tea in the musty reception room of his newspaper, the second largest in the country after the party's *Nhan Dan*, stems from the official view that the small Cambodian army built up by Vietnamese advisers and Soviet arms can hold off the Khmer Rouge on its own. "There might be some support from China for the Khmer Rouge," says Man, who edited the paper all through the war against the Americans, "but do they have any strength?"

Behind the predilection to get out of Cambodia, though, lies an almost wistful hope. Could diplomacy replace war if the irrepressible Sihanouk were drawn through negotiations into endorsing the Vietnamese-backed regime in Phnom Penh? Might Sihanouk then convince the Chinese to diminish their support of the Khmer Rouge—and return to Phnom Penh in a coalition acceptable to all sides?

Unlikely though such a solution might seem, General Man believes China may find Cambodia a treacherous battleground. "China has no trail like the Ho Chi Minh Trail in the Vietnam war," he says, using the name first applied by American military officers to the road network through eastern Laos and Cambodia down which Hanoi shipped arms to fight the Americans and South Vietnamese. "They can wage a guerrilla war, but not a big war."

Vietnamese leaders object strenuously to comparisons between their avowed desire to pull their troops out of Cambodia and the Soviet Union's withdrawal from Afghanistan. They say the Soviets, pumping in about $2 billion in aid, mostly military, aren't pressuring them at all to adopt an "Afghan-style" solution. "The situation in Afghanistan is different," says Man, not quite specifying why.

Comparisons, though, are irresistible. Vietnam's troops level in Cambodia, by Hanoi's own admission, is only a few thousand below that of the Soviet Union in Afganistan. The Khmer Rouge foe, like the Afghan rebels, operate out of refugee camps—right across Cambodia's western border in Thailand. The Khmer Rouge, like the *mujahadeen*, rely on outside aid—from China—funneled largely through Thailand. Vietnamese leader Nguyen Van Linh, like Soviet leader Mikhail Gorbachev, preaches the need to cut expenses and get on with reforms.

The Russian watchwords *glasnost* and *perestroika* are definitely not part of the vocabulary of Vietnamese officials, always anxious not to appear under Soviet influence. Still, it is almost fashionable here now for bureaucrats to show off a new "openness" in interviews with foreigners eager to hear about economic reform—or even "restructuring." For one who covered the war in the south two decades ago, an offer to meet Nguyen Xuan Oanh, advertised by a spokesman from the Foreign Press Center as a "Harvard graduate," is almost unsettling.

Could the dapper gentleman with the club tie be the same deputy leader of the old U.S.-backed regime who once briefed reporters on the potential for "economic takeoff" in smiling interviews in the Caravelle Hotel in Saigon? Known to a generation of Americans as "Jack Owen," Oanh now offers the wisdom of his Ph.D. in economics at Harvard and his capitalist indoctrination in the south to Vietnamese leaders tutored in hard-line radicalism. "Most of the reform today came from my ideas," Oanh says flatly in an interview. "They know what I have to say is not that bad."

Oanh's message: "There isn't that much difference between capitalism and socialism. We try very hard to make the best of both worlds." At the heart of the new philosophy is the idea that capitalism may serve best in what could be a long transition to true socialism.

Oanh turns neat phrases to explain the process by which Vietnam hopes to establish its own model—adapted from neither its Soviet benefactor nor its former American enemy. "We have started on a series of reforms of business administration and the management of production. We try to free the forces of production"—meaning producers should have local autonomy, even the power to make personal profits. He distinguishes between reviving the north and reforming the recalcitrant south, a freewheeling mélange of profit-seekers and peasants. "Here in the north all you have is state enterprises, but in the south you have private enterprise. We encourage the state and cooperatives in the north, but in the south we encourage joint ventures and private ownership."

Oanh, who regrets not having accepted a high-paying job with the World Bank or International Monetary Fund many years ago, now is preparing his government to apply for western loans. He hopes to convince an IMF team that the country has enough economic viability to qualify for major benefits. To do so, Vietnam must wipe out a current inflation rate of well over 1,000 percent a year, as seen in the prices of dollars and goods on black markets that flourish almost as openly in Hanoi as in Ho Chi Minh City.

From Hang Gai or Silk Street in Hanoi to Dong Khoi or Revolution Street—Rue Catinat in the French period, Tu Do under Diem, Ky, and Thieu—in Saigon, almost any shopkeeper will gladly exchange dollars for *dong*. The rates are usually higher in mercantile Saigon than in Hanoi, but either way you can begin to spend them by picking up lacquerware or brocades or porcelain at laughably low prices. In a society that cracks down on any real dissent, you needn't worry about the police seizing you in mid-deal. Your guide may even volunteer to change money for you at a rate at least three times higher than that available "legally."

By 1990, Oanh predicts, the black market in currency will be almost gone. He sets that near-magical year, coinciding with completion of withdrawal from Cambodia, as the deadline for the government somehow to have cut inflation to a mere 20 percent while holding its foreign debt to about $1 billion. As an example of how to build incentive, he's helped establish a showcase Bank for Industry and Trade in entrepreneurial Cholon, the Chinese business district of Ho Chi Minh City.

Loaning money both to socialist-style collectives and strictly private business schemes, the bank theoretically sets a nationwide precedent. "It's like the commercial banks that existed previously," says Lu Sanh Thai, bank director. "Our initial capital comes from shareholders"— with debtors paying interest rates from 9 percent for state enterprises and 9.9 percent for private business and services. "We continue to have a planned economy," says Huynh Ba Son, vice director, "but with more technicians, not administrative services."

How far down—or up—does such experimentation permeate? In both Hanoi and Ho Chi Minh City, the impression is, not very. Oanh says "small and medium-sized private business in Ho Chi Minh City now constitutes 60 percent of the city's gross domestic product," but wages have so little purchasing power that one assumes many government officials are corrupt. "Nobody in Vietnam relies only on his salary," says a shopkeeper in Hanoi who served the government until "retiring." "If you want to be rich," says a government worker with a coveted motorcycle, "you have to have two jobs."

Exactly how the government views what it acknowledges as the "chaos" of the economy remains a mystery even to those who specialize in figuring it out. Nguyen Van Linh may appear reform-minded, but no one is sure about the real views of Vo Van Kiet, the chairman of the state planning commission who served as acting prime minister before Do Muoi, a vice premier responsible for several economic ministries, emerged as prime minister in June.

The power play that put Do Muoi in that job at 71 defies certain analysis. Confucian respect for seniority, more than anything else, may be the best explanation for why Do Muoi was the choice ahead of Vo Van Kiet, 66, who seemed in line for the post. Another factor may have been Do Muoi's revolutionary reputation as a "disciplinarian," perhaps a "hard-liner," the sort to crack down on corruption and inefficiency. He promised almost at once to keep up the fight against inflation and carry on withdrawal from Cambodia—not exactly revealing, but reassuring to those who thought he might oppose economic reform.

Through it all, the bureaucracy grinds relentlessly on, propping up a new class of middle managers to whom the security of a government or party post—with guaranteed rice ration—is the due reward for years of wartime service. Southerners caught on the wrong side in the war complain they aren't eligible for state jobs and their children can't get decent educations. Economic hardship, though, cuts all ways. Faithful government workers here say the real "elite" consists of southern businessmen coddled by reformist or at least tolerant cadres. One of my guides in Hanoi spots the southerners in the lines outside Ho Chi Minh's mausoleum from the worldly suits of the men and the bright *ao dai* of the women.

Oanh, who lives in Ho Chi Minh City but flies regularly to Hanoi, hopes that a new investment law will attract foreign businessmen. Might Americans in search of a profit return once the United States relaxes restraints? Dreams of American capitalism staging a comeback here betray the disillusionment with the Soviets, whose 10,000 advisers are confined mainly to large projects that seem unlikely to provide quick relief.

Nowhere is the drive for reform more apparent than in efforts to revive agriculture, always the key to long-term stability. "Each farmer is a small capitalist," observes Oanh. "They own tractors and Hondas. They don't like the idea of being collectivized." As many as three fourths of the farmers in the Mekong River delta are wedded to private enterprise—though provincial authorities buy most of the crops they sell beyond their own villages.

The prosperity of the Mekong River delta buoys the north in time of hardship. Small cargo vessels move the rice from south to north almost in convoys. "The south had the beginnings of a capitalist country when the Americans were there," says Oanh, "so when they can't do it they feel sorry for themselves." It's time the United States got over its "Vietnam war syndrome." There have been "no stumbling blocks" to U.S.-Vietnamese diplomatic relations, "but there have been pretexts such as Cambodia"—one that Vietnamese leaders say will vanish when the troops come home.

Hanoi, May 1985

Last time I was here I'd seen a train packed with teenage recruits in green fatigues, an odd sight considering the United States had just signed the "Paris Peace" that was supposed to end the war. I'd been here for just one day on that trip—a passenger on a chartered Royal Air Lao planeload of journalists that flew from Vientiane into Gia Lam airport on the morning of March 29, 1973. We were whisked to the downtown prison where American POWs stayed—and witnessed the departure of the last batch that afternoon on a C141 before boarding the same Royal Air Lao plane back to Vientiane.

Not that I'd thought for a moment the war really was over. The emptiness of the Paris Peace was all too plain from the sound of gunfire on the roads leading out of Saigon. On this latest trip, though, the war really was over—a decade over, to be precise, and I thought

Hanoi, the hub of the great Vietnamese military and bureaucratic machine, might really be different. I expected a newness, a sense of "revolutionary progress," of change. I had no illusions about the degree of freedom, much less happiness, instilled by the ideologues who cling to power here, but at least, I thought, the city might now display some brave-new-world styles, courtesy of the Soviet Union and other East European countries.

Not a chance. In fact, the small shops on the narrow streets were just as threadbare, as half empty as I remembered them from the few fleeting minutes in which I'd been able to glimpse them more than twelve years earlier. The shopkeepers—remnants of free enterprise in a system deadened by more than 30 years of otherwise rigid collectivization—talked hesitantly, with occasional traces of real candor, through the guide supplied by the foreign ministry at my expense, though not at my request.

"I did the same work ten years ago," said a woman selling cloth in a small shop. "No, I cannot make as much money now as then," she admitted with a slight shrug. "Prices now are higher. Before, life was better."

All along the street, entrepreneurial Vietnamese peddled whatever they could—digital watches from such capitalist enclaves as Taiwan and Hong Kong, eyeglass frames, ballpoint pens, vitamin pills, pants stitched together on decrepit sewing machines hidden in the shadows. Some of the goods came in legally, but Western diplomats in Hanoi say most are smuggled. Vietnamese officials returning from overseas trips rank among the worst offenders. They routinely carry back stereo sets, motorcycles, transistor radios—items one could never obtain legitimately under the present economic system.

The influx is never enough to meet demand, and prices keep rising despite repeated government efforts to set the value on such staples as food and clothing. The great unanswered question: How can anyone afford a bicycle for sale, at the equivalent in Vietnamese *dong* of $100, when monthly wages average less than 10 percent of that figure? The presumption: Beneath a surface of great government "plans" and "objectives" and "systems" lurks a network of corruption that provides the real base of influence and power.

This theory becomes reality when you discover just how easy it is to change dollars on the flourishing black market. Wander into a *dac san* (restaurant) and chat with the smiling manager. He'll bargain briefly, then slip you a brick-sized bundle of *dong* in exchange for your dollars as long as he's fairly certain no one at a table in the front of the place is looking. Or walk around the lake in the center of the city, then stray down a street past shops showing off the best in Hanoi styles—rich, embroidered silk *ao dai*. Simply show a piece of paper revealing the number of dollars you've got, and someone will make an offer. Bargaining is the key, but if you're headed south to Ho Chi Minh City, hoard those dollars for changing there. The rates are higher in old Saigon.

The manager of a chic restaurant specializing in good wine and French-style cuisine, Nguyen Van Ngoc, will quickly try to put to rest any doubts you might have about the stability of the Vietnamese economy. But then, he has little to worry about—his cabinets are filled with bottles of French wine and brandy, both in heavy demand by the regulars from Eastern Europe and such sympathetic Western nations as Sweden and Finland. Somehow, you'll never find out just why, Ngoc's got it made, but don't think for a moment he avoided his duty to the fatherland.

From 1968 to 1971, he tells you, he was a driver on the Ho Chi Minh Trail—extremely hazardous duty when you consider how heavily the Americans bombed it. "The American planes attacked every day," said Ngoc, who came home a sergeant. "I was very lucky. Some of my friends were killed." In 1968, he said, he drove some American POWs "to the rear," meaning Hanoi. "They were treated very well," he insisted.

His brother-in-law, Hoang Huu Hy, a partner in the venture, said he was wounded in South Vietnam's Quang Nam province in 1969 while serving as a rifleman. "I feel angry at the Americans," he said without animosity against a backdrop of walls festooned with East German travel posters and a Sanyo calendar. "Now we have difficulties. Oh, we can accept them."

Contrast the luxuries savored by Ngoc and Hy with the hardships visible in the government markets. In the heart of the city, in a drab concrete structure described as a department store, crowds wait to buy pieces of paper-thin cloth at prices lower than those in private shops. Trouble is, most of the counters are bare, and displays of new sneakers and sweaters and sandals are just that—display items, not for sale.

Ask any top-ranking official for an explanation of the country's problems, and the answer is always the same. "We are not a rich country, we are a poor country," acknowledged Hoang Tung, secretary of the central committee of the Workers' Party and former top editor of *Nhan Dan*, the party newspaper. "But we have achieved things more precious than goods or clothes. We have ended foreign domination, and now gradually we settle the problems of the economy. We have unified our country and started our construction. Step by step we are building."

To get the job done, Hanoi counts on the Soviet Union. About 5,000 Soviet aid workers are scattered around the country, picking up on many projects in the south where the Americans left off. The Soviets, though, don't even begin to supply the hard cash needed to buoy the economy, and they're clearly resented.

"Lien So, Lien So," said with contempt, is a refrain you keep hearing as you stroll through the city. The words mean "Soviet Union, Soviet Union," but the tone is insulting. Let it be known that you're *ong tay*, a "man from the West," said a Dutchman working for the United Nations, and people are likely to respond with the equivalent of "good, good."

Part of the problem is practicality. What, after all, can Vietnam really do with the grand new Cultural Hall donated by the Soviets "for the workers," or with the monument of Lenin that Vietnamese and Soviet "volunteers" are building on the vacant lot nearby? The commoners in Vietnam want a better standard of living, not monuments and promises.

The Soviets sense Vietnamese resentment and, fearing confrontation, stay bottled up in a compound, away from this strange and potentially hostile environment. Once a week foreigners go for the big night out—to dance the night away at a hotel party where diplomats, aid workers, and local elitists rock and roll to Western music played by surprisingly good local combos.

The laid-back mood makes for good conversation with normally reserved Eastern diplomats and aid workers. Here you're sure to hear what it's really like to spend a tour in Vietnam, surviving on shipments from home, boiling with frustration over bureaucratic red tape, and marking the days until you're "back in the world," to borrow the old GI expression. "I don't like the Vietnamese, they're dirty," said a Czech woman sent here to teach English, of all things, looking flirtatiously at a Polish official while her husband chatted with a Vietnamese girl.

"The Vietnamese come here, yes," said a woman working for the United Nations, "but they're only the upper classes." The music blared out of the hotel dining room, audible down the otherwise quiet street where a Vietnamese woman cooked ears of corn over a small stove and sold them for several *dong* apiece.

A few blocks away, a red neon sign flashed "café" from an enticing small window. Inside were magazine blowups of western film stars of a generation ago and fading ads for French and American liquors. Not that you can get any western booze here—only bottles of Russian vodka lined a cabinet shelf.

Across the street, around the corner, another "café" competed in what is clearly the city's closest approach to a nightclub district. A couple of bureaucrats—identifiable as such by their uniformlike slacks and short-sleeve jackets—chatted at a small table, and a young couple snuggled in a corner. The bureaucrats, reluctantly answering some questions, admitted to "shortages" and "lack of spare parts" for basic equipment but said they have enough. I wondered vaguely what the 3.5 million Vietnamese still in the army, fighting in Cambodia, guarding against China, most of all keeping the country from exploding in a score of civil wars, do during leave—if they get any.

The next day, among the stalls of a sprawling government market, I saw a couple of one-legged beggars, possibly war veterans, and a small boy leading a blind woman. In one of the stalls a smiling old lady sold delicious-looking moon cakes. "Not many people can buy," she complained. "They don't have enough money. The price of rice is higher now than before."

Another woman, overhearing the conversation, said taxes were going up. "Some people don't sell anything." She got by, though, on the salary her husband makes as a truck driver. Together they scrape together enough for themselves and count on help occasionally from their five children, now in their 20s. A sixth, a son, was killed while fighting around Kontum, in the central highlands, in 1970.

"I am very sad," she said. "First his friends told me—and then the government formally confirmed it." Does she ever wonder why he fought? "It is an obligation to fight the enemy," she answered simply, impassively, before my guide, who rose to the rank of captain and has a son now serving in Cambodia, broke into the conversation. "That's enough," he stated matter-of-factly.

I wondered how the rural countryside would compare with the city.

My guide took me to Binh Da, a prosperous village in the richest rice country of the Red River delta. It was a mere 14 miles southwest of the capital, a pleasant jaunt down paved roads, through fertile land where poverty and economic hardship seem impossible. Local officials gladly confirmed the level of prosperity and happiness, and one of them pointed out the progress of the area since the B52 strikes of the "Christmas bombing" ordered by President Nixon in December 1972 before the signing of the Paris Peace.

"None were shot down here," he said, "but at night we saw fights." A mile or two away, he told me, you can see the depression in the ground where the bombs fell—now planted over with rice. "This is not a military target, but the Americans bomb it anyway. It is the mistake of the United States government to bomb the rice farmers." Beside him in the small open-fronted commune office, another official said he served six years in the south, near Saigon, as a squad leader. "I was wounded twice, but when I came back I got money from the government."

In an old pagoda down the road, the commune chairman, Nguyen Tien Ty, said he served as a battalion commander around Ban Me Thuot in the highlands but escaped without a scratch. "I hate the American soldiers," he said, parroting a government line, "but we love the American people because they support the Vietnamese people." Outside the pagoda, I noticed fighting cocks, feathers shining, beaks defiant, preening in wicker cages. Cockfights were on for the afternoon, the height of the carnival after the officials have handed out all the special achievement medals. Kids eagerly surged around the birds, and men scrutinized carefully, betting secretively on the winners.

It was an image of vitality and violence, but it's hardly typical. Off the guided tour are the "military areas," the projects that Swedish and other western aid workers say are falling far short of goals, desolate stretches of overgrown forests and farmlands forgotten in the maze of red tape of a deadening bureaucratic machine. "So far we've seen no evidence of a desire for reform," said a western diplomat based here. "They're ten years into reunification and importing more than ever. How long can the government expect people to tighten their belts? One cannot help wondering if war isn't a necessity for them—but how long can they go on like this?"

That's a question that burns into the minds of most visitors as they survey the throngs bicycling silently through the city, to work, to market, to home and family—but rarely to play. "These people seem to be motivated by war," said an Englishwoman who commutes between here and Saigon for the United Nations. "It's the only thing that interests them. There's an underlying cruelty about them. Look, their faces somehow contort." It's a harsh judgment but one that seems hard to refute in this setting of pervasive suffering and fear.

Hanoi, March 1973

The city is bustling again after months of war and fear. The women and children have returned from the countryside. The schools are opened. The streets are clogged, not with cars and motor scooters so much as bicycles, creaking buses, and trucks.

The sense of relief with the dawning of peace is not a propaganda line but a daily reality. You see it in the faces of the children waving from the sidewalks and alleys, in the relaxed poses of men and women gossiping over tea in tiny roadside stalls, in the casual exuberance of soldiers and workers playing soccer near a partially destroyed factory.

"Most of the people were evacuated to the countryside last year," says a young foreign ministry official accompanying reporters through the city on the day of the release of the last American prisoners. "They returned after the peace. During the war, the only ones left behind were the soldiers, officials from different services and workers, that's all. Most of the schoolchildren, teachers, and housewives were evacuated."

For the people of Hanoi, population 1.2 million, the war did not reach its worst phase until President Nixon ordered resumption of the American bombing of North Vietnam last April—and finally authorized the destruction of targets much closer to the heart of the city. Even then, the bombs generally hit specific targets—factories, power plants, the railroad station—and did not fall accidentally on residential areas except in isolated, highly publicized cases.

The sense of imminent death, however, was enough to frighten a populace and city administration to whom the air war had previously been somewhat remote. "The last was the heaviest," says a young girl, citing Nixon's "twelve days" of bombing in December, the Christmas bombing, before the final talks.

It was not until the signing of the Paris Peace agreement that the life of the city returned to normal—the brightest it has ever been in the memory of foreign journalists and diplomats permanently assigned here. Now, small private shops peddling clothes, shoes, bicycle parts— the necessities of daily life—thrive from dawn to dusk on streets lined with yellow-painted ornate buildings dating from the French colonial period.

"We try to repair quickly," says one of the officials escorting the foreign press. "We need space to construct our society"—and the sight of workers repairing the airport, the devastated railway repair shop, and other damaged buildings testifies to the resilience of Vietnamese society. Perhaps even more significant—and ominous for the future of the Paris Peace—is what has already been repaired: the single-track railway running 100 kilometers southeast to the port of Haiphong as well as the Long Bien bridge, extending two miles across the Red River, a canal, and a series of rice paddies.

"Last year when the river was at its highest level, we have many raids every day," says the official as our bus rumbles across the river in a line of trucks and other buses. Beside us, a passenger train carrying teenage boys in fresh, new fatigue uniforms rushes by in the opposite direction, toward Haiphong.

"To live, to work, to study, that is the example," says the sign in Vietnamese on a workers' apartment block. "Hail our great victories for peace," says another sign near the always tranquil lake of Hoan Kiem, the Redeemed Sword, in the center of the city. Around the lake, on a wide street running past stores and restaurants, traffic almost grinds to a halt at the height of the morning rush hour. Tempers flare and horns blare as a blue-and-white tram rattles by on tracks originally built by the French.

Crowds gather in front of some of the shops, and small boys wander and play by the lake near the entrance to the Ngoc Son pagoda, on a tiny island reached by a footbridge. One boy, the son of a shopkeeper, says he spent six months last year in a camp some 200 kilometers from here. Another, sitting on the railing of the bridge, did not leave Hanoi until December—the worst period of the bombing. "I do not think there will be any more war," he says. "I'm glad to be back in school again."

It is difficult, in a few hours on the ground here, to tell whether the city is "at war" or "at peace." Soldiers and security guards are everywhere, but so are civilians. "Now the movies and theaters are open again," says a foreign diplomat, remembering that power often failed as American planes dove in on generators at the bombing's height. "We would rather sacrifice everything, but we never sacrifice our freedom," says one of the signs near the lake. After years of sacrifice, it is easy to imagine the city streets jammed some day with motorcycles and cars and the shops overflowing with more than bare necessities.

Saigon scene, 1968. Statue of South Vietnamese soldier dominates Lam Son Square in downtown Saigon, Hanoi troops tore down the statue soon after they arrived on April 30, 1975. Building on right is the Rex, where JUSPAO, Joint U.S. Public Affairs Office, held briefings known as "five o'clock follies."

Saigon cop—they were known as "white mice"—directs traffic at intersection of Tu Do and Le Loi Streets outside famed Hotel Caravelle, Saigon, 1968.

Saigon cops, April 1995, stop girls for traffic offense in downtown Saigon at corner of old Tu Do Street, now Dong Khoi Street, and Le Loi (whose name remains the same since he was national hero who drove out the Chinese—see Lam Son in glossary).

Shop scene in Saigon, 1985.

Newly redecorated Rex Hotel, with sign "30.4" denoting the date of the surrender of the old South Vietnamese regime, in April 1985.

The old French-built city hall of Saigon—now the seat of the Ho Chi Minh City People's Committee—up the street from the Rex Hotel.

300 billion dollars—that's what these American presidents spent on the war, according to black and white photos in a museum on the final offensive in Ho Chi Minh City (see Chapter 1, "We Must Accept"). The presidents are Eisenhower, Kennedy, Johnson on top, Nixon and Ford on the bottom.

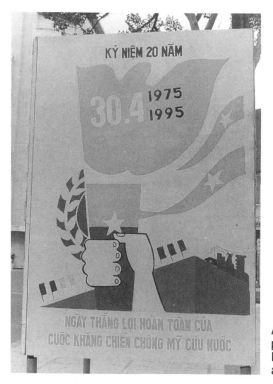

Anniversary celebration— poster gives the dates of Liberation and twentieth anniversary.

The American generals—Harkins, Westmoreland, Abrams and Weyand, with Vietnamese spelling, in black and white photos near entrance to museum mentioned in Chapter 1, "We Must Accept."

Billboard notes the twentieth anniversary of Giai Phong, Liberation, on April 30, 1975. The design is Vietnam flag—with Ho Chi Minh's picture at right.

Cathedral on Dong Khoi (formerly Tu Do) street decked out in its own way for the big twentieth anniversary. Attendance is higher than ever.

Bike piled high with rice bags in museum shows how the supplies moved down the Ho Chi Minh trail. Behind are weapons, also proudly on display.

Read all about it. Western papers for sale in Ho Chi Minh City.

March 29, 1973: French colonial-era trams run along Hanoi street, as they did in colonial period (see Chapter 3, Seat of Revolution).

More trams 15 years later, 1988. Hanoi is doing away with these relics of the past in move to modernize, broaden streets.

Hanoi Street scene: Soviet soldier eyeing two Vietnamese girls, 1985.

Hi kids! Vietnamese children mug for the camera south of Hanoi, 1988.

Armies past. Vietnamese soldier statues, nineteenth-century style, guard one of the imperial tombs outside Hue, 1988.

Guardpost with Vietnamese soldier between Hue and Danang in Hai Van Pass, 1988 (see Chapter 4, Cities Between).

Old war. American cargo vehicle provides permanent shelter for Vietnamese soldiers in Hai Van Pass between Hue and Danang, 1988.

Farmer inside Hue Citadel,
1988. The citadel was the
scene of one of the worst
battles of the war, during
Tet offensive, 1968.

The family of Duong The Tu, pen name "Le Viet," outside their apartment in
San Jose, June 1995. That's Duong The Tu and wife Nguyen Thi Mai with
daughter Bac and sons Tuyen and Vinh (see Chapter 2, "Too Dangerous to
Talk").

4

Cities Between

Danang, May 1988

They bear an uncanny resemblance to the American civilian contractor types I last saw here 15 or so years ago. Their skins are burnished red and brown under the sun, they wear sloppy sport shirts, and they look as if they are slightly hung over.

They are Soviet aircraft mechanics grabbing quick coffees and sandwiches from the snack bar by the decrepit passenger terminal at Danang air base. Vu Binh, my guide from Hanoi—you have to hire one from the Foreign Press Center whether you like it or not if you're a journalist—assures me they are not military people disguised as civilians. The Soviets, he says, are not hiding a single plane of their own in the revetments built by the Americans soon after the marines splashed ashore in 1965. Those long grey noses I see protruding from the concrete barns are Soviet-built MiGs, Binh admits sure enough, but they are all in the Vietnamese air force. Anyway, he says, these guys are just servicing the Vietnam Air Tupolevs that bind this port city on the central coast to the capital in the north and Ho Chi Minh City in the south.

The sight of Soviet mechanics is just one of the slightly jarring ironies that hits me as I return to this region that I first visited in late 1965. Dashing in and around town with my guide and a representative of the local "people's committee," I see the empty airstrip and revet-

55

ments of another base that I have almost forgotten. "We have no planes there at all," says Binh, an amiable young graduate of Hanoi University whose only memory of the war is that of going to the countryside with other children when U.S. planes were bombing around Hanoi. "We don't have enough money for it." He points to some craggy outcroppings up ahead. Then I remember. Here, near the base of what the GIs had called "Marble Mountain," was the Marble Mountain air base from which the marines had flown helicopters and observation planes.

I stare at Marble Mountain—Ngu Hanh Son, "Mountain Like Five Fingers" to the Vietnamese—as we drive toward it at sunset. From here Viet Cong guerrillas once shelled U.S. forces. Here, where we see a gaping cave in the rock, the Viet Cong ran a crude first-aid station. Around the villages to the south and west, "Dodge City" to marines who patrolled the area, the Viet Cong and North Vietnamese waged an incessant propaganda war even when they were too weakened militarily to fire more than occasional sniper bullets. My guide and I begin walking the 157 marble steps to the top. On the way we see names in Chinese characters and Vietnamese carved into the rocks. Only a couple of U.S. marines or army soldiers, it seems, paused long enough to inscribe their signatures for posterity.

By the time you finish scrambling up you can see why the marines—and the army soldiers who succeeded them after the marines pulled out—were not exactly enamored of the place. At the entrance to a cave transformed into a pagoda: plaques honoring both a "hero" who survived a battle here and a women's artillery unit said to have "destroyed 19 American planes" down below by mortar fire. From a pinnacle of marble you can see all Danang to the north, the jungles stretching to mountains to the west—and the vast expanse of the South China Sea. Inside several caves riddling the mountaintop: statues of Buddha chiseled into marble long before the Viet Cong or Americans ever fought here. None of the plaques, of course, notes that U.S. forces actually held the mountain for much of the war.

Back in the middle of town, our little entourage pauses at what used to be the Marine Press Center. Once a pad for a legion of correspondents, cameramen, and photographers, it's now Frozen Fish Factory Number 14. I tell my guide I was staying here when guerrillas staged the first attack of the Tet offensive about a mile away on January 29, 1969—a day ahead of their attacks almost everywhere else. A few blocks away: the old U.S. consulate, transformed for a while into a "war atrocities museum." Now Vietnamese go there to look at foreign videos—including Oliver Stone's *Platoon,* a popular, officially sanctioned hit showing throughout the country.

Across the river, traversed by twin U.S.- and French-made spans, is Nguyen Ai Quoc Academy, "Nguyen the Patriot," the name that Ho Chi Minh used while a young radical in France. In the old days, I explain to Binh, the ramshackle structure was "Three MAF"—headquarters of the third marine amphibious force, including all the U.S. marines in Vietnam. Now Workers' Party disciplinarians train young members there to serve as cadres.

Images and memories of a war ago fleet by as we drive through the streets of the city—home of about 330,000 people, the area's only port big enough for oceangoing vessels, and a potential light industrial center as well. Back at the Oriental Hotel, a seedy way station that I cannot recall having seen before, a couple of former guerrilla soldiers chat over glasses of lemonade about the war as they saw and fought it from the other side. Dressed in clean white shirts, they talk quietly, politely in response to my questions as relayed through Vu Binh.

Reconciliation, it is clear, is the order of the day when it comes to dealing with visitors from the erstwhile enemy camp. The reason, as authorities in Hanoi have made all too clear, is they are desperate to form diplomatic relations with the United States in hopes of picking up some aid, trade, and possibly even investment. How else can the country hope to recover from drought, corruption, and economic inefficiency? Nobody much likes—or trusts—the Soviets, who in any case don't have all that much money to throw around.

One of the old VC types, Tran Van Than, once a top provincial official with the National Liberation Front, clears up a question to which I had wanted an answer for more than 20 years: Why in hell did the Tet offensive break out a day earlier here than elsewhere? It was all a mistake, Than admits. "There were some technical problems. The calendar was a day earlier here than in the north. We got the order one day earlier." If the attack on Danang was doomed to quick failure, he points out, battles broke out "all over the province." While I was rushing from the Marine Press Center toward the sounds of rifle fire down the street, Than was "directing the offensive in that area on the southeast of the city."

Than, now 62, rail-thin, with wispy, silvering hair, has a ready explanation for the eventual withdrawal of the Viet Cong and North Vietnamese from their targets. "Our object was not to occupy, just to cause casualties," he says. "During that offensive we could bring as many as possible casualties on both the GIs and the puppet troops"—an achievement that helped shift public opinion against the war in the United States. Indeed, he maintains, "from the beginning we gained what we planned." He gives a mixed report on the fighting capabilities of the GIs. "They reacted quite fiercely," making "full use of their firepower with bombs and shelling," but they also "had to flee" some areas.

In the end, though, it was the withdrawal of U.S. units under terms of the Paris Peace, signed on January 27, 1973, by chief negotiators Henry Kissinger and Le Duc Tho, that made the difference. "From 1968 to 1975 it was clear to the puppet troops that failure would come soon so they were frightened," he says. "The balance of forces in the region changed critically after the withdrawal of U.S. troops."

These days a leader of the largely powerless Fatherland Front, a state-sponsored umbrella for different political groupings, Than looks back on a war that was "fierce and severe" beyond the U.S.-defended population centers. "When the Americans asserted the full use of their weapons throughout the province, except in the city, houses were damaged, trees cut down or defoliated."

Beside him, sipping lemonade, sits Vu Vuong Dan, 49. Now with Than on the Fatherland Front, Dan describes himself as "just a guerrilla" in the years of fighting. "I carried a rifle, guided the NLF, carried supplies," says Dan, wounded several times by shrapnel from artillery shells. In 1975 he led an attack on a province head-quarters at a town south of here that he had first hit seven years earlier in the Tet offensive.

"There was almost no fighting" in the final days before the surrender of Saigon government forces, he says. "Even one guerrilla could capture 100 puppet soldiers." He still is not sure how to view the GIs—those whom he fought and others whom he saw while in civilian clothes, on streets, in bars near the bases. "Most of the GIs were forced to come here. Our enemy was those who tried to kill the people. It was the American government—that was the enemy"—the standard line for old-time guerrilla fighters whose careers in the bush hardly prepared them for the current economic war.

Hue, May 1988

Drive north from Danang through the Hai Van Pass, twisting among steep slopes overlooking the sea, and you arrive three or four hours later in this hallowed imperial capital, scene of one of the bloodiest, longest battles of the Tet offensive. Now ex-guerrillas dream of drawing Western tourists—and U.S. dollars—to look at the ruins that are the legacy of a dynasty that briefly ruled all Vietnam before gradually falling to the French colonialists in the 19th century.

"We want to build this city into a tourist center," says Le Phuoc Thuy, vice chairman of the People's Committee—or deputy mayor—in charge of education and culture. Thuy and his boss, Nguyen Van Me, chairman of the people's committee, meaning mayor, talk of the revival of Hue while recalling their glory days battling U.S. marines and army soldiers for most of the month of February 1968. Focal point of much of the 25-day battle—and the city's appeal for tourists: the walled citadel built by the Vietnamese emperor Gia Long in the early 1800s. Thuy looks on history—ancient, modern, and future—from a distinctive perspective. "I was in the Hue citadel during the 1968 offensive in charge of the youth," says Thuy, now 46.

Thuy's headquarters for much of the battle was near the Palace of Supreme Harmony, in which Vietnamese emperors, ensconced on a gilt throne, received callers. The last occupant of the throne, the emperor Bao Dai, a puppet first of the French colonialists and then of the Japanese in World War II, fled to France in 1946. "We enjoy many good traditions that have many cultural values," says Thuy, sounding like a career tourist official. Thuy, who began his career leading demonstrations at the University of Hue in the early 1960s, sees little irony in his latter-day role venerating some of the values against which he once rebelled. The rationalizations roll quickly off his tongue as we talk in a meeting room in the French-built City Hall, across the Perfume River from the citadel.

"We show the citadel and the tombs of the old emperors so we could see what the feudalistic dynasty left behind as a treasure of the people's labor," he says. "It is the heritage of the people's sweat and labor." He appears more impassioned, though, as he describes evacuation of the citadel by communist forces finally forced to retreat before U.S. marines inside the outer walls and U.S. army soldiers from the first air cavalry division on the outside. "We went out late at night under shelling from the U.S. seventh fleet. Thousands of us left together. Many were new recruits. GIs and South Vietnamese puppet troops were everywhere. U.S. air cavalry helicopters flew every day and night."

The chairman of the committee, Nguyen Van Me, 40, was involved at the same time in an equally key military role—fighting outside the nearby U.S. air and military bases at Phu Bai and Ap Nam. "During the offensive they were shelled," says Me, mild-mannered and businesslike as he goes over the history. "After our main forces withdrew to the mountains, our agents were still working." Me and Thuy together returned in triumph to Hue in 1975, encountering almost no resistance from Saigon army forces left to fight alone when the last of the U.S. units pulled out in 1973. Named chairman of the People's Committee last year, Me now talks of a "multifaceted renovation" of the lagging economy of the city, almost as big as Danang in population, with 328,000 people.

"We are facing many difficulties," Me acknowledges, reflecting the relatively recent realism of leaders in Hanoi, but he's hoping enterprises ranging from handicrafts and fine arts to textiles and seafood will bring some measure of prosperity. Me and Thuy both blame the United States at least in part for the hardships of the city. "There are many consequences left by the war that are not easy for us to overcome," says Me, citing destruction of "natural resources, economic infrastructure," notably the forests beyond the rice paddies surrounding the city. "The Americans used dioxin, herbicides, defoliant, napalm bombs, Agent Orange. There are unexploded mines or bombs around U.S. and puppet army bases."

Thuy if anything appears more angry than Me—partly because he believes his years as a guerrilla permanently damaged his health. "I was the victim of U.S. chemical weapons," says Thuy, who shows no overt signs of illness. "I am not very healthy. I have some problems from so many years in the mountains." U.S. forces "tried every means to destroy our environment," he goes on, his voice rising in a show of emotion that he has difficulty conjuring when boasting of Hue's touristic attractions. "The forest was destroyed by chemical agents, napalm, and B52s. The damage affected the climate and the weather. Cultivated soil became less fertile. Villages were flattened."

Thuy loudly refutes charges that North Vietnamese forces executed about 6,000 residents of Hue—and dumped their bodies into mass graves—at the outset of the Tet offensive. "We executed some secret police and government officials, but the number is small." He attributes most of the deaths in the offensive to U.S. shelling and bombing. "When the puppet government returned" after the communist retreat, "they claimed all those killed were killed by our forces" but "many were killed at the same time" and dumped into what were to be very temporary graves. "It is very clear the Saigon government tried to distort the situation."

It's difficult to argue with Thuy, much less find the proof to counter this indictment, but he loses all credibility when he claims U.S. forces destroyed 80 percent of the city—including the imperial palace behind the throne room—in the 25 days they fought to recapture it. A walk through the citadel reveals most of the yellow-walled cement homes and shops as I saw them during and after the Tet offensive. An elderly caretaker, Nguyen Van Lam, says the palace was destroyed in fighting not in 1968 but in 1947. My guide, Vu Binh, who sided with Thuy when I tried to refute him in the interview, suddenly remembers hearing the palace was destroyed "in a fire"—long before most Americans had ever heard of Vietnam.*

"There was no bombing in this area," says caretaker Lam. "There was shelling." An ugly hole I recall having seen in the tiled roof of the throne room right after the offensive has long since been repaired. Along narrow streets where servants and courtiers of the emperor once lived, a tailor recalls seeing communist troops and then several days later U.S. marines outside his house. "When the National Liberation Front came, they were very kind," says Tran Viet Toan, now 54. "They didn't know anything about this area, and they always lost their way. They were from the north. No, they didn't kill civilians. They killed some people, but they were all high-ranking officers." As for the marines, "When there was no fighting, there was no problem, but in war they were very tough."

In the final days of the battle, Toan goes on, shells and bombs exploded around the nearby gate of the citadel's outer wall—miraculously still intact. Standing nearby, a former guerrilla, Thai Cong Duc, pulls up a shirtsleeve and reveals a long, ugly scar inflicted during the fighting. "We didn't prepare to stay long," says Duc, who guided northern troops as they infiltrated the city at the beginning of Tet. "At the end we were ordered to withdraw. We fulfilled our task." He grins

---

*Vietnamese officials have had singular success in getting across their version of events. Lonely Planet's *Vietnam: A Travel Survival Kit,* 1993 edition, reports that "most of the area inside the citadel . . . was flattened"—a deadpan travesty on history.

as he compares the U.S. marines and GIs with South Koreans whom he battled down the central coast. "The Koreans were very cruel. They would cut a child in two parts." It was "easier to fight against American GIs than Korean soldiers because GIs followed strictly what they learned about modern war" in training back home.

Across the Perfume River, at City Hall, leaders of the People's Committee wonder how to apply skills they learned as guerrillas to current problems. "Life is better now in the sense there is freedom," says Nguyen Nghiem, 36, a onetime student organizer, "but living standards are down, and there is lack of food and transport." Indeed, "it is very difficult to tell which is more difficult—war is human lives and hardships, and economic struggle is hardship and worry." Thuy invokes the spirit of final victory in 1975. "We are dreaming a glorious future. There can be no result without sacrifice."

Hung Dien, May 1988

The big talk fades when you go out of Hue to some of the nearby districts hardest hit by drought and economic incompetence.

In this district town, about ten miles north of the ancient imperial capital, Le Khac Phuc, 30, a math teacher, began seeing the immediate impact of the rice shortage in the region in April. "My students won't have enough rice to eat every day," says Phuc, talking in a coffee shop in the center of town. "They have to work too hard to help their parents. They cannot be intelligent. They have to go to the fields. Sometimes they are so hungry they cannot go to school. This is happening just now."

The food crisis here is typical of that in much of the central and northern regions. For the first time, the government is requesting "emergency" food aid from western countries. To many, the specter of hunger appears as a dreadful sequel to the suffering of war. "This province during the war suffered the most," says Nguyen Van Dieu, an official in Hue. "It is the worst area in Vietnam in climate and weather. We often say we are the victims of natural calamities and enemy invasion."

Around here, few people count on more than words by way of help from the government. Implicit in conversations is an undercurrent of criticism of a regime that may be incapable of dealing with the crisis. "The state has the responsibility to assist," says Tran Thi Thuan, 32, the wife of a local government administrator whom she met while they were both serving with the National Liberation Front during the war.

"We don't know what to do. The state has to be resourceful." Many former NLF soldiers, while aware of Hanoi's new realism, find the United States an easy scapegoat for their troubles. One complaint gaining credence in the drought-stricken center: Defoliation of vast swatches of jungle is responsible for altering weather patterns.

"Before the war this area was a forest," says Nguyen Binh, a one-time guerrilla, lounging under an abandoned U.S. army truck trailer in the Hai Van Pass, the pass of the sea clouds. "The trees were cleared by bombs and chemical agents. It changed the weather." Now, "there is a nutrition problem that affects productivity in this area. The farmers are in a terrible state." Towering high above him, slopes almost bare of trees testify to the impact of defoliation by U.S. forces clearing the jungle to rob communist troops of the cover from which they regularly staged ambushes.

Whatever the long-term effect of defoliation, farmers harvesting the rice agree times have never been tougher. "People are not eating enough," says Vo Van Giap, 45, pausing by a rice paddy. His five children, he says, "do not get enough to eat," and he has to trek miles into distant forests in search of firewood to sell on the village market. Giap, a onetime soldier in the old South Vietnamese army, blames only the weather for his fate—but observes the government is not doing much to help. "They don't give pesticides or fertilizer. We only get them in exchange for rice." Inevitably, farmers hark back to the wartime era when U.S. aid guaranteed food and money.

"We had more to eat at that time because we were given many things," says 35-year-old Vo Phuc Ba, who served seven years in the Saigon army. Still, he doesn't exactly look back fondly on the GIs whom he saw here. "They invaded our country. There was less freedom then. Now we can go anywhere we want"—in contrast to the constraints of wartime "areas of operations," "free fire zones," and often-mined roads and trails.

Freedom to move about, though, won't fill rice bowls. In this village, Nguyen Thi Gai, 32 and the mother of four, expecting her fifth child, reflects a pervasive, underlying bitterness. "We have to eat cassava, maize, and potatoes," she says, citing three foods that Vietnamese typically view as unsavory substitutes for rice. "There has been no aid. We need help"—a plea to which she expects no answer any time soon.

5

"Kill One ... Kill Them All"

Danang, May 1972

A steady drizzle was falling on the aluminum matting of the airstrip. The tin-roofed hangars and waiting rooms were abandoned, paint peeling and doors swinging loose on their hinges. Rusted, barbed-wire barriers were tumbling down and slashed. Across route one, endless rows of dirt-brown hootches stretched toward the grey-green of the rice paddies. Half-emptied sandbags were strewn around some of the hootches, deserted except for a few forlorn-looking South Vietnamese soldiers. An occasional jeep or truck splashed down a dirt road, veering around potholes and upturned oil drums.

It was my last view of what the Americans had once called "the Quang Tri combat base." I glimpsed it in the second week of April from the back seat of a battered French Citroën, rented for the day in the central market of Hue. We were returning from the shot and shelled remains of Dong Ha, a district center still loosely held by looting South Vietnamese rangers ten miles above Quang Tri and 50 miles north of Hue. Passing by the old Quang Tri base, built by marines in the first flush of American combat "involvement," one couldn't help but sense the nothingness, the futility of the GIs whom I had interviewed there nine months before.

"Few Americans or ARVNs [Army of the Republic of Vietnam]

really wanted to fight except for career-conscious officers concerned only in personal advancement," said a helicopter pilot in a reminiscing letter to me dated "31 March 1972," the day on which the North Vietnamese were launching their first attacks across the DMZ, or simply "the Z," for demilitarized zone. "This insane but not uncommon zeal accounted for the death and maiming of a number of my close fellow pilots," claimed the pilot, who had been smoking pot in a back room of the hangar when I met him and his crew on a deathly hot night in August. "Mature, responsible men," wrote the pilot, "allowed selfish emotion to supplant cool logic."

Neither the pilot nor his crew, at the time, had seemed particularly interested in the war itself. Their primary concern, at least then, was the army's attitude toward pot. "The nature of a marijuana 'group' is to pressure people *away* from opiate involvement," said the pilot in his letter, writing much as he had talked in our conversation. "The smokers were physically and mentally more active than nonsmokers. The smokers were more stable than nonsmokers. The best pilots were 'heads.' " The pilot's own army career had phased out about the time the army was withdrawing its last troops from Quang Tri.

"Shortly before my scheduled departure from 'Nam, I was 'busted' on suspicion of smoking marijuana," he wrote me. "The MPs apologized profusely, saying that they both smoked, that many of their fellow MPs were hung-up on skag, and that neither of them had ever been forced into such a ridiculous arrest before. . . . The shit hit the fan when word filtered to the top brass. They threatened me with court-martial. . . . I knew they didn't have a case and refused to oblige in the farce. I was held several days past my originally scheduled departure date from Quang Tri while all the heavies conspired as to my disposition. I received an official letter of reprimand from my commanding general and was scornfully sent on my way—with sighs of relief, no doubt."

So that was how the war had ended for the Americans in "I Corps," the name by which the American command referred to the northern five provinces before it reverted to the old French term of "Military Region One." There was little serious fighting in the later phases of the American war, just stupid hassles over pot and skag. The memory of the helicopter pilot's views, strengthened by his letter, somehow compounded the hideous irony of the loss of those ugly firebases, mud-caked or baked dry depending on the season, those remote blue-green hills once invaded daily by floundering marines and soldiers, those "villes" of pop-can-walled hootches built of ammo boxes and 105-millimeter artillery shells—actually very good building material if one could ignore the military-style block lettering and numerals.

How many GIs had died in I Corps? "Khe Sanh," "Rockpile," "Con Tien," "Gio Linh"—the names from the old headlines and datelines read like a ghoulish roll call. American military spokesmen say they've never "broken down the count by regions." In other words, they can tell you that 40,000 or 50,000, or whatever it is, Americans have been killed in Vietnam, but they don't know exactly how many where. Let's say a third or maybe even half of them died in I Corps—perhaps as many as 10,000 in Quang Tri alone when you consider the ferocity of the defense of the DMZ at the height of the "American war" in 1967 and 1968.*

For what did they—we—die? The question, almost theoretical and esoteric when considered at home or even in Saigon, assumes special poignancy when I recall visits to those bases and battlegrounds, desolated GI towns and villages still scarred by barbed wire and tin sheeting.

> I been going
> Downhill every [sic]
> Since I been in
> This Lost World
> But I haven't gotten
> To the Bottom yet

The writing on the walls of the latrine stall by the GI passenger lounge at Danang air base captured the mood of the final two or three

---

*"JWB," reviewing the first edition of this book in *Military Review*, charged that this choice of words implied that, "to Mr. Kirk, 10,000 dead American fighting men, one way or the other, is of very little importance—certainly not important enough to move him to dig out a 1975 copy of *Information Please Almanac* and discover that US battle deaths totalled 46,229." Neither this interpretation nor JWB's advice on source material would be valid. My point was not to make light of the suffering of GIs but to suggest the horror of the body-count war waged by American commanders, who claimed a "ten-to-one kill ratio" of American to enemy forces. (The Department of Defense says 58,153 died in the war, including 47,357 in combat under hostile fire, the rest from causes ranging from disease to accidents and "friendly fire." The Vietnam Veterans' Memorial on the Mall in Washington, D.C., lists 58,196 names.)

years of American "involvement." I wrote down some of the verses before grabbing a ride to Saigon after a farewell visit to China Beach, a tawdry GI "in-country rest and recreation center" set in tall pine trees and sand by a beach near Danang.

> Kill one, they call you a murderer
> Kill thousands, and they'll call you
>   a conqueror
> Kill them all, and they won't call you
>   anything!

The lines might not have been original, but they reflected the cynicism, the bitterness of a war that American enlisted men knew better than their officers was already unwinnable. If it was not the performance of the soldiers on the ground that ordained retreat, it was the sense of the war at home—as caught in another popular latrine-wall graffiti:

> We the *UN* known
> Do the *UN* Godly
> For the *UN* Grateful

Or, as one scribbler implored his readers, "Please don't write nothing dirty below this sign, but I have 98 days to go home and I think I'm short after a long time in this place and away from the people." He concluded, "I'm a good man, believe me, nobody wants to." Did the writers of such lines already feel they were on trial for whatever they had done in the war? If they did, it was fitting that they should finally have lost the bases for which marines and army soldiers had fought the hardest. By the time I got back to Quang Tri in April 1972, the North Vietnamese had already driven the South Vietnamese from the bases immediately below the DMZ and were about to overrun Dong Ha entirely on their way south to the provincial capital.

Chu Lai, July 1971

There was less a feeling of guilt among GIs than of deadening boredom, of daily petty suffering, of nothingness—relieved, sometimes, by terror and cruelty.

It was that way when I visited the headquarters of the Americal division on the beaches of Chu Lai less than a year before the last American troops were finally to go home. Some of the GIs had found a way to occupy themselves—and to alarm the command. They were planning to hold a "peace rally" on the beach in front of the USO on July 4th, and one of them proudly showed me a special letter distributed by the commanding general to all unit COs.

The letter, couched in typical military bureaucratic style, began with the notation, "Subject: Peace Rally." It had been reported "to this headquarters," the letter somberly began, "that a gathering of personnel to rally for peace is being planned on 4 July at the USO Beach at Chu Lai." This command, said the letter, "requested higher authority for an opinion on whether or not this rally would constitute a demonstration within the meaning" of certain army regulations formally banning them.

The verdict: "In the opinion of higher authorities, the activities planned do constitute a demonstration within the meaning of the Army Regulation and the USARV [U.S. Army Vietnam] regulation and are therefore prohibited. Accordingly those personnel who take part in this planned demonstration will be apprehended and will be punished as deemed appropriate."

But the command quickly promised to placate restless GIs with more wholesome forms of holiday recreation. "This headquarters has announced a program of entertainment for division personnel on the USO Beach during the afternoon of 4 July," said the final paragraph. "The entertainment will include floor shows, music, sky-diving etc. This entertainment is considered an important aspect of the enjoyment of this holiday by Division personnel and will be continued as planned for the benefit of those who wish to enjoy it." Just how much the GIs enjoyed the holiday is not certain, but one of them later told me there were almost as many on-duty military policemen at the USO Beach as there were off-duty soldiers. Some of the would-be demonstrators arrived with appropriate placards but were quickly dispersed.

Crusading against the war, like taking drugs, was a luxury in which soldiers in rear areas had considerably more time and freedom to indulge than did the men in the field. Several days after visiting this base, I was riding an APC—armored personnel carrier—across a string of sandy dunes speckled by small bushes and rocks nicknamed the "Gaza Strip" by Americans who had fought over the land for most of the war. The Americans had "rome-plowed" the strip several times, exposing the bare earth with great plows to uncover mines and Viet Cong bunkers, but they still had failed to drive out the "enemy."

A young lieutenant, adviser to a battalion of South Vietnamese RF or regional force soldiers, described the problems—and the senselessness of the mission. "This morning an RF executive officer lost his leg, and so did another ARVN soldier," said the lieutenant. "We found booby traps that were put in yesterday." In the previous two months, he reported, his RF battalion had killed only six Viet Cong soldiers and captured twelve. "Very seldom will they engage in an open fight," he said of the VC.

So we were riding on APCs to avoid the mines while the South Vietnamese trod gingerly, carefully on the ground—usually precisely in the footsteps of the man in front, who tried, as much as possible, to step only on well-used, open paths. Beside me on the APC was a young sergeant from Long Island named Andrew Hritz. "We haven't seen any kids this mission," he observed, contemplatively, as our APCs trundled down a small road. "That's a sign there's VC in the area."

Occasionally, at odd intervals, we passed the burned-out remains of old homes, identifiable by a few sticks, ancient gravestones, cement foundations, perhaps a teakettle or piece of china. "This was a prosperous area, you can tell that," said Hritz, relieved for the moment of the tension by a fleeting thought of homes and families. "Be one in there— a booby trap. Trip wires across the opening. Or they'll put strawmat over the hole—cover it with dirt and grass—with wires across. You won't see them until you step into it. It's a sure foot blown away. Friend of mine lost his foot that way."

We watched listlessly, broiling in the sun, as some of the ARVN reluctantly pulled a stone away from a hunk of concrete in a hollow. "Could be for a mine or a weapons cache," said Hritz. "But probably it was a hiding place." The ARVN tossed away the stone, then picked up a badly tarnished piece of brassware, a minor spoil of war. "I'm past the point of thinking anymore," said Hritz, broad-shouldered, blond, who once had a football scholarship at a large midwestern university but volunteered for the army after failing to make the team. "You're just here, everybody helps everybody else to get home in one piece."

Hritz sounded almost saddened as he ruminated over the times he had spent on the Strip. "Most of the guys here count their days, but I don't—makes them seem longer. This whole outfit here is gettin' short. They all want to go home."

That night, sleeping by the APCs on the beach, some of the other soldiers talked about the war. "The army could pull out, and it'd be just *titi* time before the place was overrun," said a sergeant named Terry Zimmerman, a Texan. "Unless the ARVN really shape up, they're just freeloading with the U.S. here, doing as little as possible." Another interjected with his own observation. "These people here figure they have their whole life fightin' this battle. Why rush it?" Zimmerman was still talking about the army. "You're not seeing anything, riding around losing people for nothin'," he said, "because you're not getting anything."

Next morning, early, we were again "sweeping the area" on another arc back across the dunes. At some point around breakfast we trundled by a barbed-wire refugee camp. Hordes of children ran out in hopes of GI handouts. Soldiers threw down cigarettes, and boys aged six or seven picked them up and lit them. Some of the children rubbed their stomachs, and the GIs tossed out C-ration cans. Dozens of kids pounced on them at once, and a wild fight broke out over one stray can of applesauce. The GIs shrieked with laughter as a dozen boys punched and kicked each other for the can. "Git 'im, git 'im," one of them yelled, until a couple of old women broke up the melee.

Not all the soldiers were so anxious for peace. "The way Nixon talks, all he wants is his POWs back," said another young sergeant, our APC commander, as we roared out of the "ville," down a long dirt road toward what the soldiers called the "redball," route one. "That's a good idea," said the sergeant, a North Dakotan named Robert Jackson. "But what did all these fifty thousand guys die for? I think there's too much politics, really. Now they can't do anything because of fucking world opinion. All they want really is an agreement. We're blowing up booby traps and watching ARVNs get their legs blown off."

You sensed the bitterness, the hardness as the sun rose higher over the dunes and slowly penetrated our fatigues. "We should all be in the rear," said a spec 4 named Stephen Pulles, from Minneapolis. "We're just having people killed for nothing. There's no sense staying here, with opinion the way it is. We'll never win. We should all be in the rear until we pull out. Now it's too late because of world opinion."

It was also too late for a young POW whom we picked up at a firebase by the road. Blindfolded, hands bound behind his back, he was ordered to climb to the top of the APC and return with us to the Gaza Strip, to the place where he'd been captured a couple of days before. I tried to sense what he was thinking as we bounced back along the same road. Light froth was forming at the corners of his mouth, but there was no other sign of the terror he must have felt. Our platoon leader chatted with me about life in some small Texan town, where his father edited a weekly paper.

Then, after we had turned off the road and wandered into the dunes, he ordered the GIs on the APC to put on flak jackets and helmets. South Vietnamese RF troopers on the ground began to "recon by fire"—fire blindly into the bush. It was here, around here, that they had picked up the POW.

The ARVN pulled the POW off the APC, took off his blindfold, and ordered him to lead the way into the dense grass and brush beside our trail. A few seconds later we got a radio report. They'd found a Soviet-made SKS rifle, a "Kilo Sierra," it was called, after the initials KS. "Shit, is that all?" one of the GIs muttered. "They should kill that sunuvabitch."

From the APC I could still see the bruises on the POW's neck and arms, where he'd been beaten. He was now about 50 feet away. The lieutenant was telling me how mines were set. "They'll melt the explosive from a dud round and use the fuse from the blasting cap," he said. "They can put it all in a Coke can and set a trip wire." We saw the ashen remnants of cooking fires near us. "Looks like a couple of VC slept here last night," said the lieutenant. In the midst of our talk we heard the dull roar of an explosion a hundred feet or so away, in the trees where the POW was looking for mines.

The report came back over the radio. "Found a cache with two M60 machine guns," began the American adviser who had walked with the ARVN patrol into the low shrubbery. "We got a booby trap. Two wounded." Beside us on the APC was Spec 4 Ronnie Cloud, our medic, a black with a cross stuck into one pierced ear. "A Vietnamese girl put the cross in my ear," he explained laconically. He had a twisted black shoestring necklace with a wooden image of a black power salute on the end. He kept his hair long. One other thing I had noticed about him. He never moved as we were driving out, just sat there motionless on top of the APC, as if he were somehow an extension of it.

Now Cloud was talking quietly in response to my questions. "Some dink POW led the ARVN to the same point yesterday," he said, "and two guys lost their legs." We got another report on the radio. The ARVN were carrying out one of the wounded, but they refused to move the other. He was the POW. He had "multiple wounds" on his abdomen, the radio crackled. "I'm going to have to go in and get the VC," the lieutenant on our APC announced. "The little people don't want to get him." Now the medic was annoyed. "I patched up three mother-fuckin' dinks before, and they shot them," he told me, showing some sign of emotion for the first time in the day. "Yeah, I'll patch this one up too."

So we rumbled through the brush, pushing the branches to either side, sitting loose and high on the APC, hoping we'd get blown far and clear if we hit a mine, and we stopped about 20 feet from where the POW was lying. The medic jumped off, brushed past some ARVN, and started working on his chest. "He's dead," he announced simply, after a few seconds of attempts at artificial respiration. "Tripped on his own wire." The lieutenant looked down at the bloodied body of the POW, at the gaping, garish-red shrapnel wounds in his chest. "I'd say they blew his shit away," he said in a monotone. "OK, let's get out of here, let's get back," he snapped at the GIs on the track. But before we could begin our ride to route one, he called for a medevac chopper. "Wounds to the abdomen, urgent dustoff," he said, as the wounded ARVN lay on a poncho.

Several minutes later the bird came in amid great swirls of dust. The lieutenant was trying to explain over the radio why he had only one wounded when we had originally reported two. "The little people," he said. "It was their boy, and they want to leave him." We were, in fact, in the middle of an old graveyard. A slab of concrete bore a name, Bui Ly, and a year, 1958. Behind us one of the GIs began shooting idly into the brush. The lieutenant whirled around. "Tell that dude to knock it off or I'll have his ass."

The incident had aroused the GIs from their lethargy. "Evens the score a little," said a kid named John Kakamo, who'd been a steelworker in Fort Wayne. "I don't find this place boring. There's always something happening." Finally we were moving back toward the redball, route one, the same road we'd traveled twice before that day. None of us talked much. I kept thinking of the POW who'd been sitting in front of me on the way out and of the flecks of foam on either side of his mouth.

The Rockpile, June 1969

It had been that way for years. Between the Tet and May offensives of 1968, while the generals still prattled about "searching and destroying," the GIs grumbled about the waste of war. It was that way when I visited the marine firebase at the foot of the Rockpile, a vicious crag jutting up like an angry fist from the Cam Lo valley just below the DMZ, defying the bravado of the bravest young men who tried to scale it. The marines, by the time I got to the Rockpile in mid-1969, were pulling out.

Almost daily, truck convoys rolled through the bases below the DMZ carrying marines to the third marine division headquarters at Dong Ha. Some of them grinned and offered the "V" sign from the backs of the trucks, others shook their fists in black power salutes, but almost none evinced much confidence in the future of the region for which they had been fighting and dying for more than four years. "Charlie's gonna kick ARVN's tail," said Lance Corporal Edward Davis, slouched in a folding chair by the Rockpile. "Every time we was out in the field, I never seen ARVN out there fighting." Davis, black, from Los Angeles, thought the marines should have gone all the way to Hanoi rather than fight an enemy who could retreat beyond the borders of Laos and North Vietnam.

"Now it's just going to be a stalemate," said Davis. "They're gonna come to some kind of agreement, and no one will win." Davis was no longer certain, however, whether or not it mattered how the war ended. "This is their country," he said, surveying route nine, once a rutted dirt road, mined and often ambushed, now a paved all-weather highway, militarily "secure," at least by day. "I don't see why we should be out there fighting for them. The people up here could care less who wins the war as long as they still got their buffaloes and rice."

Other marines shared much the same view. "I think we should have taken all of North Vietnam," said a lance corporal from Virginia named George Siegrist, sipping on a can of beer he had opened to celebrate his imminent departure. "In this war here Charlie hits us, and then he runs back to safety across the DMZ. That's a useless war."

Useless or not, the fighting went fitfully on. Marines admitted the tempo had declined markedly since the large-scale engagements of last year and the year before, but they pointed to a long, low-lying range, known as Mutter's Ridge, a mile or so beyond the Rockpile. "They hit us with everything on our last patrol through there," said another lance corporal, John Rice, from San Jose, California. "We lost 18 guys killed and 20 wounded."

Rice waved languidly toward a rise only a few hundred yards from the camp. "We had a couple rifle cracks there the other night. They're waitin' for us all the time." Another marine, who had been listening to our conversation, predicted, "Charlie will try to kick us before we leave" and then would mine the road and bridges. "But they'll have a helluva hard time. We're ready for them." That kind of big talk was typical of marines throughout the war —even though many of them suffered from the same morale and drug problems, in the latter stages of the conflict, as did the army troops.

It was difficult sometimes to imagine a war really was going on as I visited the small bases below the DMZ in the period of American withdrawal. "Alpha One" was the name of the easternmost base, a windblown, bunkered circle of sand several hundred yards in from the sea and several miles below the mouth of the Ben Hai River, the formal boundary between the two Vietnams.

From Alpha One, the sand gradually yielded to overgrown, flooded stretches of green bush, once-fertile rice paddies now shell-pocked, mined, and inhabited only by occasional patrols of North—or South— Vietnamese troops. The next base, two miles inland, on a deserted brown-dirt road leading to the Ben Hai, was "Alpha Two." From the observation tower on Alpha Two, headquarters for a South Vietnamese armored squadron, one could see the flag of North Vietnam flapping wanly in the hot afternoon breeze at the other end of the bridge, a couple of miles away, linking North and South Vietnam.

"Must be 30 by 20 feet," the senior American adviser on Alpha Two, Major Eddie Story, remarked as the red flag with the yellow star stretched on a puff of wind and then fell limp in the ensuing calm. Flag-watching was a favorite pastime for Story, a Tennessean who'd spent the previous four months on Alpha Two. "There's nothing going on around here. We have occasional reports of infiltration, sometimes ambushes, and they fire mortars at us once in a while, but no real big action."

Story had seen the lights of what he thought were trucks moving by night down the highway north of the bridge where the flag was flying. As he was talking, an American observation plane flew low over the DMZ, and jet fighters above it unloaded bombs just south of the river.

The explosions kicked up smoke and debris from the paddies along the banks. Earlier in the day, one of the spotter planes had crash-landed into the dirt of Alpha Two after its engine had died over the DMZ. Both the pilots had escaped, but the wreckage still lay in a crumpled heap beside the observation tower. "That was the most excitement we've had in months," said Story. "You can't tell, though. They could be getting ready for something once the marines have left."

Khe Sanh, July 1968

The turning point of the war, as everyone who read about it in a newspaper or watched it on television knows perfectly well, was the fighting earlier this year, the period of the Tet offensive. It's hard to judge the significance of Tet. You could interpret it, as many reporters do, as a fantastic defeat, or you could accept the view of the American commander, General William Westmoreland, the picture soldier, that it was a great victory over the enemy.

As a matter of fact, Tet falls into neither category, since the war was so complicated by international politics and diplomacy, but it rates, undeniably, as a turning point. With Tet the Americans realized, if they were going to keep fighting at all, it was not going to be to win. At the same time, the North Vietnamese and the Viet Cong sensed the necessity, after Tet, of lying relatively low, fighting to demoralize their foes but not sacrificing depleted forces until the Americans finally negotiated their own withdrawal.

No confrontation illustrated the paradox of the war more precisely than did the siege of this large marine combat base on route nine in the northwestern corner of South Vietnam. When I first visited in late January, three divisions of North Vietnamese were just beginning to lay down their epic siege. They were rocketing the base every now and then, but marines still walked above ground in daytime and patrolled beyond the perimeter.

With the onset of the Tet offensive in the northern provinces on January 30, the North Vietnamese sharply tightened their squeeze on the base. They not only attacked it frequently on the ground but dug in so close that marines could no longer patrol outside the barbed wire surrounding it. And they rocketed, shelled, and mortared it so often that no one moved outside his bunker except when he had to—and then at a dead run.

The fad at the time was to compare the siege of Khe Sanh to that of Dien Bien Phu nearly 14 years before, but the marine regimental commander at Khe Sanh, Colonel David E. Lownds, said he had never read Bernard Fall's book on the French debacle. It was just as well. The two were not comparable at all. The Americans had all the airpower they could use—an asset the French had desperately needed—and with it some two months later forced the North Vietnamese to begin retreating. By the time the siege was lifted, in early April, the marines had lost nearly 300 dead, and the bodies of thousands of North Vietnamese lay strewn on nearby hills and valleys.

And yet the marines, in the end, lost Khe Sanh. That is, three months after the siege was over and American troops could punch through to Khe Sanh on the ground, the marines decided to abandon the base, exposed in the middle of a longish valley dominated by hills from which gunners could fire down on them. Marine commanders, wisely enough no doubt, concluded they could deploy their forces more quickly and more adeptly from small outposts on top of the hills—or else by sending in large task forces to accomplish specific goals.

The way the military briefers described it, the new approach made eminent sense not only in theory but also in practice. The marines, it seemed, had finally awakened to the realities of how to fight in Vietnam. Still, revisiting the base on the day the marines revealed they were leaving, you hardly found anyone below the rank of lieutenant in agreement or sympathy with top-level strategy.

"It was just a waste," blurted Sergeant Richard Morgan, a battalion intelligence scout from New York. "Tactically they couldn't stop the gooks from infiltrating anyway. They just went down further south. . . . This whole country's a waste. You gotta set up positions around the villages and brainwash the people, but there's nobody left to brainwash around here."

Marines at Khe Sanh kept asking why they fought, what was the meaning of it all. "I feel like they're defeating the whole purpose of holding it in the first part of the year," said Lance Corporal William Laines, an Alabaman. "They made such a big thing, how it was the strong point blocking all the gooks coming through Laos." Laines looked back on the marine stand there as "something we accomplished" but asked plaintively, "Why didn't they blow it up earlier, before we lost all our friends and fellow marines?"

We were standing in a jumble of sandbags and upturned earth, the remains of bunkers blown apart by North Vietnamese shot and shell. Occasionally we heard the distant thud of artillery fired from across the Laotian border six miles away and jumped in a bunker until the explosion on or near the base. I told one marine the news of the pullout. He stared at the dirt for a moment, then replied in an angry burst, "Tell it to the dead."

6

"Peace Is at Hand"

The American GIs were leaving, but Vietnamese were always skeptical of promises of peace. So often, for the past two generations, from the period of the first uprisings against the French colonialists, through the Japanese occupation and the "first" Indochinese war, they had been misled and deceived. Yet, when Henry Kissinger, during the peace talks in Paris in the fall of 1972, declared that peace was "at hand," it really seemed as if Vietnam were on the threshold of a new era, not just another turn in the old war. As the peace talks dragged on and American B52s and F111s swept over North Vietnam, including Hanoi, in the Christmas bombing of December 1972, Kissinger's promise again seemed to have been merely an empty act of diplomacy. Then, when the Vietnam peace agreement was finally signed in Paris on January 27, 1973, Kissinger was temporarily vindicated.

In the end, however, that agreement, like the one reached in Geneva in 1954, was a transparent act of deception, a gesture that saved face for the war-weary Americans but did not prevent the killing of another 60,000 Vietnamese in increasingly fierce fighting before the year was out. In the months before and after the agreement was signed, I traveled around Vietnam asking Vietnamese what they thought of it all. I had often talked with Vietnamese about their views on war and peace but was still moved by the almost desperate yearning they invariably displayed for relief from suffering.

No hamlet was more representative than My Lai, which I visited five years after the massacre—and several days before the last American troops were going home under terms of the agreement. In different ways, however, the people of Cai Lay district, in the upper delta, and the denizens of the urban sprawl of Saigon also reflected the agony of a populace long accustomed to lies and broken promises from diplomats wherever they debated their fate—in their own country or in Paris, Geneva, Washington, Moscow, or Beijing.

My Lai, March 1973

"Certainly," the leathery-faced man remarked as we squatted on the road in the middle of the barren hamlet, "I'd be glad to tell you what happened. Why not?" It was slightly more than five years since the massacre, on March 18, 1968, of some 100 Vietnamese civilians by a platoon of American troops, but the aged farmer recalled it all as if it had been only yesterday. "It was really a bloody thing," said the man, talking to two Americans—this reporter and David Barton, a volunteer hospital worker who had lived in the area for a couple of years and spoke Vietnamese.

"There was blood all over these trails," he went on, pointing vaguely toward a narrow footpath leading into a clump of trees lining the famed irrigation ditch where the bodies were thrown. "The people who were wounded were coming right out here. Sometimes the people said to me later, 'You were there, why weren't you killed?' but I was out tending my cattle. Anybody who left their bunkers during the shooting was killed."

Somehow that was how it had happened at My Lai. This, the fifth anniversary, had more meaning than most others. By now, the Americans—the soldiers, that is—had finally left Vietnam, and the people of the hamlet might ponder what it had all meant, the constant apprehension punctuated by occasional moments of terror. But that morning, five years ago, oddly enough no one had been particularly afraid, the man insisted. "Nobody was around that day," he explained. "The soldiers of the National Liberation Front had already left—had gone to another place. That's why the people weren't afraid."

True, the Americans had been firing artillery rounds in the general vicinity since about six in the morning, but they were always doing things like that, that was nothing unusual. "The other side wouldn't fight here because the fields were all in the open," the man pointed out with simple logic. "When the people saw the American troops entering the hamlet, they thought there was no more danger and came from their bunkers and were shot." The old man spoke in low tones, sometimes rolling a cigarette, glad to pass the time on a warm spring day.

"We know there's supposed to be a ceasefire," he was saying. "We're still afraid of the Americans—afraid of more artillery, more bombing. I have to think that people who kill like that are very cruel. There isn't any other way to think. So many people were killed. Six in my own family—a son and daughter-in-law and four grandchildren."

It was now around ten in the morning, and the narrow black-topped road stretching around the Batangan Peninsula, through the middle of My Lai and the village of Song My to route one, was busy. Children were scampering after their water buffalo, women were carrying kindling wood and produce from the fields, and South Vietnamese soldiers were wandering by every now and then, some on motor scooters or trucks or jeeps, others on foot. Another man, much younger than the farmer, interrupted him. "The Americans came to help the government fight the communists," he said, but the old man wasn't satisfied with such a stock explanation.

"If they came to fight the communists, then why did they kill all the people like that?" he asked. The younger man had no ready answer. "To tell the truth," he replied, "I don't know. The Americans came to help, but they killed. I don't understand. There should have been a commander responsible for them, to keep them from sending people into a village like that."

Barton remarked that there had indeed been an official investigation of the entire incident and that one lieutenant in the end had been convicted but still for some reason could stay in his home or quarters and drink beer and play cards. The younger man shook his head. "It was a whole company that fought here," he said. Something in Barton's remark about an official investigation was especially distasteful to the older one. "There've been a lot of people who have come here and asked a lot of questions, but we don't see the results. There's been more war."

Even now, the old man pointed out, no one could live in the hamlet, no one could rebuild the devastated homes. Government troops often fired from the road or from a small outpost on a hill overlooking the entire area. The younger man expanded on the theme. "You know," he

said, "there were two massacres that day." The second one somehow
never got publicity.

Barton recalled that American military investigators had acknowledged the other one but never bothered to arrest or prosecute anyone.
A hundred more people were killed in the second massacre down the
road, said the younger man. "I hid in a bunker while my wife and some
others went down the road that way. The others, those who went the
wrong way, were killed." An edge of wonder crept into the man's
voice as he tried to convey the enormity of the event. "They didn't kill
just people," he said, as if the killing of people mistaken for enemy
troops might by itself have been understandable. "They killed animals
and children—everything."

"I don't know what to say, what to think," said the older one. "I just
have to live. I come to tend my cattle. There's been a lot of war. We
have to accept it." Some soldiers drove up in a truck and stopped
beside us. At first I thought they had come to order Barton and me to
leave, to return to the provincial capital of Quang Ngai some five miles
to the west, but they were just idly curious. "Aren't you afraid of being
captured by the Front?" asked one of them, grinning. "The communists
kill people. They are only 50 meters away. There is no security here."

The communists lately have not fired much, but the soldier's remark
indicated one of the essential ironies of My Lai—and the entire war.
For all the killing and suffering, this hamlet is just as "insecure" now
as it was on the day of the massacre five years ago. Nothing has
changed, nothing except that My Lai in effect no longer exists. The
former citizens of the hamlet, those who survived the scourge, live
down the road in Song My or in a typically crowded refugee camp
across the river from Quang Ngai. They return to farm the fields only
in daytime, if at all.

On a slight pile of earth near the road another farmer and several
boys talked about what had happened. "I left in the morning when I
saw the first helicopters. Otherwise I would have been killed. I lost two
nephews. The soldiers shot the wounded too. How do I know why they
killed? A lot of the people had come in from farther out on the
Batangan Peninsula because of the fighting out there. We weren't worried." But the people should have known, the farmer went on, rambling
in a low voice. "There were lots of people who had already lost people
in other battles." One of the worst aspects of the massacre, he added,
as if recalling a long-forgotten detail, was the stench that hung over the

hamlet. "We couldn't come back for two or three days, everything smelled so bad. It was really hard to bury people."

My Lai today looks almost like a picture of pastoral peace. The breeze gently sways the pine trees as the boys tend their cattle in fallow fields. Only an occasional distant plane breaks the silence, a reminder of the constant fact of war. "I just see neither one side nor the other has gotten anywhere," said the farmer. "The government side, with the Americans, has really fought strong with artillery and bombing, but you never see the other side. They're here, though." The farmer described himself as a person of the country to whom the main problem was survival. "The big people may have decided on a ceasefire, but for us it's all the same. All we want is to be able to eat, to work our fields, and the big people won't let us do that."

A year ago, said the farmer, he had again had to flee My Lai in the face of war. This time armored personnel carriers and planes had annihilated a new cluster of buildings occupied by men of the National Liberation Front at the start of the offensive of spring 1972. The rubble of the foundations and the floors of the buildings were still clearly visible on either side of the road. "We used to have sweet potato fields and lots of coconut trees," explained one of the boys sitting beside the farmer, "but when the bombs fall, they cut off the trees right at the trunk."

Another boy, sitting quietly through the conversation, said that he too had been at My Lai that day five years ago. He had lain at the bottom of the ditch, shielded by the dead bodies of his mother and father and five brothers, while the soldiers were shooting. "I've been living with friends near the market down the road and taking care of cattle. I had to get someone else to come back with me and help bury my family."

The boy was seven then, twelve now. What does he think of the American soldiers five years later? Why did they come to Vietnam? Were they really cruel people? "We can't talk to the Americans," he replied. "They don't speak our language. They were cruel, but we don't know why they came here or why they killed. All I know is my family was killed, and I feel a tightness in my chest."

Nor has the suffering ended for the people of My Lai. The refugee camp where most of them now live is an enclave of crowded, steaming tents pitched behind barbed-wire barricades guarded by South Vietnamese policemen. Although these people are by no means prisoners, in the technical sense, they often cannot enter or leave without the permission of the guards, and they cannot go out at night at all. More saddening, however, they do not have enough to eat. "It's too far to go to the fields," said a gnarled old man sitting in one of the tents. "And we have only half a kilo of rice per person per day."

The men and women, passing most of their days in the dark shadows of their tents, have little better to do than to sit and talk—and remember. "It seems like just a couple of days ago, but it was really five years," said one man, reminded of the anniversary of the massacre. "Yes, I was there," he went on somewhat contemplatively. "I was only beaten, but I lost some relatives. Then we went to the new place, but we had to run away a couple of times a year during the fighting, and finally we came here. It's been a year since we could work our fields."

A woman interrupted. "We've had to run without enough to eat." Another young man spoke up. "We don't have any chance to work. The government doesn't let us go back when we wish. If we want to go someplace near here, we don't need permission, but we need permission to go and work the fields." An old woman: "We really want to go back now, but they're not letting us. They say there's no security. So we stay in this one tent—64 or 65 of us in each of the tents."

During our talk another man, a greying, tough-featured farmer, sat down and began berating us for posing so many questions. "Many reporters have come to ask us about the situation, but we have seen no results. You come and ask people how many were killed that day. If you want to ask such questions, that is all right, that is your business, but we need help. Many reporters have come and written about us, but they haven't helped a bit. You make us very angry. We feel a tightness in our chests."

There was nothing more to say. The farmer was right. We were outsiders intruding on their suffering, asking the same familiar questions but offering nothing in return for the replies. The tragedy of My Lai was not just the death of 100 or so Vietnamese civilians. It was the loss of an entire hamlet—and a legacy of bitterness and hatred and hopelessness, the tragedy of Vietnam.

Cai Lay, November 1972

They were the "Tu Kiet," the "Four Brave"—four who died fighting a foreign enemy, who gave their lives for their family, their village, and their country rather than flinch before certain executions. Even their names, typically Vietnamese, reflect their nationalism—Duc, Duong, Thanh and Long.

Beheaded by the French in 1885, they live in the "hearts and minds" of the people of this upper delta district some 60 miles southwest of Saigon. The leading officials and businessmen of the district, as well as peasants in remote villages and hamlets, contribute annually to the Tu Kiet society, which exists to maintain a pagoda built five years ago in honor of "the Four Brave ones" of Cai Lay. Duc, Duong, Thanh, and Long—their cement gravestones lie beside each other behind the pagoda, painted with blue, yellow, and red inscriptions, but villagers insist loudly their spirits never died. "Their eyes did not close after they were beheaded," explains Le Van Truong, a tailor with a small shop in the central market near the pagoda. "Therefore the people believe they are saints."

The myth of the Four Brave has gained credence lately as a result of the yearning for peace among peasants in a rural region periodically afflicted by guerrilla warfare and propagandizing. Lately, as the warring factions grope tentatively toward what may prove a stopgap ceasefire agreement, the people of Cai Lay have turned toward the spirits of the Tu Kiet for guidance on what will happen next in the faltering struggle for peace. "Every day I spend quietly in the Tu Kiet pagoda burning incense and praying for peace," says Nguyen Van Huong, who has watched over the tombs of the Four Brave ones for 20 years and serves as caretaker of the pagoda. "I do not know what kind of peace the Four Brave ones wanted," says Huong, a thin, quiet man who speaks softly, almost haltingly, in his home several blocks away. "They died for the independence of their country. They wanted peace for their people."

The story of the Tu Kiet seems particularly relevant today because actually they surrendered to the French rather than subject their communities to complete annihilation. French officers were holding all the people of their villages as hostages in exchange for the Four Brave. If they refused to yield, the story goes, the French would behead every one of the villagers. If the Tu Kiet gave themselves up, the villagers would go free, and only the four, as leaders of the prolonged local revolt against the colonialists, would die. For the Tu Kiet, it was more important to relieve the immediate suffering of their people than to fight for a lost cause.

The symbolism of their surrender is implicit in the words of the aged caretaker as he talks of Vietnam's continuing, endless agony. "The people here just want peace, no more killing, no more hostility," says Huong. "We should live neighbor-to-neighbor, brother-to-brother." Every day the doors of the Tu Kiet pagoda are open for mothers, fathers, sisters, and brothers offering prayers for relatives killed in the war or still fighting for one side or another. "The people are praying for peace much more now than before," Huong reports. "They come all day long, even the high district officials."

Once the members of the Tu Kiet society organized a ceremony in which they prayed for peace and threw two old bronze coins to determine the will of "the Four Brave ones." If both the coins landed on the same side, it meant there would be peace. "The Tu Kiet answered our prayers," says Huong. "The coins fell the same way. There will be peace soon." Sitting beside Huong, one of his relatives nods her head and talks excitedly. "The Tu Kiet have reappeared through other people. They say the war lasts too long and is too hard. They tell the people to prepare for peace."

But what kind of peace? Neither Huong nor the woman seems to know. "It is up to the politicians in Saigon," Huong murmurs. Among rural peasants the "modalities" of a peace formula drafted by American presidential adviser Kissinger in talks with North Vietnam's Le Duc Tho seem as unreal and academic as an exercise in calculus or nuclear physics. In the countryside, in contrast to urban Saigon, one gets the impression that the populace wants only peace without qualifications—and does not care particularly which formula the negotiators finally agree to adopt.

"I always pray for an end to fighting because the civilians are caught in the middle," says a woman in a small hamlet several miles south of here. "Sometimes I listen to speeches on my radio," adds the woman, who has a son in the South Vietnamese army. "It all goes in one ear and out the other. All I want is for my son to return home."

In the next hamlet, a man named Nguyen Van Hai recalls a series of battles along the road last May and June. "All the families had to leave," says Hai, who lives with his wife and eight of their nine children in a one-room home dominated by a small Buddhist shrine. "All the people here want is a ceasefire and peace. If it happens here with the control of the international observers, then it should make no difference if the communists occupy the area. My family will stay on no matter because we have lived here for generations. As a poor citizen, I know nothing about high politics." Hai, whose eldest son serves in the army, gleans enough news from Saigon Radio to believe "the big politicians are working for peace." He hopes it will happen soon, "before the communists attack here again."

Even if the war ends, the memory lingers on for Hai in the form of bits of shrapnel from artillery shells that exploded in his small rice paddy. "The pieces cut into my feet sometimes," says Hai, wincing instinctively. The pervasive influence of the war on the hamlet, typical of hundreds like it in the Mekong River delta region, emerges in the structure of a tiny food shop 100 meters from Hai's home. "Ammunition for cannon with explosive projectiles," say the block letters on the wooden slats, once used for crates of 105-millimeter artillery shells.

Despite an external appearance of disinterest in the form of a peace settlement, the owner of the shop displays a sense of tradition that explains much about the villagers' tolerance for unending suffering. "In ancient China, two warlords fought for a decade," he says, proffering Coca-Cola and a sticky local candy. "One won because he had the full support of the people. The other lost because the people hated him." The shopowner runs through the whole elaborate tale of the warlords, but he seems quite ambiguous on the crucial point of which warlord symbolized which side in Vietnam. Such ambiguity typifies the outlook of the peasants, who never know who really is fighting—or spying—for whom.

Although the road itself is secure by day, there always are rumors of propagandizing and flag-raising by Viet Cong agents in nearby hamlets. Not infrequently the National Liberation Front resorts to terrorism, even in broad daylight, against those who somehow seem too dangerous or too closely allied to the government hierarchy in the district headquarters.

It was that way in the hamlet of My Kiem, just a mile or so from the district center. "We came here two years ago because our village was unsafe," says a young woman named Thai Thi Huynh. "My husband slept here at night but went to the old village to work in the day. He was in charge of death and birth certificates." Several mornings ago, two young men knocked on her door and asked for him. "He was not in the house but next door with his brother and a friend. They had not been together for a long time and were celebrating by drinking wine and eating cake." The two men in uniform, both carrying Chinese-made AK47 rifles, walked into the house next door and sprayed fire around the room. Huynh's husband and brother were both killed. So was her 15-month-old baby, who happened to be playing there at the time.

"They tried to kill me too, but I ran away. They were agents from our old village. I do not know why they wanted to get my husband." We are talking in the same room in which Huynh's husband died. An old woman points to the bullet holes in the furniture. Another woman picks up a piece of wood that splintered from an ancient chest. Among the tall shade trees hanging over the thatched homes, villagers gather silently, impassively, hoping to overhear the conversation. Yellow-and-red-striped South Vietnamese flags are painted on the doors or roofs of almost all the houses—proof that the Saigon regime controls the village in case both sides finally agree to a ceasefire-in-place. Huynh, however, does not think in such terms as "government control" or "Viet Cong control" or even "ceasefire-in-place." All she wants, she says, is a ceasefire with no more killing.

"Then I can return to my old village and farm my land. I listen to the radio and know that a ceasefire will happen soon. I want a ceasefire to bring independence for the country and peace for the people. It is too late for my husband, but I want a ceasefire that will let everyone do his job with no more killing, no more shooting. I want a ceasefire under any circumstances, with no more hostility." Some of the villagers smile slightly and nod in agreement. "We are afraid the VC will come back because of the killings," says a gold-toothed man sitting in front of one of the houses. "Peace depends on those in high positions in Saigon, the politicians and intellectuals," he adds, smiling. "We are only the poor people, we can do nothing."

Saigon, November 1972

It is 6 P.M. on the ninth anniversary of the overthrow of Ngo Dinh Diem, and Ha The Vinh is sitting in his coffee shop near the racetrack listening to the evening news. Vinh hears the voice of President Nguyen Van Thieu warning against a "country-losing surrender" to the North Vietnamese, against falling for the "cunning tricks" of the communists, against signing any kind of ceasefire that might compromise the country's "independence" and "right of self-determination."

Vinh has operated his coffee shop at the same corner since fleeing from North Vietnam in 1954. As a refugee, he is almost certain to agree with Thieu's stubborn stand against the ceasefire formula negotiated by Henry Kissinger and North Vietnam's Le Duc Tho in Paris. "What kind of ceasefire are they talking about?" he asks, sipping a cup of thick *café den*. "If there is any ceasefire, we must have conditions. We cannot accept a leopardskin ceasefire. We, the non-communist element, would not accept it."

There are, Vinh explains, communists who work secretly in the government. "They might hang their flags in the offices of the government and declare them communist-held regions. That is the problem with agreeing to a ceasefire-in-place." Vinh admits his outlook may be prejudiced by his personal experience in North Vietnam, but he claims that most of his customers share the same view. In fact, it is difficult to find anyone in this war-weary capital who really welcomes the prospect of signing a ceasefire agreement of the sort proposed by Hanoi and Washington.

Thieu may not be popular, but the people of Saigon clearly share his general distrust of the terms of any agreement that permits the North Vietnamese to continue to occupy portions of the country within striking distance of the capital. The crusade against a ceasefire has assumed almost a carnival tone with the blossoming of thousands of South Vietnamese flags on cars and taxis, outside hotels and shops, on windows and walls.

I visit a crowded alleyway near the docks on the Saigon River, expecting that here one may listen to the voices of the dispirited, the disillusioned, yearning for an end to the war—and perhaps an end to Thieu as well. In the first house I enter, one Pham Van Lieu, a greying dockworker, gladly offers his opinions. "The people suffer too much in this war so now everybody wants peace. Peace depends on the government. If it is a good government, it can make a good peace. If it is bad, it will make a bad peace. Good peace is peace which can bring reunification of the country, north and south, so people can go from place to place with freedom. Bad peace is a peace which still encourages the hatred of the two sides."

Lieu's brother, Tran Du, also a dockworker, is somewhat more explicit. "If North Vietnam accepts the plan proposed by Thieu, then peace can come—if not, peace could not come and there will be no ceasefire." Du explains that he wants a form of peace under which "anybody can do anything he likes." In other words, "If I make much money, I can spend it, and nobody can control my family expenses." Du doubts if a ceasefire would really bring about this kind of peace. "This government is good because it can fight effectively against the communists," he says simply.

In talking to the dockworkers, however, one soon senses that the prospects of peace, or ceasefire, is hardly uppermost in their minds. For them the agreement is merely a thought sometimes mentioned on radio broadcasts. As long as the North Vietnamese and Viet Cong are not actually attacking Saigon or its outskirts, they are far more worried over such matters as rising prices.

"I can make only a little money now," says Pham Chi, 45-year-old father of eight children. "Everything is too expensive for me." Chi looks with feelings akin to nostalgia on the era of Diem, whose assassination on November 1, 1963, is still hailed as a climactic point in the revolution of a clique of Saigon generals. "During the Diem regime, everything was cheap," says Chi. "I listened to Thieu's speech on the radio about the peace settlement, but it was much too long. I forgot everything. Anyway, the people have no power to work for peace. Only the government can decide. It's their business, not mine."

One reason for the indifference with which many Saigonese view the negotiations is that, except for brief periods during the Tet and May 1968 offensives and during occasional rocket attacks, the city has remained calm. To a superficial observer, Saigon seems to thrive, with crowded markets and restaurants, busy streets and shops. One is aware of the great contrast between rich and poor, between stately French colonial-style villas and squalid slums gleaming with tin roofs, but one hardly envisions Saigon as a city at war.

"The people here have not awakened to the danger confronting our country," complains Senator Vu Van Mau, a distinguished law professor who heads a slate of anti-government Buddhists in the Senate. Paradoxically, although Mau has often opposed Thieu in the past, he too criticizes the ceasefire plan as one that would not solve the war, would give the communists too much territory, and would subvert the independence of the central government under a super-government election council.

"The unanimous aspiration of the people of Vietnam is to want peace," says Mau, receiving me in the office in the front room of his home in the center of Saigon. "We want peace, but we must study the modalities very carefully. If we do not, then the ceasefire will raise many more problems than it will solve." How, he asks rhetorically, "can you conceive of a ceasefire in place? You will just have countless problems, so the ceasefire cannot be won, realistically speaking. If you display flags to show territory, you cannot show flags in the jungle and the mountains. So how can you have a ceasefire?"

The elite of Saigon, whether for or against the government, complain openly of American "sellout" and "betrayal." They reiterate the criticism of President Thieu that Kissinger should not sign a treaty on behalf of Saigon, and they claim that Kissinger does not understand Vietnam. Kissinger is "a learned man, no doubt," says Nguyen Van Huyen, the Senate president. "He has traveled widely and seen many people." Senator Huyen smiles somewhat ironically. "It is another matter, however, whether he knows what is right for Vietnam."

The sense of disillusion with the United States relates in part to the extent to which the disillusioned are dependent on American largesse for money and position. Thousands of Saigonese, if they do not actually work for Americans, realize their shops and restaurants would soon close or lose much of their business if the United States withdrew entirely as the result of a ceasefire plan. It has already happened along Tu Do, the main street running from the stately French-built cathedral through the center of the city to the Saigon River. Empty bars, crammed with "waitresses" ready to ply their customers with drink and good cheer, reflect the departure of fun-seeking GIs and money-laden contractors.

"Business is no good for months," says a bargirl named Phuong. "First the GIs go home and then the police close us. When we open again as restaurants, no good. Still, no customers." At the desk of a luxury hotel down the street, a clerk asks me if I think the United States will really make a deal with Hanoi. "Nobody likes," he assures me. "Everybody is afraid." Outside the door of the hotel a host of taxi drivers wait for the chance to overcharge the foreign guests. "I am for President Thieu," says one of them. "No like Kissinger"—which he pronounces "Keesger."

Those who are really rich (the bankers and realtors and big store owners) are all making plans to hoard their money and get out of the country. Every day, says a customs officer, the well-to-do of the city send out crates full of paintings, lacquerware, heirlooms, and the like to New York, London, Paris, Switzerland —the gathering places for Vietnam's *émigré* population. "One thing's for sure," remarks a jaded American official. "If there really is a ceasefire, all of these people will be ready to leave the country at a moment's notice in case the North Vietnamese have the chance to attack the city."

But attack on Saigon itself at this point seems unlikely. While the rest of the country may suffer, with or without the signing of an agreement, Saigonese fantasize themselves as above the war, thanks to military defenses as well as diplomatic guarantees. It is because the capital is relatively secure, even in the midst of war, that many Saigonese fear an arrangement that might jeopardize the position of the government and provide the communists with the chance to assume power by *coup d'état*.

At the same time, the yearning for peace also seems genuine among those who have suffered personally. "I know nothing about politics," says a woman who has lost two sons in battle. "Only President Thieu knows about that. I want only peace, that is all. I want a ceasefire, but I do not know what would happen later." Beside her sits her son-in-law, an air force sergeant. "Everybody wants peace," he says, "but the communists should not be allowed to keep territory in which to regroup for later attacks. I agree with President Thieu's viewpoint."

7

"We're Here to Win"

Both Vietnamese and Americans were doubtless misled by the promises of real peace at the conclusion of an agreement in Paris, but there was no greater deception than the repeated pledges of victory at the outset of direct American involvement in the war in 1965. Perhaps no single group of Americans was more grossly deceived than the black GIs, to whom military service initially provided an opportunity, a hope for escape from slights and slurs encountered in civilian life. My first assignment in Vietnam, in September 1965, was to interview black GIs for a magazine article—a project that compelled me to visit major American bases soon after their first occupants had arrived.

Soldiers of the Big Red One—the first infantry division—were still living in tents by the highway between Saigon and Bien Hoa when I saw them that month. An American general, addressing troops before a performance of "Hello Dolly" starring Mary Martin on the tarmac in front of hangars at Danang, read of great triumphs against "Charlie" as the result of an operation he was launching in the nearby hills. (From my own subsequent perusal of *Stars and Stripes*, I gathered that his men spent most of the next few weeks flailing around in the jungle and returned with very little to show for the operation, typical of scores to follow.)

Black GIs often spoke of their own special racial problems, but their war was not that much different from that of everybody else. In their early exhilaration, black soldiers exuded a sentiment shared by many if not most members of the American military machine in Vietnam. Sometimes their remarks sounded like propaganda for the war effort.

Similarly, in the closing phase, in the depths of their own depression and demoralization, blacks did not differ radically from white GIs in their criticism of the war. Thus the story of the evolution of black attitudes—the contrast between those at the beginning and end of the American involvement—really illustrates a total shift in national mood and outlook. Yet, in many of its details, the black story *was* different, particularly as racial tensions erupted in the later stages.

Danang, October 1965

A sea breeze blew a blast of hot air and sand across the wide white wastes that stretch inland for half a mile from the South China Sea just below Danang. First Lieutenant Tommy D. Gregory, 26, bit on a grain of sand, spat it out, and smiled. "Well, now, I wouldn't say these were ideal living conditions," said the lieutenant as he looked across the tent encampment of the third marine division's third tank battalion. "But I didn't join the corps to lead an easy life. That's not why I came to Vietnam either. We're here to win."

Gregory, a coal miner's son from Birmingham, Alabama, began dreaming of a career in "the corps" when he was a twelve-year-old student in an all-black school. "The history of the marine corps was what impressed me," said Gregory, the battalion liaison officer. "It's a real distinctive organization, and I wanted to become a part of it."

For Gregory, like most of the blacks with American forces in Vietnam, the civil rights problem, Dr. Martin Luther King, and Watts are names in occasional headlines in *Stars and Stripes*. Even in the lower enlisted grades, blacks in Vietnam have discovered that the armed forces offer a degree of equality they might not expect in civilian life. Private First Class John Smith, 21, of Philadelphia was trudging through thick jungle in War Zone D, a Viet Cong stronghold northwest of Saigon, when I talked to him.

"This jungle is their home," Smith remarked softly as he pulled a stubborn piece of vine from around his grenade launcher. "The only jungle I know is that asphalt jungle." A lanky six-footer, Smith grinned and walked on. "But I don't mind it here, not much, anyway. I'm thinking of staying in the army. There's things about it I don't like, but it's all right." Smith's sentiments were echoed by many blacks to whom I spoke in four weeks of interviews throughout South Vietnam. While they did not usually articulate racial factors, clearly many have found opportunities in the service that elude them at home.

"Frankly, I never encountered that much prejudice even to talk about," said Sergeant Willie G. Waters, 33, of Greenville, Texas, a helicopter crew chief based in Saigon. "My platoon has Puerto Ricans, Mexicans, blacks, and whites. You just can't make any difference and run a platoon successfully." Blacks suspect discrimination in some cases, but most agree the armed forces have gone far in eliminating the problem. "There really ain't no way of telling if a man's acting out of prejudice," said Air Force Sergeant Jimmie Robinson, 28, of Gadsden, Alabama, crew chief assigned to F104 fighters at Danang. "People come from different places and act differently. But they always have to follow orders, so it don't make much difference in the end."

To career men like Lieutenant Gregory, the racial issue seems strangely remote and academic. "I think it's a matter of difference that'll be worked out in time," said Gregory. "I never encountered any trouble myself. I always figure, if I want something, I'll get it. And I will, too." Gregory never doubted, for instance, his ability to get a commission. He enlisted in the corps after graduating from Alabama Agricultural and Mechanical College in Huntsville in 1961, made private first class in boot camp, and four months later entered officer candidates' school in Quantico, Virginia, finishing in the top 20 percent of his class with a regular commission.

As liaison officer for his battalion, Gregory coordinates relations with regimental headquarters, South Vietnamese forces, and other marine units. He spends most of his time behind a makeshift desk in a tent but occasionally goes out on patrols and quite often visits other headquarters. "There's been a lot of cases of marines shooting other marines around here. I run around finding out what other units are doing." He added with a wry smile that he was proud to say that no marines in his battalion had accidentally shot at, or been shot at by, other marines.

Like Lieutenant Gregory, Army Captain Lewis W. Wright believes in America's mission in Vietnam. Captain Wright, 32, flies a UH1B helicopter, one of the workhorses of the jungle war. He recalled an occasion in June in which his unit flew some 200 ARVN troops to Dong Xoai, 50 miles northeast of Saigon. "It turned into one of the hottest battles we had gone into. The next day I had a chance to go to the battleground and see the destruction—women, children, and babies lying dead on the ground. The thing that really struck me was the senselessness of it all. I think I saw more dead women and children than soldiers."

Wright said the Viet Cong had attacked an ARVN post and lined up the soldiers and their families and massacred them. "My answer to those who sympathize with the Viet Cong is that if they were able to see for themselves, as I did at Dong Xoai, there wouldn't be any question in their minds as to who is cruel and who isn't. I think people who accuse the United States of wrongdoing in this war are really being unfair."

Wright does not view the conflict "in terms of winning or losing." He believes the American buildup in Vietnam "has contributed a lot to stopping the fighting." The "ideal solution would be if the people of South Vietnam would be allowed to determine the kind of government they want without threat of force or outside pressure." In his opinion, the American military push has raised "the morale of the South Vietnam forces" and infused "a new spirit in the people."

The number of black officers in South Vietnam is relatively small, no more than two percent of the total. Blacks who want commissions, however, have discovered they will probably be judged more fairly and objectively by military reviewing boards than by most civilian corporation officials in the United States. "Just pass the right tests and say the right things," said Navy Lieutenant Jon A. Shelton, 26, who graduated from the Naval Academy at Annapolis in 1961 and is now with the U.S. Naval Advisory Group in Cantho, a Mekong delta center 50 miles southwest of Saigon. Shelton mans a desk in an old French yacht club overlooking the docks of South Vietnam's river assault group. He lives with several other officers in a French-built house across the road and claims Cantho is "one of the nicest towns in Vietnam."

Shelton, third of five sons of a Washington, D.C., Pullman car inspector, spent two years on an attack transport ship before going to Vietnam in May as assistant fourth naval zone adviser. He is proud of the South Vietnamese with whom he works. "They're the best in the Vietnam navy. They're better educated, they have high morale, almost no desertions. Basically we're winning in the delta." The outcome will depend on "who can stay here the longest—if you sit around and wait, they're going to take it all."

Captain William Cummins, Jr., with the fifth special forces at Bien Hoa, 20 miles north of Saigon, doubts if "you'd find a better opportunity for the black man than in the army." Cummins, who got a regular army commission as a "distinguished military student" at Morgan State in Baltimore, completed special forces training, cold weather mountain school, the pathfinders' course, and airborne training before getting orders to Vietnam. "The ultimate aim for a career officer is to be in combat. Here's where the war is going on. Here's where you're needed the most. That's why I'm here." His current assignment as a green beret in Vietnam, he says, is "the greatest I've ever had."

Gripes are more common among enlisted men than officers, but not always for racial reasons. "I volunteered for the peacetime army," said one private first class, manning a radio on a patrol. "This is war, man. I want to go home." The armed forces say they no longer calculate the numbers by race, but blacks are estimated to fill about 20 percent of enlisted ranks in Vietnam. Their numbers are especially high in airborne outfits like the 101st airborne division and the 173rd brigade, where some battalions are as much as 35 percent black.

Like white troops, blacks accept their fates in Vietnam with varying degrees of eagerness, apathy, or dislike. Outright discrimination is a rare complaint.

Corporal Henry Whaley, 25, of New Haven, Connecticut, was leaning against the turret of a marine corps tank when I encountered him. The tank was on a bluff near Danang, and he was looking through a pair of field glasses toward a village. "You see those people over there? It looks like they're running." Whaley and a second lieutenant on the tank surmised that they were VC returning from ambush points—though they weren't carrying weapons. "Can't shoot 'em unless we're sure," drawled the Tennessee-born white lieutenant.

Whaley looked through the field glasses again and spotted some other marines herding VC "suspects" through the village. "It's not bad here," he said, putting down the glasses. "I sure wish I was home, though." He watched a crowd of peasant women follow their "suspect" husbands and sons out of the village. The sounds of the women wailing for their loved ones carried across the rice paddies. "I guess you have to do it this way," he said. "Otherwise, you'll be doing it in the United States, but it'll be rougher then."

Sergeant Robert Jenkins, 27, expressed somewhat deeper convictions—the result of a dozen years of marine corps service. Jenkins, who lied about his age and joined the corps at 15, believes "they should take all the demonstrators at home and bring them over here." Better yet, "they should let them fight for the VC." He is convinced "those kids are just afraid to join up and fight" and the best cure for them would be a dose of action.

In charge of administration for his company, Jenkins thinks the United States and South Vietnam forces have finally taken the initiative. "In August I didn't think either side was winning," he said, looking over the sandy stretches of wasteland near Danang toward the bristly mountains where the Viet Cong are known to hide. "We first had orders not to shoot until they shot at us. Later we were told to go out and get them like we're supposed to. So now we're gonna get them."

The life of a typical marine is tough. Night and day, they sweat under scalding sun, flounder in muddy foxholes, are constantly on patrol in search of VC. "Every marine knew what he was in for," said Jenkins. "If they didn't want this kind of life, they could have joined the air force. It's pretty tough, but then think how the Vietnamese live. They have it even tougher." As for discrimination, Jenkins said he never really encountered it—"at least in any way that counted very much."

The envy of the troops in the field are the airmen and sailors, who at least are assured of relatively comfortable bunks at night and three hot meals a day. "But it isn't that easy," said Staff Sergeant Otis Boler, Jr., a jet aircraft mechanic at Danang. "You're always worried about your plane. You check over and over again to make sure nothing goes wrong." Boler, a 30-year-old Philadelphian, had just finished "pre-flighting" a B57 bomber when I spoke to him. "I can think of places I'd rather be," he said, "but I have to be here so I make the best of it."

Boler had dreamed of becoming a pilot when he decided on the air force 13 years ago. "First of all, I didn't have the education, so I became a mechanic. It's the next best thing. Eventually I hope to become a crew chief." The roar of jets sweeping up and down the runways behind him occasionally made conversation impossible. "You get a chance to take a test just like everybody else," he yelled above the sound. "A lot of us that are fairly intelligent just don't have the get-up-and-go, but I've seen several black pilots, and I think there'll be more of them."

There's no question in the mind of Air Force Staff Sergeant Johnson

Rooks as to which service is basically the toughest. "The air force has better people," said Rooks, whose wife and two daughters live in Savannah. "The army will take people the air force won't look at." Rooks, 31, is a loadmaster on a C123, an all-purpose cargo plane that lumbers through the skies above South Vietnam with the dependability of a Mack truck.

"I've flown all over Southeast Asia," said Sergeant Rooks. "I've been to Bangkok—I love that place—and to Singapore and the Philippines. They work the hell out of us. Like yesterday I worked sixteen and a half hours. We were carrying chickens, ducks, pigs, ammunition, rice, passengers, everything. It's the only plane over here that can carry a decent payload—10,000 pounds—and still get into a short strip. My plane's been shot at five times. Yesterday they hit the air force letters. You don't generally feel it as such. You hear a big crack, and then you know your plane's been hit. But it's hard to knock one of 'em down. It's a pretty swell plane."

Sergeant Rooks is just as proud of the pilots as he is of the C123s. "I think we've got the best over here. I've got even more confidence in them than the plane." As for the VC, "We've got them whipped only they don't have sense enough to know it. The VC efforts are fruitless and stupid. All they're doing now is dying and not gaining anything."

While many black servicemen involved in the war agree with Rooks, some have quite a different outlook on the wisdom of America's involvement. The dissenters may be in a minority, but their views are significant, especially when contrasted with those of other servicemen in Vietnam and Americans at home.

An air force sergeant, for instance, said that two months in Vietnam were enough to give him "a very bitter attitude toward the whole conflict." The sergeant, who asked that his name not be used, said the United States "shouldn't be here." Many Vietnamese, he believes, are simply "making money out of us" and did not really care who won. "I've seen so much cheating going on, it's just amazing." The sergeant denied discrimination in the air force but said, "For some blacks, with all those civil rights problems at home, it's hard to understand why we should be fighting here." At the same time, he criticized American students for "going about their protest the wrong way" and "not knowing much about the war."

An army private whom I saw unloading goods from a truck at Bien

Hoa had somewhat the same view. "I don't know why I should be work-ing here," he said, "when we've got enough to keep us busy in the States." He repeated the common criticism that America was involved in a situa-tion that's "none of its business" and that the South Vietnam government was "so weak it doesn't deserve to run the country." The private, who also asked that his name not be used, admitted his view was not exactly popular in the barracks. "They've been listening to too much propaganda. I think some of those students are right when they say we should pull out and let the Vietnamese settle their own problems."

The armed forces have encountered some serious cases of dissi-dence, but it is difficult to say whether or not racial questions were involved. Three soldiers, all black, in the first air cav got sentences ranging from two to ten years for attempting a hunger strike and refus-ing to go with their units to South Vietnam. Another soldier, Johnnie L. Jackson of Washington, D.C., was sentenced to six months for disobeying a sergeant in the States—and got three years for joining the others in the hunger strike and refusing to get off the ship.

I happened to see Jackson and the three others just before their general court-martial in An Khe, present home of the first air cav. "I don't think we should be in Vietnam at all," said Jackson, pointing to his wrists. "You see these handcuffs? That's how the army treats you." A military police sergeant—a black—ordered Jackson to shut up. "You can use my name," Jackson shouted to me. "Go ahead and use my name." Then, just to make certain, he yelled out, slowly, "That's J-A-C-K-S-O-N!" The sergeant cursed and asked me to leave. "I can't do nothin' about him, but you can help by not leading him on."

Both North Vietnam and the National Liberation Front in the South have tried to capitalize on America's civil rights struggle in broadcasts aimed at persuading black troops not to fight. After one of the court-martials, the Vietnam News Agency in Hanoi put out a story that concluded, "The new repressive acts further testified to the increasing fear of the U.S. imperialists in the face of mounting anti-war move-ment among U.S. troops." Radio Hanoi, Radio Peking, and the VC's Liberation Radio regularly report and comment on civil rights prob-lems in America.

Yet common cause unites black with white troops in Vietnam more closely than at military installations in the United States. One white air force sergeant told me he believed the average black worked harder than did the average white airman in Vietnam. "They want to prove they can do the job," he said. Diehard white southerners cooperate with blacks on duty with only occasional complaints. Some of them say blacks are "lazy," but most don't really notice if a black or white troop is assigned a particular job. Black officers are respected, and the sergeants appear as well-liked or disliked on average as white NCOs.

The armed forces' authority to give orders accounts for the degree of integration achieved in the years since President Truman's landmark decision to break up black units, but social segregation still exists. In the mess halls, in the barracks, even in tents in the field, blacks tend to mix with blacks and whites with whites. There are innumerable exceptions, but the rule remains. Blacks explain they don't feel at ease with whites, and a white said, "It just seems to work out that way." At the airmen's open mess at Tan Son Nhut, white airmen almost always congregate on one side of the room and blacks on the other.

The situation is even more acute in Saigon, where hundreds of soldiers and airmen flock nightly to bars, restaurants, shops, and movies. Almost every bar along Tu Do Street in downtown Saigon is for whites only. Blacks who wander in are greeted with curious, often hostile, stares. They complain that sometimes they are not served, and usually the girls will not talk to them, much less go out later.

Across the Saigon River, near the docks, a row of brightly lit nightclubs caters especially to blacks. It's there that black troops gather, talk to the girls, get drunk, and have their good times, at least in Saigon. Fights have broken out—but few of a racial nature. Blacks say they feel at home with their friends in the bars near the docks. "I just like to have a couple of beers and relax," said a sergeant in slacks and sport shirt. "I don't want to feel that I'm not welcome."

The bargirls say the blacks generally treat them well and are big spenders when they have the money. The bars are slightly more run down than those on Tu Do, and the girls are not quite so good-looking. The blacks blame the white troops for social segregation in Saigon and in other new soldier towns such as Danang, Nha Trang, Hue, and Vung Tau. "I'll tell you exactly what happens," said a black airman in the Playboy bar, once the scene of a VC bomb blast, now dimly lit and subdued behind crossed-iron screens. "The white guys tell the girls, 'If you drink with colored guys, we won't bring you any business.' The girls don't care who they drink with, but they want the business so they do as they're told."

There is another side to the story. The Vietnamese, like other Asians, are deeply color-conscious. They have developed a carefully graded scale, placing people with dark skins at the bottom. "They think anyone with a very dark complexion is ugly," said an American who has spent a number of years in the country and speaks fluent Vietnamese. "Some of them wouldn't drink with blacks even if the white Americans didn't care at all."

Whatever the reasons, social segregation exists in military towns in Vietnam as in Germany, Japan, Korea, and other places where large numbers of American troops are based. So far, the issue has given Radio Hanoi and Liberation Radio little to crow about, but they did report one fight involving black and white marines in Danang. American senior officers are clearly nervous and reluctant to discuss the situation. "After all, there's not much we can do," said a lieutenant colonel in the army. "We can tell soldiers what to do on duty, but we can't order the bar owners around." The problem is not yet serious. Many troops—black and white—who do not get to Saigon are not aware of it. There is the potential for unpleasantness, however, and military leaders claim they are powerless to combat it.

Upset as they are by social discrimination, black troops try not to let it affect their work. I spoke to several in the Casanova, on the same block as the Playboy. They talked in enthusiastic terms of the American military effort. "The people at home don't know what's going on here," was the gist of their remarks. "We're putting all we can into it," and "Listen, we're working as hard as anybody," were other observations. But when we got to the subject of social discrimination, their attitudes changed at once. "Don't see why this has to go on. . . . It's stupid if you ask me. . . . We're in the fight the same as everyone else."

And they are. "I volunteered to come here," said Sergeant Willie Waters. "The main reason was, I'd never been in combat. I wanted to make sure I was capable of leading men under those conditions. This was the only war we had." Waters, who flies in a helicopter almost every day, thinks he knows more about the war than about the civil rights issue. "For the 190 years we've had an army, we've never lost," he said emphatically. "The American soldier is the easiest soldier in the world to teach. It won't take us forever and a day to learn how to fight this war. We're going to win it in the end."

Saigon, July 1971

Turn left off one of the main streets leading to the gates of sprawling Tan Son Nhut air base and you find where it's at in Saigon. It happens on "Soul Alley," where the brothers get together, get close, real tight and rap, let it all out, and none of the rabbits or lifers, as career military men are known, dares bother them. Check it out, dig it, around five or six of an evening when they start getting back from their jobs as clerks and communications specialists, security guards and drivers, or whatever else the army makes a man do in this country. The brothers, almost all of them enlisted men in olive drab fatigues, stroll down the alley while soul blares from the bars and clubs, and some of them settle down for a game of cards in the few hours before night falls. Then, around midnight, Soul Alley empties as they retreat to their rooms in the cement block apartment houses and homes with tin roofs that crowd the neighborhood.

"Technically, we're not even supposed to be here," says one of the brothers, talking to an intruder in the shadows of a small shop purveying cold canned soft drinks, stolen or purchased for illegal resale from the base exchange at Tan Son Nhut. "We're supposed to be living on the base. It's the only way we can get away from the harassment, the 'man,' the 'lifers.' Here we can live the way we want and do what we want. It's home to us."

Soul Alley, in fact, is home to only a small percentage of black GIs in Vietnam—200 or 300 at most, including deserters and AWOLs, some of whom have been living in the maze of surrounding walkways for months and even years. Soul Alley attracts hundreds more blacks for a few hours, an evening, or a weekend before they return to their quarters and duties at posts surrounding Saigon. Even if the majority of the approximately 20,000 blacks in Vietnam have never visited Soul Alley, almost all of them have heard of it and view it as a symbol of their desires and needs in what many of them describe as a white man's army fighting a useless war.

"You get to live with the Vietnamese. You stay in the same houses with them," says a GI, explaining the symbolism, the sense of identification, inherent in a place like Soul Alley. "You find out the problems the Vietnamese go through to live from day to day. They're striving, the same as our people. They want to progress, same as we do. Here's President Thieu staying in his palace making money, and these people are hustling for bread. Check it out. Same as President Nixon in the White House, and the blacks gettin' nothin'. There it is."

The GI, who goes by the soul name of Brother Rap, articulates better than most of his friends the underlying attitude of thousands of blacks now serving in Vietnam. Only a few years ago, in September 1965, asked to write an article on racial problems among GIs in Vietnam, I'd interviewed black soldiers from all services, in all regions, and discovered their attitude was almost universally enthusiastic and highly motivated. They had gripes, like most GIs regardless of racial, ethnic, or social background, but basically they liked the army, were grateful for the opportunities it provided, approved of the war, and thought we were beating "Charlie," as the VC were then known. (Now GIs refer to the VC as "gooks," "dinks," and "slopes." The term "Charlie" for VC is distinctly old-fashioned.)

Indeed, I had found former black GIs more vocal than white soldiers in defense of the war. "The army's tough, but it's good for us," a black GI from Philadelphia told me in 1965 while on patrol in jungles north of Saigon. "We can get rank here where we can't even get jobs on the outside."

Brother Rap is not impressed by my experiences of nearly six years ago in interviewing black GIs. "The army treats us like dirt," he says. "If you're white and you're in the army and you don't dig black, you can be real mean. You can put false charges against us. You can give us little details." Another GI, previously silent during my conversations with Brother Rap, interrupts. "The army's the most prejudiced place I've ever been in," he says, and then unhesitatingly gives his name: Spec 4 William Gary, 23, from Chicago. "I don't mind saying who I am. Anybody wants to know who I am and how I feel, they're welcome to it." Gary, like most of the blacks I meet, bitterly criticizes the army for small, seemingly petty daily offenses rather than for having sent him here in the first place.

"You can go on sick call and you're black and they give you some detail," says Gary, toying with a chain of beads with a black cross around his neck. "You go see the IG [Inspector General] or chaplain, and they won't do a damn thing for you. You sit around down here minding your own business, and the MPs come on lookin' for you, sayin' you're AWOL."

Whether or not such complaints are entirely justified, they are representative of the changing, angry mood among black GIs. Not all of those whom I interview, from the mountainous jungle-covered northern provinces to the flatlands around Saigon, complain about racial discrimination as such, but not one of them believes, really, in either the army or the war. They are clearly attuned to both racial and student problems in the States and aver, almost to a man, that they'd rather join their brothers "in the real war back in the world" than go on fighting in Vietnam.

The attitudes of black GIs to some extent parallel those of white soldiers, many of whom are also extremely embittered by their military experience, but resentment among blacks penetrates much deeper. Whites talk of returning to more or less conventional lives—homes, families, jobs, and school. Blacks tend to discuss "revolution" and "liberation" from the "system" and react swiftly, sometimes violently, to racial slights and slurs. Blacks and whites, more so than at any time since the end of formal segregation in the armed forces more than 20 years ago, tend to cluster in their own cliques and rarely talk or socialize with each other. Blacks assert their identity and independence in hairstyles, dress, language, music—just as they hang together on Soul Alley, their own neighborhood, whenever they have a chance.

"If you pulled all the blacks out of Vietnam, you'd have the biggest revolution you've ever seen in the United States," says another brother whom I meet in one of the bars off Soul Alley. "You better believe when Nixon pulls us out there won't be no more United States. The blacks know demolition. The blacks know how to shoot. We're gonna use all that stuff back in the world"—the term GIs often use to mean "back in the States." These words may appear exaggerated, but blacks in Vietnam have begun to organize just as their brothers have done at home. During our conversation one of them pulls out a plastic card printed on one side in red, black, and green stripes. "That's the flag of the Black Liberation Front of the armed forces," he says, noting his own name above that of the president, Bobby Wilson, on the back.

"Bobby Wilson never talks to people," says the brother, in response to my suggestion that he arrange an interview. "He's here, though. We know him." The GIs rated the Black Liberation Front and the Black Panthers as the two most influential organizations among black GIs in Vietnam.

"Go to Troop Command, Company D, across from the Pacesetter

Service Club at Long Binh," one of the GIs on Soul Alley advises when I ask where I can learn more about these organizations. The next day I hire a taxi and drive down the crowded four-lane highway from Saigon to Long Binh, the large logistics and command center 15 miles northeast of Saigon. I wave at the MPs at the gate, and they wave my car into the post on the incorrect assumption that I'm a civilian employee on contract with the government.

Rather than look at once for the Pacesetter Service Club, I ask the driver to stop in front of the Long Binh Jail, "LBJ," as it's generally known. (If you're black, you get put in a big box at the LBJ," Brother Rap told me at Soul Alley. "You sit in there all day with the sun beating down. You might spend your whole time there. The LBJ is a real black man's university.")

As I walk toward the barred front gate of the stockade, a jeep stops and three men get out, two whites and a black. The whites are guarding the black, who's just been sentenced to three months' confinement. "What for?" I ask the black GI. "It would take me all day to explain," he says, then raises his fist in a black power salute and disappears through the gate with his guards.

A white sentry tells me to see the stockade commandant before asking more questions. I go to the headquarters, a neat grey frame structure with clipped green grass in front, and see three blacks painting the walls. "We're parolees," explains one of them, Sergeant Charles Trigg, 24, of Racine, Wisconsin. "We do outside jobs while serving our sentence." Trigg has no particular grudges against the guards inside the LBJ but talks about the circumstances of his arrest and conviction. "They gave guys promotions to say I was AWOL," he says. "My CO told me, 'If you stay in my unit, I'm gonna git you.' I was held in pretrial confinement for two and a half months. They accused me of being militant, a junkie. The first sergeant of my unit had a map of the U.S. with 'Wallace Country' written on it. That shows what kind of people they are."

Before Trigg can go on with his story, a colonel walks out the door and tells me I can't talk to parolees. He directs me to the office of the brigade public information officer, who carefully writes down a series of questions I want to ask the LBJ commandant, who later refuses to grant me an interview.

Then the brigade information officer tells me to visit the main information office at USARV—U.S. Army Vietnam—headquarters on a small knoll a mile or so away. At USARV, a lieutenant colonel informs me of a new regulation that an information officer must escort all reporters at all times on army posts in Vietnam. He orders a young lieutenant to accompany me to the Pacesetter Service Club. I expect the lieutenant to interfere with my questions, or at least to inhibit the blacks whom I want to interview, but he politely sits a few tables away from me during private conversations.

"The colonel put me out of my unit because I was a suspected Black Panther," says the first GI I meet, Spec 4 Bernard Barges, 20, of Columbus, Georgia. "The policy was to send all suspected Panthers into the field. I had a lifer looking for me. He really wanted to get me. I've been transferred eight times in nine months, and I never did anything." Another 20-year-old spec 4, Ernest B. Stokes, from Chicago, joins Barges and me for coffee. "We had a Black Panther meeting right outside the door of the service club," says Stokes. "It was a peaceful, calm meeting. Everybody was discussing their feelings. Nothing was happening, but the MPs came down there and broke it up. If there's too many blacks in a crowd, they think we're making trouble."

Barges says one or two men lead all the blacks in every company and try to unite them against slurs from whites. Sergeants from rural southern or tough urban backgrounds are apparently the ones most likely to bait them. "They had a racial riot at the enlisted men's club a while ago," says Barges. "The whites wanted to play country music, and we wanted soul music. Seems like every time we tried to play soul, some sergeant came along and turned it off and put on something else."

The riot was not particularly serious, but it was typical of the increasing number of clashes between racial groups in the wind-down period of American involvement in the war. A few whites and blacks fought each other, crowds gathered, the MPs came, and, in this instance, the incident was over. "The next night the colonels had guards lined up on either side of the street with M16 rifles." Racial clashes of this sort occur much more frequently in rear areas, where soldiers often live in boredom, with not enough to do, than on firebases and patrols in the bush, where GIs are primarily concerned with survival against an elusive foe.

Like the brothers in Soul Alley, Stokes and Barges both urge me to go to Company D, Troop Command, in a row of dingy wooden barracks across the red dirt road in front of the service club and ask some of the Black Panthers about racial incidents and provocations. "You can tell the Panthers by the black tams they're wearing on their heads," says Barges, walking me out of the service club and pointing me in the right direction. Trailed by my lieutenant escort, I enter one of the barracks and find a GI who calls himself "Brother Lacey" sitting on a bunk in his darkened cubicle. "The tam is just like a symbol of what we do," says Lacey. "A lot of guys wear peace signs on their caps, so I think we should wear black berets when we want. The CO gave five guys extra duty for wearing them." Another GI, "Brother Money," walks into the cubicle and reveals the existence of still another black organization known as PUFF, People's Union to Fight Fascism.

"The pressure in this company is rough," explains Brother Money. "We need PUFF and the Panthers to hold us together." Brother Money and Brother Lacey both agree the young whites are not particularly to blame. "The old whites are the trouble," says Money. "The only beef we got is with the old lifers, black or white. You don't have any black lifers to turn to. They think just like the old whites. They're all Toms." Money notes the black lifers refuse even to engage in the black handshake, known as the DAP, Dignity for Afro Peoples. Black GIs, wherever they meet in Vietnam, customarily exchange the handshake by banging their fists together a number of times in an elaborate ritual that infuriates most commanders and noncoms, who view it as a departure from conventional military discipline. "The Toms are afraid the man will think they want to get on with us if they go in for Dapping," says Money. "They're more white than the whites."

"They hate to see the blacks can get together," says a third GI, Sergeant Fred Wilkerson, 22, of Macon, Georgia, the only one in the group who doesn't hesitate to reveal his full name. "They don't think we can get together without violence." One gesture that particularly annoyed white superiors was a daily formation called by the blacks in honor of all black GIs who've died in Vietnam. The idea, says Brother Money, "is to show the man we sympathized with all the blacks out there in the field dying for nothing." The army finally persuaded the blacks to cancel their impromptu demonstrations by sending a black civilian employee around to talk to some of them.

"He said how dangerous it could be if we continued to organize," says Brother Money. "He told me he had no sides. He didn't belong to anything. He had no right to be talking." The blacks agreed to call off some of their meetings, but their anger never faded. "This is the last war we fight," says Money. "The last generation in America sang songs and poems. The next time will be guns and rifles—at home."

Besides deepening anger and resentment among black GIs, the war also is having another effect that frightens enlisted men and officers alike—and knows no racial boundaries. Blacks and whites freely admit that more than half of them have adopted the heroin habit in Vietnam and are not sure what they can do about it. "They need to get everybody out of the 'Nam because there's too much dope," says one of the blacks at Company D. "Eighty percent of the young people in 'Nam are on dope. They're all getting strung out on heroin."

Another GI informs me that heroin is available for $2.50 a vial from Vietnamese outside the post gate—or $50 on post. "For $20 you can get ten vials. In the States one vial costs $160. Over here it's 97 percent pure. In the States, it's only 15 percent." GIs often begin their addiction by smoking marijuana cigarettes laced with heroin and then advance to snorting and skin-popping without marijuana. Almost all GIs smoke marijuana, which few regard as a serious problem. The real menace, GIs contend, is heroin, an almost unshakable habit once it really hooks you.

The blacks at Company D, however, resent the white man's complaint that black GIs are responsible for the drug problem. "They say the young blacks are the cause of drugs here," says Brother Money, "but it's the young whites and the Vietnamese who sell it to them." Money charges that noncoms often deter black GIs from entering the army's "amnesty program" for breaking the habit. "Say I go up there and go through the program," says Money. "Then I come back here and the sergeant's been tellin' everyone I've been on drugs though he's not supposed to tell anyone. . . ."

Before Money finishes his thought the door of the cubicle swings open and a major stands framed against the light in the corridor. "I'm the information officer for the support command," he informs me. "Where's your escort?" The polite lieutenant, who has remained outside the room, identifies himself. The major rebukes the lieutenant for not having informed him I am here and then forbids further interviews in the barracks.

"They're afraid we gonna say something," says Brother Lacey. "We don't have any privacy at all. That's how they jump on the blacks." As I'm about to leave, Money signals Lacey, and Lacey puts on a recording of "Whitey's Got a God Complex." Blacks from other cubicles appear in the hall. They begin giving each other the black hand-shake, temporarily blocking the major, the lieutenant, and me as we begin to walk down the hall of the barrack to the front door. "Hey, I want to talk to the reporter," say a couple of blacks, and the major says anyone who wants to talk to me can see me in his presence in the company headquarters.

Two blacks follow us to the orderly room, where I ask more questions. The presence of the major does not bother them particularly. "The blacks get treated worse than the whites," says one of them, Spec 4 Donald Brooker, 22, of Philadelphia. "When I first came, I try my best to straighten up. The lifers try to make me screw up." Brooker says he never even smoked pot before arriving in Vietnam. He doesn't admit having experimented with hard drugs, but he blames service in Vietnam for having inculcated the habit in his friends. "The main reason people use drugs is not just to escape reality but to get away from the stress and strain," says the other GI, Private Anthony Austin Dumas, 21, of San Francisco. "It gets so bad here, it's the only way to relieve stress."

Brooker and Dumas basically confirm impressions I've already picked up in dozens of other interviews. I wonder, though, how GIs feel just before they leave Vietnam. Could it be that they're a little happier then—willing, possibly, to forgive and forget some of the suffering they've endured in their year here? I ask for permission to visit the 90th replacement battalion, the unit through which all GIs must pass on their way from duty in the southern half of South Vietnam to the United States. USARV headquarters grants my request, and four days later assigns the same lieutenant to escort me to the 90th. I find several hundred GIs spending their last hours in Vietnam before boarding the "Freedom Bird" for the ride to the West Coast. Not all of them are looking forward to peace on the home front after their year at war.

"We're gonna lose here," says Spec 5 Gregory Brigham, 22, of Albemarle, North Carolina. "There's too much going on 'back in the world.' That's where we're fighting the big war." Almost to a man, the blacks I meet at the end of their tours are planning, one way or another, to support their brothers in the States. "I'm gonna throw all my medals right on the White House steps," says Spec 4 Charles Doswell, 21, of Richmond, Virginia, who spent most of his year here in an artillery battery. "I got a bronze star, and I don't know what for."

Only two or three years ago most GIs, black or white, would have been glad to have had a bronze star on their records, deserved or not. Now, however, medals and rank seem to have lost much of their meaning, especially for blacks, who regard them as white men's status symbols. "Medals can't help you get a job these days," says Doswell. "Nobody cares anymore." Sergeant Bobby Dozier, 21, of Charlotte, North Carolina, echoes Doswell's views. "It's just a political war," he says. "A bunch of people are makin' money off it." Doswell and Dozier both promise, after they return to the States, to join "some kind of black organization." Not one of the blacks whom I interview has the slightest desire to reenlist in the army after his current tour.

"Don't fight a war," warns Spec 4 Mack Hart, 22, of Chicago. "That way you can't lose a war. This war doesn't make any sense. Nobody knows what the hell we're over here for." The futility inherent in Hart's remark summarizes the attitude of black GIs as they look back over the history of this seemingly endless struggle. As far as most blacks are concerned, the war is already over and lost. Now they anticipate a larger, much more important struggle for themselves— "back in the world."

Jacqueline Kennedy with Prince Sihanouk during trip to Phnom Penh,
November 1967. In background, wearing sunglasses, is Lord Harlech. Barely
visible through Sihanouk's left hand, wearing glasses, is Charles Bartlett,
columnist.

Helicopter lifting off from jungle region in Fishhook during American invasion of
Cambodia, May 1970.

Vietnamese refugee casts a worried look while sitting on boat carrying him down Mekong from Cambodia to South Vietnam after invasion of Cambodia. He's sitting among family possessions.

Family of two kids run down and killed by American armored personnel carrier huddle under rubber tree, Memot rubber plantation, Fishhook, Cambodia, May 1970, as described in Chapter 1, "We Must Accept."

Vietnamese refugees killed by Cambodian troops in town of Prasaut, east of Svay Rieng, Cambodia, on route 1, April 9, 1970. Refugees were fleeing Cambodia for Vietnam. This scene described in Chapter 11, A Prince's "Oasis."

More gore, body shots from same massacre in Prasaut, April 9, 1970 (picture taken the morning after).

Relatives of massacred Vietnamese sit among the bodies in the Prasaut massacre.

Vietnamese refugee kids, Cambodia, Spring 1970, looking unhappy about their lot, with mother looking over them.

On the move—Cambodian villagers crowd bullock carts to get out of the way of widening war, Spring 1970.

Gory find—skulls and bones turn up as Cambodian soldiers look for victims of Khmer Rouge. This grave is in Prey Veng, 1985 (see Chapter 11, A Prince's "Oasis").

Officer candidates in new Cambodian army train on Chinese-made weapon, 1985.

Statue in Neak Loung, where Route One crosses Mekong southeast of Phnom Penh, of Cambodian and Vietnamese soldiers shows alliance between Hanoi and Phnom Penh after expulsion of the Khmer Rouge at end of 1978.

Border crossing, from Cambodia to South Vietnam. That's Canadian cameraman Maurice Embre on the right, 1970.

Prince Sihanouk, November 1967, makes a show of returning three American sailors whose patrol boat wandered into Cambodian waters. He's in Phnom Penh. Note American flag, though he'd broken with U.S. three years earlier.

U.S. army soldier, on Navy PBR (patrol boat river, see glossary) in the Mekong in Spring 1970. The boat was part of joint U.S. army-navy riverine force.

Chopper comes into landing zone, door-gunner at the ready.

ABC News correspondent Steve Bell and cameraman during Cambodian invasion, May 1970, landing zone Valkyrie.

GIs take a break, LZ Valkyrie (could be anywhere in war).

This GI's got a monkey in his hand.

KKK (see glossary), CIA-trained Cambodian troops, identifiable by their American M16s and American boots, relaxing on the way to war, May 1970.

GIs give the peace sign, around 1970.

GIs stand over body of dead enemy POW, killed when looking for mines at their command during patrol on "Gaza Strip," near Chu Lai, July 1971. This scene described in Chapter 5, "Kill One . . . Kill Them All."

Medic stares at body of dead POW, "Gaza Strip," near Chu Lai.

Black GI raises both fists in double black power salute.

Checking into the Long Binh jail. That's where GIs were sentenced for various misdeeds.

Couple of black GIs, airing their gripes, Long Binh, 1971, as recounted in Chapter 7, "We're Here to Win."

Laotian soldiers man
fighting holes at key road
junction north of Vientiane.

Laotian soldiers at firebase at Sala Phoukhoune, 1969.

Desolate mountain base, Muong Kasi, in Laos, 1969.

Ready for war. Lao soldier with grenades ready to fire, 1969.

Village kids stare balefully at the author's camera near key junction in Laos, 1969.

Street scene, Vientiane, Laos. That's old Hotel Constellation, hangout of journalists, on left. Owner Maurice had the Heineken franchise for the country. Note beer van in front.

Opium smokers in Laos, around 1969. They did inhale.

Crowd surges across street from Hanoi Hilton, as the prison for American POWS was known, for look at the final release of American pilots, March 29, 1973 (see Epilogue).

Last of American POWs, captured pilots, and navigators, line up after getting off the bus that carried them from Hanoi Hilton to Gia Lam Airport, Hanoi, for the ride home on C141 Starlifter.

Last of POWs ready to leave Hanoi's Gia Lam Airport on C141 Starlifter, background with Red Cross on tail.

8

"The Whole Thing's Pointless"

The attitudes of GIs did not turn seriously until President Johnson stopped the bombing of North Vietnam and agreed to enter into peace talks with Hanoi and the National Liberation Front in late 1968.* Until then, in visits to the field, GIs spoke optimistically, if grudgingly, of what they'd accomplished in Vietnam and often seemed rather proud to have done their time. Many of them angrily criticized demonstrators back in the States, notably those who were avoiding the draft by going to college.

The change in GI attitudes in 1969 was so sudden that I wasn't aware of it until a free-lance journalist named Ewing Carruthers told me of conversations he'd been having with GIs on firebases near Saigon. The "V" sign had suddenly assumed a new meaning—as a symbol for peace rather than victory. GIs who obviously were not at all concerned about winning were flashing it at bases all over South Vietnam.

In the spring of 1969, during a series of massive demonstrations in

---

*The NLF's Provisional Revolutionary Government was formed in March 1969—and formally assumed the NLF's place at the table. South Vietnam was the reluctant fourth participant. For a clear account, see Allen E. Goodman, *The Lost Peace: America's Search for a Negotiated Settlement of the Vietnam War* (Stanford: Hoover Institution Press, 1978).

Washington, I visited GIs outside Tay Ninh, a provincial center northwest of Saigon not far from the Cambodian border, and watched as some of them fired machine guns and cannon at the conical form of the legendary Black Virgin Mountain, as the Americans called Nui Ba Den, literally Mount Black Lady, for years a favorite VC hideout. Most of the soldiers did not sympathize much with the demonstrators, but the overwhelming sentiment was that war was a waste, that "we aren't fighting it like we should," that "we should go home and let the dinks fight their own war."

GI morale from 1969 onward deteriorated rapidly, so much so that I spent a month in the northern provinces in 1971 reporting on GI attitudes. By this time the GIs, in more danger from hard drugs than from the enemy, by and large applauded the demonstrators. "I wish I was there with them," was a commonplace remark. The senselessness of the struggle, at this stage, was nowhere more apparent than among the dull, desolate hills west of Danang.

Danang, August 1971

It is late afternoon on the dirt brown outcroppings and pale green brush of Charlie Ridge, and the 18 or 20 remaining men of the first platoon and headquarters of Delta company are slowly emerging from under their poncho liners, which they have strung up as tents to protect themselves from the sweltering dry-season sun. "Who's going on that patrol?" asks Spec 4 Garrett Gentry, a tall Californian with a shock of sandy hair. Gentry is "pig man"—M60 machine gunner—and he is nearing the end of twelve months in the field. He would prefer to do as little patrolling as possible.

As if to answer the question, Sergeant First Class Louis Tartaglione, first platoon's craggy, gravel-voiced leader, announces he's heard people by the stream, a bare trickle hidden by thick underbrush at the base of the spine on which Delta has encamped for the night—and, it seems, the day as well. No one really believes there are people by the stream.

Sergeant Tartaglione, a Brooklynese known as "Tag" to the troops, avers, at 36, that he's "too old for this war," and it's quite possible he's confused by the sound of falling limbs or the rustle of small animals. Still, since someone must go on patrol down there, two or three GIs absentmindedly pick up M79 grenade launchers and squeeze off a few rounds. "If anyone's there, it'll scare 'em away," one of them remarks as eight or ten men, not including Gentry or Tag, get their stuff together for the walk down the slope.

The shadows are lengthening as the patrol—cursing, chattering, bunching together, breaking all the rules that sergeants are supposed to teach their men—hack their way through elephant grass and bramble that snaps back and claws at faces, sleeves, arms, and legs. Some ten miles to the east, across a flatland of rice paddies and peasant hamlets, one sees the jagged cliffs of Marble Mountain, on the coast just south of the turgid base town of Danang, built for 40,000, now teeming with 400,000, most of them refugees from peasant hamlets destroyed in more than six years of war.

To the southwest, beyond more rice paddies, broken by ugly gashes of earth occupied by South Vietnamese and American troops, lies the "Arizona Territory," a dangerous no-man's-land pocked by shell holes and booby traps, fought over incessantly by soldiers of all kinds—American, South Vietnamese (regular, regional, and popular force), VC, and North Vietnamese. South of the Arizona Territory, running almost to the sea, rises a range of slate-grey peaks, once the scene of daily firefights between U.S. marines and North Vietnamese, now largely left to the latter except for intermittent air strikes and haphazard patrols.

The marines, after having campaigned up and down the northern provinces of South Vietnam since 1965, finally vanished a few months ago. Army officers now walk the graceful tree-shaded grounds on the Han River in Danang from which marine generals directed operations from the beaches of Chu Lai to seasonally muddy or dusty firebases along the DMZ. An army colonel lives in a house atop "Freedom Hill," a barren outcropping just west of Danang air base, from which a marine major general led a 22,000-man division.

The colonel, Rutland Beard, a well-groomed Washingtonian in command of a brigade of 6,000, sends his forces over precisely the same country once traversed by marines—the lowlands, the Arizona Territory, Charlie Ridge to the west, and some of the mountains beyond. "We should have been out of here two years ago," says Beard, an Army War College graduate who would doubtless have been relieved for expressing such heretical views in 1969. "Let some other people police up the world," he adds, during a visit to one of his firebases, a patch of dirt on a steep promontory west of Charlie Ridge. "We have enough problems in CONUS [continental United States]. We should clear up the mess at home."

Later, over a drink in an air-conditioned officers' club, also built by the marines, Colonel Beard, who commanded a battalion south of here on his first Vietnam tour in 1966, revises his statement to conform with national policy. "I feel that I have accomplished my mission if we can get out of here with as few casualties as possible and still accomplish the task we're assigned"—the defense of Danang and environs, including one of the three largest air bases in the country and supply, support, and logistical facilities for U.S. forces spread up and down Military Region One, the five northernmost provinces. Except for occasional isolated forays, the colonel readily concedes, American troops have ceased pursuing the enemy much beyond the first few ridgelines. Among some 70,000 GIs in the entire northern region, no more than 8,000 are beating the bush at one time—and the number may be considerably less than that by the end of the year.

Yet, if there *is* any war, that is, an American war, involving American troops and costing American lives, it is mainly here in Military Region One, once known as "I Corps," whose mountains and rice paddies have absorbed more American blood than the other three regions combined. "We've lost 18 men in our company in the month of July to booby traps," says Sergeant Tag, biting off his words in a Brooklyn accent that's safely survived 17 years of service, including a previous tour in Vietnam. "All we get out of it was killing two dinks in an ambush."

Half a dozen GIs were sitting around an old shell hole eating C-rations when one of them tripped on a hidden wire, setting off a booby trap concealed in the hole. Three men were wounded—two of them partially blinded, one with possible brain damage. "There all night and nothing happens," says a rifleman, recounting the incident as we pause by the stream. "Sit here and watch a buddy get blown away. The whole thing's pointless. We'll never win."

It is, in reality, a desultory kind of struggle, punctuated by occasional explosions and tragedy, for the last Americans in combat in Vietnam. It is a limbo between victory and defeat, a period of lull before the North Vietnamese again seriously challenge allied control over the coastal plain, as they did for the last time in the Tet, May, and September offensives of 1968. For the average "grunt," or infantryman, the war is not so much a test of strength under pressure, as it often was a few years ago, as a daily hassle to avoid patrols, avoid the enemy, avoid contact—to keep out of trouble and not be the last American killed in Vietnam.

"I mean, what does it accomplish, what does it gain?" asks the Delta company forward observer, a captain who attended OCS after graduating from the University of Southern California in Los Angeles. "Even if we kill 500 dinks, to me it's not worth it." The FO—forward observer—calls in artillery strikes on suspected targets in the nearby hills, but he does so with notable lack of relish. "I just saw three dinks down in that rice paddy. One of them was carrying a shiny tube. They were probably VC, but maybe they were civilians with an old shell. I don't think it's right to look for some excuse for shooting at them." Although the FO is an officer, a captain, he articulates the views of the GIs with whom I go on patrol down the ridge.

"The dinks are just playin' with us, waitin' for us to go home, then they'll beat the shit out of the ARVN," says the rifleman in front of me, reiterating a view held by many of his superiors. "It's a lifers' playground, a chance for the generals to test their strategies," the GI enlarges, in thick Georgian tones, as we scramble up from the stream bed, only to stop again a minute later so our pig man can test-fire his machine gun. "Git them cows down there," another GI yells, grinning while the M60 spews a torrent of bullets into the bushes in front of us. The cows, grazing on a rise half a mile away, amble off at the urging of a boy who hears the shots. A couple of grunts idly curse all the lifers, the CO, the NCOs, anyone vaguely responsible for issuing them orders and threats. "If the lifers don't get you," says one soldier, explaining why we don't radio a false location and rest instead of walk, "then the VC will."

Their chatter is hardly unique. In a month visiting units in the field and rear areas around Military Region One, I found literally no young GIs in favor of the war, none who didn't think we should get out, few who didn't hate the lifers almost as much as the "dinks," a term sometimes used to describe ARVN as well as enemy forces. For all the complaints, though, cases of refusal to fight or go to the field are quite rare—perhaps an average of two or three per battalion per month. Virtually every GI in the bush theoretically yearns for a softer job somewhere else, but almost all of them allow time slips by faster here, the "lifers don't hassle you so much" over petty matters of haircut and dress, drugs are less available and duty not so dull as in the rear.

Nor are there more than slim odds these days that a combat GI will die despite the danger of mines set and reset daily by VC sympathizers—often farmers or small boys selling PX Cokes by the road at 50 cents a can. Casualty figures in July receded to the lowest ebb in six years: eleven killed one week, 29 another, approximately 70 for the month, the first since 1965 in which the number of American KIAs was below 100. (The U.S. command now emphasizes low American casualties with the same enthusiasm that it once accorded such statistics as enemy "body counts." At a briefing in mid-August, for instance, a military spokesman proudly disclosed a weekly average of 19 American KIAs for the previous two and a half months, "exactly half the average of 38 KIAs for the year to date." These figures, he noted happily, were low compared to an average of 81 killed each week of last year.)

Specifically ordered to hold down casualties, commanders rarely invade traditional enemy base areas among shadowy crags and valleys to the west, and they carefully disengage from battles in the lowlands if heavy losses seem inevitable or even conceivable.

"There's no longer that intense aggressiveness," laments Lieutenant Colonel Lee Roberts, who enlisted in 1948 at 19, attended OCS after having been turned down for West Point, and now commands a battalion from a mountain firebase 20 miles southwest of Danang. "Instead of going on lengthy sweeps our companies set up defensive positions from which they send out patrols," he explains, sipping coffee from a paper cup in front of his sandbagged command bunker overlooking an undulating velvet-green valley. "If they get into contact," he says, surveying his AO (area of operations) through baleful slate-grey eyes, "they back off and call in air and artillery."

"What we're performing is defense-in-depth," summarizes the information officer at the headquarters of the Americal division, which includes the 196th and two other brigades. "We're interdicting enemy supply routes and infiltration of troops to the lowlands." Off-duty, in the officers' club behind the headquarters, built on rolling sand dunes at Chu Lai for which marines fought bunker to bunker in 1965, a couple of ROTC lieutenants joke about the Americal's notorious past. First there was exposure of the massacres at My Lai, a few miles to the south, followed by the case of a former brigade commander charged with mowing down civilians from his helicopter and, late last year, revelation of the use of a chemical defoliant, Agent Orange, capable of inducing cancer. Then in June, the commanding general was relieved in the aftermath of an attack on a firebase in which 33 GIs were killed—the worst such disaster of the war.

"I'm afraid to tell anyone back in the world I'm with the Americal," says one of the lieutenants, laughing. "No one has much pride in the division. That's one reason morale is so bad."

Despite the image, however, the mission of the Americal, and the attitude of its men, is no different from those of the only other full-strength U.S. division in Vietnam, the 101st airborne, based at Camp Eagle, midway between Danang and the DMZ. Just as the Americal defends Danang and the coast to the south, so the 101st patrols the lowlands and hills beyond the one-time imperial capital of Hue, for political and cultural reasons South Vietnam's most important city after Saigon. Once regarded as the toughest of U.S. divisions, the 101st now appears as wary of combat, as reluctant to fight, as lax in discipline as the Americal. Commanders evoke its traditional nickname, "Screaming Eagles," but GIs these days prefer to call it, not without a certain touch of reverse pride, "the one-oh-*worst*."

"I have seen the Screaming Eagles in action—in the jungles and air and assisting the people of northern Military Region One—and can testify that the outstanding reputation enjoyed by the 101st is completely justified," brags the division commander, Major General Thomas M. Tarpley, somewhat defensively perhaps, in a letter on the inside front cover of the division's slick-paper color magazine, *Rendezvous With Destiny*. The cover itself, however, testifies to the war-weariness of the men whom Tarpley tries to praise. In a watercolor sketch of defoliated trees etched against glowering grey clouds, three GIs are standing on a truck, reaching toward a crane helicopter hovering above them. Black peace symbols adorn drab army-green canisters containing 155-millimeter artillery shells, and the twisted limbs of three leafless trees form the initials FTA—Fuck the Army.

Already a legend around the 101st, the cover evokes the mood of the grunts whom I accompany on a couple of patrols by a stream along which the VC slip men and supplies into the lowlands. The platoon leader is a gung-ho career soldier, a first lieutenant out of OCS, airborne, ranger, and jungle schools, who inwardly regrets he's arrived in Vietnam a couple of years too late for "the real war." He has been here only three weeks, and he wants to play by the rules. Maybe, if he succeeds, there's still enough time for him to get a regular, as opposed to reserve, commission, a promotion to captain, and command of a company in the field, if not exactly in full-fledged combat.

"Shoot to capture, not to kill," the lieutenant, an athletic lifeguard type with close-cropped hair and finely sculpted features that remind me of a carving of a Roman centurion, earnestly abjures his troops, in an upstate New York twang. The men, saddled up for a RIF [reconnaissance in force] through abandoned rice paddies and hamlets erased except for occasional cement foundations by air and artillery strikes, grin and snicker. "I shoot for KIAs, not POWs," retorts Spec 4 Robert Latchaw, a wiry Pole from South River, New Jersey, laughing at the lieutenant's naïveté. "Whaddya want us to do, shoot an ear off?" jibes "Doc," the medic. The lieutenant, unfazed, insists he's following policy set down by "higher higher" headquarters. "We're not after body counts anymore. We'd prefer information. KIAs don't talk." With that, we sally forth through tall grass toward a stream near which our platoon sergeant, remaining behind with a squad, swears he saw "two dinks running that way."

It is clear to everyone but the lieutenant, though, that we're not seriously pursuing the dinks. "Just walkin' around don't accomplish nothin'," says Latchaw, a churchgoing Catholic with a wife "back in the world" who sends him weekly packages of "world food," good canned stuff to supplement the boring, bland diet of C-rations. "I been here nine months, and I ain't been in no firefight yet. Most I did was spend 100 days in the mountains during the monsoon without changing my clothes once." We are, by this time, beside the stream, filling canteens, after an hour-long stroll broken by frequent halts for rest and talk. If there are any VC in the area, they are as eager to keep out of our way as we are to keep out of theirs.

All of us, that is, except for the lieutenant: next morning, around ten, he leads another RIF toward the stream, this time aiming for the "draw," the ravine down which the water tumbles from the last ridgeline into the lowlands. Before we begin it seems like another easy walk in the sun, but our point man is still hacking away with his machete several hours later. (Murmurs from the grunts behind me: "I want to be back in Kentucky rabbit-huntin'." "When I get back to the world I don't *even* care if I see another forest—I'm stayin' in the city.") The lieutenant sends a Chicano named Quito and the Kentuckian into the bush in hopes of finding an easier route. They return a few minutes later. "Gettin' too theek," says Quito. "Might see some dinks we don't want to see." We plunge straight ahead, find a trickle of flowing water, fill canteens, keep going another hour until we stumble on the same stream we reached, lower down, on yesterday's patrol. Some of the men flop in, lying on their backs in the fast-running water, cleansing bodies, fatigues, socks. We would be easy marks for an ambush. No one is standing guard.

Across the stream we see clear signs of VC movement—footpaths leading across open clearings. For the first time we spread apart, a routine precaution. Behind us rise the slopes of the ridgeline, burned off by a fire ignited by one of the Delta Tangos—"defensive target" artillery rounds—called in by the lieutenant a couple of nights ago. We follow the path along the stream, wade in the water for a while, then emerge about where we'd been the day before. A couple hundred yards from the bank a neat path cuts a straight line through the bush—the kind of trail along which guerrilla soldiers could run full-speed if necessary, dropping for cover at the sound of approaching helicopters. "We're going to work this area really well," the lieutenant advises his men, who remain sullenly silent. "We're gonna set up ambush positions in here and set out a couple of claymore mines. We'll get them as they fall back from fighting the ARVN."

As soon as we return to our original position, the lieutenant announces his plan to our platoon sergeant, a hard-talking midwesterner who's been with the unit only a couple of days but knows how to handle eager young officers. The sergeant reminds the lieutenant a resupply helicopter is about to arrive, that it'll take a while sorting out the stuff, burning off the waste. He says he's found a "beautiful NDP [night defensive position] over there by the trees." The lieutenant hesitates, wavers. He senses that his men, from the new sergeant on down, are against him. "We don't have enough men for an ambush," the sergeant argues. "We get into a fight, we'll get waxed." The lieutenant finally settles for placing a single claymore on the trail this side of the stream.

That night we hear the crackle of small arms from near the ARVN position, a mile or so away. Helicopters circle overhead, muttering machine gun fire, and artillery and mortar rounds thud across the fields. Next morning, the lieutenant is beside himself with anger and frustration. "Should have sent out that goddamn ambush," he says, not looking at the sergeant. "Could have gotten the bad guys running away. Godammit, we gotta get moving. It's late already. This happens again, I'm gettin' everyone up at five o'clock." It is ten-thirty before the men are ready. Then the lieutenant gets more bad news, this time over the radio. The battalion commander, on a firebase a couple of miles away, is ordering the entire company in to guard the base perimeter: "just routine rotation." In vain the lieutenant pleads that he needs "a couple more days to work the area by the stream." His men curse him silently. "Godammit, if no one was looking, I'd frag the sunuvabitch," says one of them.

The threat of fragging—explosion of a fragmentation or hand grenade—in this case is probably not serious. The GI who makes it not only walked point the morning before but willingly went on patrol again in the evening to plant the mine. An Iowa farm boy, he criticizes the war on the grounds, "We're not fightin' it like we should." Since we failed to invade North Vietnam, H-bomb Hanoi and Haiphong, and declare "free fire zones" of VC hamlets, he says, "we oughta quit wastin' time and go home." Like most of the grunts in the field, he may lack motivation but he's not really bored.

It is mainly in the rear, among the troops whom the grunts disdainfully call the REMFs for Rear Echelon Mother Fuckers, that talk of fraggings, of hard drugs, of racial conflict seems bitter, desperate, often dangerous. At the combat base at Quang Tri, the last provincial capital below the DMZ, I walk into a dimly lit single-story barrack one afternoon hoping to find perhaps a couple of GIs with whom I can talk—and count 16 of them reclined in the shadows of a lounge shielded by blankets and curtains hanging from the windows. "Welcome to the head hootch," says a thin, hollow-cheeked private first class of 18 or 20, waving me to a spot on the couch after I convince him I'm a reporter, not a criminal investigator. The GIs proudly explain that their hootch is a meeting place for potheads from all over the base, but I don't smell any marijuana in the air. "How many of you smoke skag?" I ask. They all raise their hands.

Why have they "graduated" from pot to heroin? They are, for the most part, white, with ten to twelve years' education, a few with records of juvenile delinquency or petty crime in civilian life. While some might not perform well under any circumstances, all of them seem hopelessly demoralized both by the war and by their immediate surroundings. "I was supposed to be a heavy equipment operator, but all I do is pick up beer cans," says one. "They haven't got anything for us to do," says another. "They just want to keep us busy." Several are aimless drifters, too strung out for work, awaiting court-martial or undesirable discharges, demotions, and restrictions. Many, if they report for duty at all, put in only a few hours a day before finding some excuse to return to the hootch—or else they just go back with no excuse at all.

It's far from clear whether the men are more at odds with their commanders and sergeants or the war in general. "They tell you to do something, then they yell at you for doing it," says the equipment operator. "They harass you about haircuts and beards and burn you for sleeping on guard when you've been working all day." Most of their complaints are petty, often unjustified, but they also suffer from the same sense of futility, of pointlessness, that affects thousands of other GIs in the midst of withdrawal of American troops. "The gooks are winning this war," says one. "The ARVN are afraid to fight. They run away. The gooks can have the place when we leave."

While we are talking, one of the heads slowly stirs a plate of "hard times," all-but-powerless marijuana seeds and stems. "It's what I got left. It's gettin' so hard to score marijuana around here, guys have to turn to skag"—which doesn't smell, comes in much smaller quantities, and is easier to hide. Another GI idly tells a story, verified by his friends, of ordering more than 300 vials of heroin at two dollars a vial from a Vietnamese "cowboy" on a motorcycle at the gate of the base. "I gave him $200 for a hundred and grabbed the rest and ran," says the GI. "He drove away grinning, and I knew *I* was the one that was ripped off. It was all salt and sodium acid." The next day the GI, armed with an M16, bought 200 vials from a trusted pusher in a nearby village. "I sell it here for five dollars a vial," says the GI, a personable fair-haired midwesterner who served six months of a five-year jail term "back in the world" before enlisting in the army.

Late that night a couple of the GIs—a black and a Chicano—invite me to a pot party at a helicopter hangar on the other side of the runway. The air in the little room in the back of the hangar is heavy with the sweet smell of "dew." The helicopter pilot tells me he's been "stoned ever since getting to Vietnam," that he performs better that way but is "scared shitless of skag." Beside him is a doctor, an army captain, silently smoking pot in a corncob pipe. Some of the helicopter crewmen pass freshly rolled cigarettes around. A couple other GIs stand lookout, glancing from time to time over the walls to see if MPs are coming.

One of the chopper pilots argues convincingly for legalization of pot—says it's not habit-forming, is no more harmful than beer. He doesn't know it, but several of the enlisted men in the room have laced their marijuana with heroin. Some of them plan to go to "the party after the party"—an all-night get-together in one of the perimeter bunkers for speed freaks, pill-poppers who get them by mail from home or else buy them on the local market, often at ordinary pharmacies.

It is difficult to quantify the use of drugs in the rear. It is obvious, though, that a relatively high proportion of the REMFs, perhaps 20 percent, are on the hard stuff, as opposed merely to marijuana, while in the bush only a marginal few indulge. ("We see a guy using it out here, we take care of him, or the CO sends him back to the rear," one of the men on Charlie Ridge tells me. "Otherwise he'll be high some time when we're under attack. You can't hardly walk if you're high all the time.") The use of drugs in base camps accounts for widespread thefts and also is a major factor in fraggings. GIs on drugs will steal almost anything, ranging from stereo sets to food from the mess hall, to sell in exchange for heroin, peddled by small boys and women, cowboys on Hondas, even South Vietnamese soldiers operating near Americans.

Addicts resort to fraggings—or threats and intimidation —whenever commanders order shakedown searches, restrict them to quarters, or otherwise attempt seriously to cut down the flow. At each camp I visit there are tales of incidents in which GIs have blown up orderly rooms, sometimes wounding or killing the wrong man, or merely exploded grenades outside windows for shock effect. One of the favorite techniques is to set off a tear-gas canister, a harmless antic that creates momentary chaos and serves as a warning of more violence later. At the rear headquarters of one of the battalions of the 196th brigade, on a road leading to Freedom Hill outside Danang, the battalion's new executive officer, in the midst of a crusade against drugs, walks into his quarters one day and finds a grenade pin on his pillow—a symbol of what may happen to him if he keeps up his campaign.

"It's like a war, you take chances," says the exec, Major John O'Brien, a bluff, outspoken man with a strong Massachusetts edge to his voice, who served ten years in the enlisted ranks before attending OCS. The major, on his second tour in Vietnam, arrived here in June totally unprepared for the new mood among GIs in the rear. He found heroin vials, empty and discarded, around battalion headquarters, in the latrines, under barracks. At least 20 of more than 100 men assigned to his battalion "rear" were perpetually too high and too weak to perform.

At the same time, numbers of others were not only opposed to the use of drugs but also willing to work with him to prevent it. "We had a couple of meetings just brainstorming," says O'Brien, who, unlike many career officers, seems capable of talking with young GIs on an informal basis. "We were receptive to any ideas anyone wanted to offer. The situation was so desperate, we had to be open to everything." The result was a balanced combination of force and propaganda.

"As of this date I'm declaring war on drug abuse in this battalion," begins the mimeographed "Open Letter to All Drug Users," posted on bulletin boards around the battalion area. "I will seek out and find every drug user and pusher" in the battalion. The letter recounts what many of the GIs already know —that the major, assisted by a special "drug squad" of half a dozen men, has already confiscated more than 100 vials filled with heroin. "Things are going to get a hell of a lot tighter before the problem is satisfactorily resolved," the letter promises. "There will be more shakedowns and inspections. The flow of traffic in and out of the compound is going to be dramatically reduced. My officers and senior NCOs are now authorized to conduct unannounced search of any man on this compound." The letter invites addicts to turn themselves in voluntarily to the army's amnesty program, under which they can spend several days in a special ward getting over the immediate physical effects of the habit—or else face prosecution and court-martial.

Major O'Brien has no real illusions, however, about the long-range efficacy of his program. He thinks he's drastically reduced the use of heroin in his own compound but points out a couple of cases in which addicts went through amnesty "withdrawal" only to pick up the habit again a few days later. He doesn't like to talk about the grenade pin left on his pillow for fear that publicity might encourage a fragging but points with a grin at a copy of his open letter, scrawled with defiant notations. "Happiness is a Vial of Smack," says one of them. "Major O'Brien is a Smack Freak," says another. "Stay a Head." Perhaps overoptimistically, the major views the comments as a good sign. "It shows they're worried. At least I'm getting a response."

Major O'Brien's program, I discover, is the exception, not the rule. By far the majority of the commanders and executive officers whom I meet are simply not aware of the scope of the problem in their own units. They tend, in many cases, to rely on the word of their NCOs— many of them so conservative, not to mention so hooked on alcohol, as to distort their whole attitude toward the drug problem. Another complication is that officers and NCOs also must cope with racial conflict in the form of protests against authority by young blacks who claim the army discriminates against them. Racial tension, like drugs, is of secondary importance in the field, but it threatens to explode in base camps where blacks have time to form their own Panther or anti-war "liberation" organizations and chafe under petty harassment by lifers who often, in fact, do reveal instinctive, subconscious, if not explicit forms of prejudice.

The racial question is so sensitive at Camp Baxter, on a road lined with military installations and Vietnamese refugee shanties near Marble Mountain, just south of Danang, that military officers don't want to let me on the base. Finally the camp commander, Colonel Joseph Otto Meerboth, a greying West Pointer, agrees to let me talk to GIs but asks me to "come back tomorrow" when I show up for my appointment. As I am escorted toward the gate, he orders military policemen to seal off the post to intruders and search the barracks for half a dozen blacks, whom he's convinced are plotting a major racial disturbance. The next day, Colonel Meerboth explains that the blacks, transferred four days ago to another base, returned without warning to pick up their possessions and that one of them, at least, is "extremely dangerous."

"He's organized an extralegal confederacy," says the colonel, who admits having had little experience with either drug or racial problems before his assignment to Camp Baxter last fall. "The traditional method for rendering extralegal confederacies ineffective is to dismember them. Last night I brought in three of these men one by one, talked to them, and told them they had to leave. They have been escorted elsewhere." Colonel Meerboth's decision, however, has not necessarily conquered the problem, characterized by intermittent demonstrations, a couple of killings, secret meetings, and threats, spread over the past eight or ten months. At the service club, where he reluctantly permits me to interview GIs, both blacks and whites criticize the transfer of the troublemakers and claim the one singled out by the colonel as the ringleader was actually instrumental in keeping the blacks from staging an armed, open revolt.

"A white man just don't understand the problem," says Sergeant Clarence Chisholm, a graduate of Tuskegee Institute who was drafted into the army and works as a communications specialist. "Whenever you try to explain what's happening, you're branded as a militant." Chisholm, due to rotate home from Vietnam in a couple of days, charges the white officers and NCOs with practicing de facto segregation by recommending transfer mainly for blacks and leaving the camp, once 20 percent black, almost entirely white. Some of the white GIs I meet agree with Chisholm's interpretation. "Our sergeant told me, 'It's open season on blacks,' " says one of them. "The thing is this Colonel Meerboth cannot control this compound," says another, shouting excitedly in the middle of a circle of white soldiers who rush to the service club to talk to me when word gets around "there's a reporter there."

The GIs charge all the "undesirables"—Black Panthers, drug addicts, whatever—were transferred to three or four nearby units reputed to be dumping grounds for those not wanted elsewhere. The black "ringleader," I learn, has gone to Chu Lai, where he's now on permanent guard duty with the 277th supply and service battalion. "I'm scared to go there," says another GI, a Chicano, who's also been transferred to the 277th but has returned to Camp Baxter to pick up his stuff and has somehow escaped the colonel's notice. "I hear they're *all* skag freaks down there."

Intrigued, I go to Chu Lai the next day to meet the colonel's nemesis, Spec 4 Loyle Green, Jr., a tall, polite onetime student at Malcolm X University in Chicago, who once had visions of attending OCS and making a career in the army but has since decided "to help the brothers back in the world." "They gave us five hours to pack our bags and leave after they notified us of our transfers," says Green, whom I meet in battalion headquarters. "We started to protest, but there was nothing we could do. We were railroaded to Chu Lai. The majority of the transfers were from minority groups—blacks, Spanish, Indians."

Green attributes his transfer to his role in leading a sit-in in front of Colonel Meerboth's headquarters in protest against the pretrial confinement of a black GI charged with assaulting a white. "It was so tense that a lot of blacks had gotten weapons, but it was going to be a peaceful protest." The blacks, he notes, simply turned their backs, got up, and left when the colonel emerged to order them to disperse. Then, says Green, there was a plan to destroy the entire compound, large enough for several thousand men. "I talked to a couple of the blacks and told them there was no way. We were already infiltrated by informants. We had the weapons and grenades to do it, but we would have lost in the end."

Green, seen by Colonel Meerboth as a "persuasive speaker" and a "natural leader," appears less than militant in his outlook. Rather, he displays a sensitive judgment of power realities, an understanding of the limits to which black GIs can go, and determined, passive defiance of white authority. One factor that may have cast him as a sinister figure, in Meerboth's mind, was the funeral service in March for a black killed by a white in a brawl in the middle of the camp. "The blacks didn't want the chaplain to speak," says Green. "We had two or three hundred there. We just turned our backs to the chaplain while he kept rattling on. We chanted 'Black Power' and put up a liberation flag. It had a black fist in the middle with the words 'Black Unity' in black letters on top, with a red background. The colonel stood there shaking his head. I told him we didn't want any American flag there. No blacks are American. I don't consider myself an American. I consider myself a black."

Green, like many of the black GIs, wears the black power band, made of black shoelaces, around his wrist. A black power ring, in the form of a clenched fist, gleams from the index finger of his right hand. In defiance of authority, he is growing a full beard, in addition to the regulation mustache. Ironically, in view of his anti-white, anti-war outlook, he has never been disciplined, court-martialed, or reduced in rank. He does not refuse to go to work, as do many blacks, particularly those on drugs. "I was a clerk-typist and a driver. It was challenging at first, but there wasn't enough to do"—an explanation, combined with opposition to the war, that may account for most of the army's problems in the rear.

Unlike Green, however, most of the GIs whom I meet at the 277th headquarters in Chu Lai seem depressed, openly, dangerously rebellious, possibly on the verge of armed revolt. One of them, interviewed in the presence of the battalion executive officer, tells me the blacks have a "secret arms cache" and plan to start using it "if things don't let up around here." The exec, Major Robert DeBiasio, who has been trying to work with the blacks to find the causes of their problems, listens without interrupting. Later he tells me he doesn't think this GI is kidding. "We've searched those barracks time and again and found nothing much. I think they have the arms underground somewhere. The only way we could find them would be to order everyone out of the barracks early in the morning, keep them under guard, and go over the whole area with a mine detector."

Major DeBiasio may face a tougher problem than does Major O'Brien at Freedom Hill. At the 661st ordnance company, GIs estimate that 20 percent of the more than 1,00 troops don't work at all. The commander, a pleasant, open man with eight years enlisted time behind him before he went to OCS, may be afraid to impose tight discipline. He arrived several months ago, after the fragging of his predecessor, who escaped un-harmed but severely shaken. "We have some outstanding young men here," the CO blandly observes, venturing that only a dozen men in the entire battalion "use drugs on a somewhat irregular basis."

In view of the CO's easygoing tolerance, it is not surprising that many of the troops whom I meet at the 661st focus their complaints on their sergeants rather than on the officers. The most feared of the NCOs is a black, a 33-year-old Georgian known for his skill as a boxer and judo expert and nicknamed, as a token of both respect and dislike, "Karate Joe."

Karate was sipping beer with another NCO, a white sergeant from Tennessee, when I interviewed him in his hootch. He's afraid to go to the enlisted men's club. He doesn't want the men thinking he's trying to harass them off duty. He's stopped counting the times he's found grenade pins on his pillow or been threatened verbally. "It doesn't even bother me anymore," he says, but it is clear he is intensely unhappy. "My first tour here, we were all together. We worked as a team. I was doing the same thing then, running the ammo supply point, humping ammo into helicopters to take to the field. I never had no problems with the men. This time they don't really care no more." Karate shouts and curses his men to work, but he's beginning to feel he's engaged in a lost cause. "You discipline them so much and eventually the CO gets started on getting them 212s"—discharges on grounds of unsuitability or unfitness for service. "I just don't know what the answer is," he says, clenching his beer can. "It's not the same army anymore."

*   *   *

The only real answer, as far as this war is concerned, may be to keep withdrawing the men on an accelerated timetable and send only volunteers for the remaining advisory and rear-area jobs. Wherever I go in the northern provinces, whether in the field or in the rear, I find the problem of motivation so overwhelming as to defy rational solutions and programs other than withdrawal. Below Charlie Ridge, in the Arizona Territory, I talk with a young captain on his first tour. He is a West Point graduate, in command of a troop of armored personnel carriers—an ideal position for a career-minded military man. He has been here only a week, but already he is filled with doubts and questions.

"They train you, send you to schools," says the captain as we begin a bumpy ride through fields planted with mines and booby traps, "but nobody's prepared to see a guy killed or wounded. I had the most sobering experience of my life yesterday—I saw one of my men wounded with shrapnel. He's the first guy I've ever seen wounded. Once we've decided to get out, and then keep fighting, it seems kind of worthless." That night, after the APCs have formed a defensive circle by a small river, a lone guerrilla fires an AK47 rifle from a couple hundred meters in front of us, sending bright red tracers over our position. The GIs leap onto the tracks, answering with machine gun fire and M16s. Helicopter gunships arrive, spraying the bushes with bullets. Against the black backdrop of the sky and mountains, it is an eerie late show, and it lasts for an hour.

"They got some nerve opening up against all our firepower like that," says one of the GIs as the guns fall silent and we stretch out to sleep on cots behind our track. "Far as I'm concerned, they can have this whole country. We was fightin' to win, that'd be one thing, but we're just wastin' time." It is a typical GI commentary, one I hear countless times around Military Region One at the butt end of a bad war.

9

"John Wayne Would Have Dug It"

For a brief period in 1972 the Nixon-Kissinger policy of withdrawal from Vietnam amid "Vietnamization" and negotiations for peace appeared in serious question. The North Vietnamese and Viet Cong on April 1, 1972, opened their greatest offensive since Tet 1968, this time sending tanks as well as infantry across both the demilitarized zone and the Cambodian border northwest of Saigon. President Nixon responded to what has gone down in history as the "Easter Offensive" by resuming the bombing of North Vietnam, which the air force had already been doing in secret on a limited scale for several months, and shelling the coastline.

American information officers, who had been eager to publicize military activities at the beginning of the war, prevented reporters from visiting the air bases in Thailand on the spurious grounds that they were technically Royal Thai property. And they claimed they did not have the aircraft to fly us to navy carriers from which planes were also flying over North Vietnam—even though such facilities had always been available in the early years of the war. They did, however, finally relent to the extent of letting us onto navy cruisers and destroyers off the coast of South Vietnam, thus enabling me to glimpse the combat from an entirely different perspective.

The views of navy officers and sailors, the latter perhaps influenced by bitterness that erupted in fighting and near-mutiny at several American bases, were much the same as those of soldiers and marines on land. There were differences, though. The days at sea produced their own kind of boredom, and the sailors could never glimpse or immediately sense the suffering of the land they were assigned to bombard.

For all the anti-war sentiment, however, there were always the buccaneer types who would volunteer for any kind of fight anywhere—if the price were right. After the last American warplanes had ceased bombing Cambodia, in August 1973, I met a couple of them flying a cargo plane and eager for more action. Their outlook reflected the thinking of thousands of Americans who came to Indochina on lucrative contracts. Some of them, as they lounged in luxury apartments and villas and piled up enormous bank accounts, even believed in what they were doing.

Aboard the USS *Providence*, May 1972

Through binoculars on the signal bridge one discerns specks of people walking along a beach littered with sampans and hootches. Beyond the beach rise green rice paddies and woods fading rapidly into a distant skyline of bluish peaks and haze. Occasionally, one also sees white or black puffs of smoke hovering on the horizon, but for the most part the view of Quang Tri, the first South Vietnamese province to fall entirely to the North Vietnamese in the current Easter Offensive, is deceptively tranquil.

It is only at odd interludes, in fact, that the air force spotter plane swinging lazy circles some ten miles inland finds a target worth a shot. Then, if he does happen to see a bunker complex or supply dump or barge, he radios the nearest ship—at the moment one of three cruisers, including the *Providence*, or a dozen destroyers patrolling a 200-mile stretch of coast south from the DMZ. An officer in the combat operations center, two decks below the main deck, "sights" one or more of the ship's five guns with a computer, then calls a petty officer in one of the two turrets and tells him to load.

On the bridge, Captain Kenneth G. Haynes, the skipper, a Texan whom most of the men seem to like, watches while one of the ship's six-inchers, the largest gun on board, roars and sends a 130-pound projectile over the shoreline a couple of miles away. Several minutes later, Lieutenant Commander Gerald Anderson, assistant weapons officer, standing on the deck below, shouts back the good news from the FAC (forward air controller), the term for the propeller-driven spotter plane. "Several trucks destroyed, several structures destroyed, several secondaries," says Anderson. Haynes, who has already noticed the cloud of smoke rising from the explosion, smiles approvingly.

"That's pretty good," he says with an air of understated modesty. "You have to remember we're firing at 50-gallon oil drums at ten miles." His smile broadens. "It would appear we've stopped effective movement of their supplies. This morning we've also been shooting at three tanks." He doesn't yet know what happened to the tanks, but later one of the enlisted men on the signal bridge offers a somewhat irreverent account. "We chased this tank right down the road. We must have fired 50 rounds and never touched it. Finally the men inside all jumped out and hid in a hootch. Then one of our rounds got them all in the hootch and tac air [fighter planes] got the tank."

The memory of the tank chase provides a moment of humor on an otherwise dull day. Since arriving on line off Vietnam on April 28, the ship's crew of more than 800 officers and men have been standing watch six hours on and six off, a wearisome routine that slowly tightens nerves and frays tempers. Captain Haynes attempts to boost morale by providing free soft drinks and keeping the ship's gedunk—snack stand—open 24 hours a day, but the men still yearn for the ease of the four and twelve routine in their home port of San Diego. Besides, few of the younger officers and almost none of the enlisted men share Captain Haynes's view that the *Providence*, lobbing an average of 40 to 50 shells a day into Quang Tri province, is "here to see the war end honorably."

In the surrealistic half light inside the six-inch gun turret, the sailors who load and ram the shells and powder reflect the underlying unease of the crew. "It's a rotten game, it's making no progress, it's just making people miserable," says Seaman Glenn Stillman, a bearded Mormon from Bountiful, Utah. Stillman, like most of the sailors, hopes that President Nixon's decision to mine all of North Vietnam's harbors will somehow shorten the war, but he is not optimistic. "He's made a decision forcing them to make a decision," he says, standing beside the gaping breach of an unloaded six-incher. "This war could build up anytime."

The turret captain, standing by a phone near the entry to the turret, gets the order to load from the combat operations center. The bullet, or projectile, and powder casing arrive separately by hoist from below the gun. Stillman and another seaman pick the bullet from the hoist and place it in the breach. A third seaman then rams it into the gun itself by turning the switch on an electric hydraulic system. They follow precisely the same procedure as the powder casing emerges from below. Finally, the breach block closes and the petty officer in the combat operations center pulls a trigger that detonates the powder and fires the projectile.

Stillman complains somewhat querulously about his work. "It's too hot and I'm only getting five and a half hours' sleep a day." It is partly because the *Providence* is an old ship, commissioned at the Boston Naval Yard near the end of World War II, that it lacks the new machinery needed to transfer bullets and powder automatically from hoist to breach. When the ship was refitted in the late 1950s, it was provided with what her official history calls "the highly sophisticated and effective Terrier missile system and a nuclear capability." The history does not mention her basic conventional weapons—less than entirely up to date.

Captain Haynes argues that the missile system, occupying the space of two gun turrets in the aft portion of the ship, "would be nice to have" for shooting down enemy aircraft, but no one seriously expects the opportunity to arise. (In any case, says one sailor, eight practice rounds fired by the missile system were all duds. Purse-lipped officers refuse to comment.) In the wardroom, relaxing on a sofa in front of a coffee table decked with *Life* and *Business Week* and *U.S. News & World Reports*, an intense, crew-cut lieutenant commander seriously criticizes the navy's failure to outfit its ships with enough of the newest, best guns.

"The United States is making a big mistake in not having more gunships," says the officer, who did a previous tour on a ship blockading the southern coast of Vietnam from enemy munitions traffic. "Take a look at these destroyer escorts we have around here. They have a single gun on some of them. If we're to have a navy and remain number one, we should have more ships with more guns." Another lieutenant commander admits the navy needs more ships to do the job but still praises the guns on the *Providence* for their accuracy. As evidence, he says that one of them "destroyed a truck today from ten miles."

How much do such success stories really mean? On the *Providence*, as in almost any other American military setting, the answers may vary according to rank and dedication to service. At the apex of the pyramid on the *Providence*, Rear Admiral William Haley Rogers, commander of the entire "cruiser-destroyer flotilla" off Quang Tri, believes implicitly in the efficacy of shore bombardment. "Cruisers have large guns and are very good at it," says Admiral Rogers, a tall, swarthy man who wears a blue jacket with the emblems of a couple of his previous commands. "I can't think of anything more important than what we're doing now in terms of the defense of South Vietnamese cities south of Quang Tri."

Discussing the weapons at his disposal, Rogers talks as persuasively as an air force pilot advancing the need for bombing or an infantry commander explaining why you can't win a war without ground troops. It is up to young ensigns and lieutenants, few of whom plan to make a career in the navy, to point out some of the more obvious flaws in official logic. "Until a year ago we had the infantry over here, and we didn't interdict enemy supply lines," says an ensign from upstate New York. "Now we're interdicting the supply lines, but there's no infantry. If we'd done both at the same time, we might have won."

The crux of the ensign's argument is that mining the ports of North Vietnam will hardly win the war for South Vietnam if the South Vietnamese are incapable of fighting effectively on the ground. As for whether or not the shelling of Quang Tri province will permanently impede the flow of supplies farther south, the ensign assumes the question is meant as a joke and laughs good-naturedly in reply. "I guess the war will go on for another ten years. I happen to be rather conservative. I think we should have taken all these steps five years ago."

The lack of a real sense of purpose disturbs many sailors who might otherwise entirely favor the war. "I'm for fighting the war," says Signalman Third Class William Dunn, a fair-haired Californian who's been on the ship for the past two years, "but I don't know if it's being fought right." As far as Dunn is concerned, the ship ought to have carried out more raids like the one off Haiphong on May 10 nearly 19 hours after President Nixon went on radio and television announcing that "all entrances to North Vietnamese ports will be mined to prevent access to these ports and North Vietnamese naval operations from these ports."

Dunn, manning a telephone on the bridge of the *Providence*, knew the ship was heading toward Haiphong harbor when he spotted a beacon on a headland south of the entrance to the Red River channel. "We weren't any farther out than maybe four miles. I put everything together and figured we were making a raid on Haiphong." The *Providence*, all its lights out, was sailing full speed ahead, at approximately 30 knots, in a line with two other cruisers, the *Oklahoma City* and the *Newport News*, and two destroyers, the *Buchanan* and the *Hanson*. "We saw a merchant ship lit up like a Christmas tree. It began moving out to sea as we came in. All the lights inside the harbor were on, too. It looked like downtown LA."

The North Vietnamese may have caught the cruiser-destroyer striking force on their radar, but basically the raid came as a surprise. The ships, within 200 yards of the first buoys marking the channel, cut their speed to 18 knots, turned, and then began firing broadside toward the shoreline. Four minutes later North Vietnamese coastal defense batteries began returning fire. "All you could hear was the whistle of the shells," says Signalman Apprentice Joseph Stankiewicz, who watched the engagement from the port side. "Then all the lights of the harbor went out at once." The battle, the first multi-cruiser strike since World War II, lasted only 15 minutes, but it seemed much longer. "You could see these muzzle flashes on the beach. You get the feeling, if anything hits, it'll land in your lap."

The *Providence* fired some 60 rounds at a barracks complex, a fuel storage point, and some of the coastal defense sites. Then, still in line with the other ships, it turned, resumed full speed and left as quickly as it had come. Stankiewicz and Dunn heard some of the enemy shells landing in the water, but none of the ships was even scratched. "Everything was just fantastic," says Dunn. "It was the most beautiful operation I've ever seen. This ship just turned fantastically. I'm glad I got home to talk about it." The next day Captain Haynes went on the public address system to compliment and praise the crew: "You gotta be doing this for fun, because it's a crazy way to make a living."

Captain Haynes now tries to minimize the raid. "Just another fire mission," he says, but in retrospect its purpose appears to have been far more important than any of the men quite imagined at the time. The aim apparently was to soften North Vietnam's defenses before American planes began dropping the mines into the channel. "I wish John Wayne could have been there," says Quartermaster Third Class Steve

V. Schlemmer, who joined the navy "to get out of this stuff." Wayne "would have dug it," and "Billy Graham could have been there beside him."

For the men of the *Providence*, the strike off Haiphong may very well have been the climactic point of their tour. The ship, almost immediately after the raid, began sailing south and may remain here for weeks. Without either the excitement, the tension and danger of battle, or some of the ease and amenities of home, as the officers are aware, men grow restive and unhappy, lax and lazy. "All we're doing now is banging holes in the land, making a few Olympic-sized swimming pools," says Schlemmer, whose father was a naval aviation mechanic in World War II. "It's far enough where the guilt of killing people doesn't bother me, but it's still cutting into my sleep."

Not that the shelling of Quang Tri is entirely a one-sided gambit. Sometimes, particularly from around the mouth of the Cua Viet, a river ten miles south of the DMZ, enemy gunners have the temerity to fire back. The men on the deck wear flak jackets and helmets whenever the ship sails within ten miles of the Cua Viet, once a waterway for American vessels carrying supplies for bases near the DMZ. Living up to their reputation, the North Vietnamese fired some 30 rounds one day at the *Newport News* while it was shelling bunkers and storage depots of one kind or another around the Cua Viet. None of the enemy rounds found its mark that day, but shells have hit several destroyers over the past month.

Even this danger, however, may recede as North Vietnamese gunners begin to conserve their ammunition. Nor is there much chance that the cruisers will strike again at any of the North Vietnamese ports since they now run the danger of sailing over the mines. The only other possible threat may be that of Soviet minesweepers, accompanied by destroyers and cruisers, attempting to cut new channels into the ports. On the *Providence*, however, neither Admiral Rogers nor Captain Haynes regards this possibility at all seriously. "You could take any situation and postulate it," says Rogers, "but I can't think of anything that's occurred that would cause the Soviet Union to go to war. I don't think we've given them any reason to make a confrontation."

Assuming Rogers is correct, one may predict a long, dull tour for the men on the *Providence*, plus some 40,000 on the other 64 ships now cruising the waters off Vietnam with the rather large exception of the pilots flying from five different carriers. "It can be pretty miserable here," says Captain Haynes, "but we have a job to do." In the six-inch turret, Seaman Stillman agrees—and disagrees. "This is such a low level of human existence, I don't see why we should go on playing games like this."

Phnom Penh, August 1973

They were two American adventurers, Don Douglass and Fred Compton, and they'd come to Cambodia in search of a war. They were pilots for an odd little company named Southeast Asian Air Transport, and they flew a lumbering old DC4 approximately four times a day to a town named Kompong Cham, some 50 miles northeast of here on the Mekong. That is, they flew four flights a day when the ground crews weren't working very hard and didn't load or unload the plane quite fast enough. "Godammit, tomorrow we want to make five flights," growled Douglass, a onetime Massachusetts cop who, in his spare time, had learned how to fly. "We get paid a certain guarantee, and then we get more if we fly over a certain number of hours. We don't like sitting around on the ground."

Douglass and Compton belonged to what you might call the hard-hat faction of the expatriate American set. They didn't really say so, but they clearly believed in fighting communists. They thought bombing was a good thing, and they'd signed on with Southeast Asian Air Transport not only for the pay, which was high, but for the cause. "I want to help these people," said Douglass. "They're not gonna get anywhere without airpower. I could do a lot of other things, but I like following the wars. I don't like your nine-to-five Stateside routine. I want something different." One could, if one wished, condemn Douglass on a number of different grounds, ranging from ignorance to insensitivity to worse, but somehow I found him more ingenuous than anything else, and I couldn't help but laugh when he excitedly told me exactly what he'd *really* like to do as long as he was in Cambodia.

"They've still got one old MiG17 in their hangar over there," he confided. "The engine's out, but they're repairing it. I ran into the general of the Cambodian air force the other night—told him I'd like to fly it once they got it into shape." There was, it seemed, nothing that Douglass would not do with the MiG, the last of a squadron or so bequeathed the Cambodian government by the Soviet Union before the downfall of Prince Norodom Sihanouk in 1970. "Bombing, strafing, it's a lot of fun. I flew a MiG in Nigeria in 1971. They bought it from the Egyptian government. The Russians were madder than hell about it, but there was nothing they could do. It took me five days to learn how to fly it, three days on the ground and two in the air." Compton, the captain on the DC4, had yet to fly a MiG but was eager to learn. "They'd need another guy to fly it. Don could show me how. I'm ready. I'd do anything they wanted me to do with it. I think it'd be a real kick."

I'd met Don in the bar of the Monorom Hotel the day before. Relatively new to the war, he did not seem to harbor the anger of most pilots and contractors, as well as CIA and State Department types, regarding the press. "Hey, I fly every day to Kompong Cham," he told me. "Come out to the airport and take a ride in my plane." So I was in the jump seat, looking over their shoulders, as we circled the town. "We go around like this because the bad guys are out there. We can't come in straight and low or they might take a shot at us." I'd been reading in Cambodian government handouts all about the bad guys outside Kompong Cham. They'd long since captured the road to Phnom Penh and just a couple of days previously had seized the town of Skoun, a bunkered, bombed-out enclave at a key junction. Now they were only a few miles away. I was anxious to get into Kompong Cham to do a story about a town under siege.

The apron by the airstrip was crowded with two or three transports when we landed. The civilian planes, such as the DC4s owned by Southeast Asian Air Transport, carried in rice and other foodstuffs and left with tobacco or raw rubber, once shipped by highway or boat to Phnom Penh. The military planes, notably a C123 just turned over to the Cambodian air force by the United States, were hauling reinforcements for the town's defenses. Even so, one had difficulty conjuring a sense of real crisis. The few soldiers by the entrance to the airport lethargically waved almost anyone through the gate without bothering to check credentials. No bunkers were visible in the open green fields stretching beyond the road to a series of low-lying hills.

"You think the enemy will attack?" I asked one of the soldiers through my interpreter, who had flown up in the same plane with me. "Our men are out there to stop them," the soldier replied, but I had the distinct sense the Khmer Rouge—"Red" Cambodians—could walk through the defense like a sieve. A few mortar or rocket rounds could close the airport. Kompong Cham, population 80,000 or so, now swollen with refugees, lay like a ripe melon, ready to fall at the slightest pull.

"They can't hold it without bombing," one of the American pilots told me. "They may have to hire mercenary pilots—sign up Americans and buy some fighter planes and have them fight the war for them." The suggestion indicated the desperation of Cambodian government forces only a few days after the United States, in mid-July, had finally ceased all bombing as a result of a rider on a congressional appropriations bill. The Khmer Rouge might not win in the first week, but they could quickly expand their control over the countryside, capturing towns and bases that had eluded them in more than three years of fighting since Sihanouk's downfall.

Yet the town, when my interpreter and I finally got there after a five-mile ride in the early monsoon rain, did not seem to have changed much since I had last been there, two years ago. Old French-built cars and Japanese motor scooters and American-made military vehicles still rolled leisurely down the broad, tree-shaded streets. The governor's mansion remained as a symbol of power and security in the center of a grey-green-brownish kind of park. The general, at that particular moment, was conferring with some aides, but he was glad to talk to me.

"The enemy came from the highlands, like the water coming from the higher to the lower region," he remarked as the rain poured down on the roof. "There are enemy troops, but we have stopped them in many places. They cannot attack us." What if they hit the airfield— the only entry for all the necessities of war and daily life now that both the road and river routes were closed? "Around the airfield, there are no houses or villages," said the general, with the social ease and glibness that somehow seem to characterize all senior Cambodian officials, nurtured on French colonialism and the postcolonial social milieu of the capital. "If the enemy comes near the airfield, we can use our air strikes"—as delivered by the Cambodian air force's newly acquired T28s, single-prop jobs whose "T" stands for trainer.

The general was unfailingly courteous, but his briefing was pathetically similar to dozens of conversations I had had with Cambodian officers over the past few years. One only had to talk to people around the town to confirm an initial impression of military weakness and ineptitude.

"They overran three positions two miles from here last night," said a merchant sipping thick coffee in a little café in the center of town. "We don't think there are enough soldiers to defend us. If they keep on attacking, the enemy will easily get into town, and we will have to run away." The coffee shop was crowded with tradesmen, clerks, bureaucrats, and young officers. They were still there, in Kompong Cham, because they had no way to get out, no place to go, no exit. They listened and smiled and joked about our conversation. If the town were in danger, you couldn't tell it from their faces.

But Cambodia is that way. You never know, when you encounter troops in the field, if they feel they are under pressure or not unless the bullets and shells are actually flying. And even then you can't be entirely sure. A few hundred meters behind the front lines you are quite likely to see soldiers lolling in hammocks or chatting and joking as if the war were a hundred miles away. It was the same way in Kompong Cham that day—except that the scene, if anything, was more relaxed, almost charming, as the rain gradually stopped and the sun filtered through the haze.

I'd originally thought of staying overnight in the governor's mansion, at the invitation of the general, but by late afternoon I had gleaned about as much from Kompong Cham as anybody would care to know. My interpreter and I found the same motorbike-taxi driver who had met us at the airport and drove out of town on the same tranquil road, weaving our way around occasional bicycles and bullock carts, grinning at peasant farmers who grinned back at us with open, typically Khmer countenances. It was the end of the working day at the textile factory, and we were caught for a moment in a wave of small vehicles of varying descriptions, but the road was soon quiet again, and my interpreter asked if I would like to see the ancient temple complex before turning down the last stretch toward the airport.

"It is as old as Angkor Wat," he assured me. "Maybe you won't have another chance to see it again." The driver veered onto a mud road, past some crumbling, blackened walls, then under an arch and around a large pond. The ruins, perhaps somewhat restored but never rebuilt as completely as the temples in the Angkor region, rose mysteriously beyond thatched peasant homes. We didn't have time to stop and look as we might have wished. We wanted to reach the airstrip in time for Don and Fred's last run back to Phnom Penh. Besides, there would always be another chance, another trip. The ruins could wait.

But we were wrong. The ruins couldn't wait. Three or four days later the Khmer Rouge did what everyone except the general had anticipated. They rocketed and closed the airport. Then they advanced on the ground, overrunning the factory and the temple area and a university campus, also near the airport. They overran outpost after outpost until the Cambodian defenders, reinforced the day we were there by two fresh battalions, controlled only the center of the city and still couldn't prevent infiltrators from exploding grenades in the market and sniping at the governor's mansion. Cambodian T28s bombed and strafed, but they could hardly replace the American F4s and B52s on which Cambodian commanders had always depended to postpone their final defeat. American military planes were airdropping supplies over the center of the city.

Don and Fred had to fly their DC4 elsewhere. No more easy milk runs for eager young pilots out to see the war. Nor did I hear anything about the last MiG17 in the Cambodian air force. I assume it's still in the hangar, where it may form the nucleus of the next Cambodian air force if Prince Sihanouk returns to power.

10

"Such a Nice Man"

Others also served. They weren't exactly soldiers. Nor were they militia or "people's self-defense force" types. They were generally described, for want of a better term, as "paramilitary." They were all over Indochina, on all sides of the conflict, but the most famous were the "advisers" and whatnot hired by the Central Intelligence Agency to run the war in Laos. They had no precedent in American history, these daring, often middle-aged men in PX sport shirts and slacks, who had learned their trade while in the army's special forces or the marine corps, among other places. They theoretically did not carry weapons but naturally thought nothing of breaking this rule while training hardy tribesmen, jumping with them into combat—or spending weeks in some of Indochina's densest jungles or scaling its craggiest peaks.

If the CIA in Laos had any equal, it was the CIA's Phoenix program in Vietnam. There, CIA agents not only encouraged the Vietnamese to coordinate and pool the intelligence-gathering efforts of various agencies but also schooled them in the recondite arts of intimidation and torture. (The CIA in Vietnam, incidentally, didn't really approve of straight killing. "The dead don't talk," CIA people sometimes reminded the Vietnamese, who may have been overly anxious to do away with their victims in the process of torturing them.) The Phoenix operation in Vietnam, however, was the brainchild and plaything of

141

button-down bureaucrats, notably the cool, taciturn William Colby, rewarded in 1973 with the post of director of the entire agency.

For real romance, for adventure that was stranger than much of the fiction that later emerged from the war, you couldn't beat the secret war in Laos. One of the most colorful warriors in this struggle was a tough guy named Tony Poe. I never got to meet him—though I heard a lot about him in a month of reporting on his bizarre doings. Lance Woodruff, who runs the Indochina Media Memorial Foundation in Bangkok, tells me Tony was madder than hell after my article about him finally appeared—but may have mellowed somewhat over a long semi-retirement up-country.

Bangkok, June 1971

He's a round-faced, cheery man with a cherubic smile and a charming family. He's a satanic killer with a glowering sneer and a penchant for preserving the ears of his victims in formaldehyde. He's a classic Dr. Jekyll-and-Mister Hyde, and he's been waging the most secret phase of America's secret war in Indochina for the past ten years.

He's just plain Tony Poe to the boys at the Napoleon Café and the Derby King on Bangkok's Patpong Road, a watering ground for Air America pilots, CIA types, journalists, and other assorted Indochinese hands, but his real name's Anthony A. Poshepny. He's a refugee from Hungary, an ex-marine who fought on Iwo Jima and a dedicated patriot of his adopted land, the United States of America, for which he's risked his life on literally hundreds of occasions while ranging through the undulating velvet-green crags and valleys of China, Laos, and Thailand.

He also shuns publicity and *hates* reporters, as I discovered in a month-long search for him beginning in Bangkok and extending to the giant American air bases in northeastern Thailand and to the mountains of northern Laos. The search for Tony Poe ended where it had begun, in the lobby of the Amarin Hotel, a luxury lodging run by the Imperial Hotel of Tokyo, on Bangkok's Ploenchit Road, a six-lane-wide avenue jammed with traffic running from dawn to dusk through a residential and shopping district supported largely by rich *farang* (the slightly demeaning Thai term for anyone from a western country). There, before leaving Bangkok for the last time, I picked up a note, signed simply "Tony" in a flowing scrawl, stating that he had to decline my request for an interview. "I beelieve [sic] that you can appreciate my reason for not seeking public commentary," wrote Tony in formal-statement style befitting a public official—and obviously suggested, if not dictated, by one of his superiors with the Central Intelligence Agency.

"C-I-A?" asked the cute Japanese girl at the desk of the Amarin, carefully enunciating each of the letters, smiling slightly with glittering white teeth, raising her eyebrows flirtatiously. "Oh, no," she said, covering a shy smile with a delicate left hand. "Tony Poe is airplane pilot. He works for Continental Air Services. You mean Continental, not CIA?" An assistant manager, also Japanese, showed me the card Tony had signed only a few days before my arrival at the Amarin at the beginning of my search. Tony, it seemed, generally stayed at the Amarin, only a few blocks from the modernesque American embassy on a tree-shaded street off Ploenchit Road. He was a familiar, beloved character to the hotel staff—the opposite of his public image as a sinister, secret killer and trainer of anti-communist guerrilla warriors.

"Anthony A. Poshepny," read the top line. "Air Ops Officer— Continental Air Services." So Tony, with a record of more combat jumps than any other American in Indochina, had used Continental as his "cover" while training doughty mountain tribesmen to fight against regular communist troops advancing year-by-year from both China and North Vietnam. The revelation of Tony's cover surprised me since I had assumed he would declare himself a bona fide U.S. government official—perhaps an adviser to border patrol police units, the traditional cover under which CIA operatives masquerade in both Thailand and Laos. Nonetheless, Continental was a logical choice. Like Air America, Continental regularly ferries men and supplies to distant outposts throughout Indochina.

The next two lines on the form were even more revealing, in terms of what Poshepny was doing at the present. Following "Going To," Tony had written, "Udorn," the name of the base town in northeastern Thailand from which the United States not only flies bombing runs over all of Laos but also coordinates the guerrilla war on the ground. And where was Tony "Coming From"? According to the form, his origin was Phitsanulok, a densely jungled mountain province famed in Thailand for incessant fighting between communist-armed guerrillas, most of them members of mountain tribes, and ill-trained Thai army soldiers and policemen. Tony sometimes vanished into the wilds of Phitsanulok, where the jungle was so thick and the slopes so steep as to discourage the toughest American advisers, on a mysterious training venture not even known to most American officials with top-secret security clearances, much less to the girls behind the desk of the Amarin.

"Oh, he's such a nice man," one of the Japanese girls assured me when I asked how she liked Tony, who, I'd been warned by other journalists, might be inclined to shoot on sight any reporter discovered snooping too closely into his past—or present. "He has a very nice wife and three lovely children," the girl burbled on, pausing to giggle slightly between phrases. "He comes here on vacation from up-country."

The impression Poshepny had made on the girls at the Amarin was a tribute both to his personality and his stealth. As I discovered while tracing him from the south of Thailand to northern Laos, he already had an opulent home in Udorn for his wife, a tribal princess whom he had married a year or so ago. Mrs. Poshepny, a tiny, quick-smiling girl whom Tony had met while training Yao tribesmen for special missions into China, liked to come to Bangkok for shopping while Tony conferred with his CIA associates on the guarded third floor, the CIA floor, of the American embassy.

It was ironic that I should have learned that Tony stayed at the Amarin while in Bangkok, for it was only by chance that I had checked in there at the beginning of my search—and only during small talk with the desk clerks that I found one of Tony's registration cards. The day after my arrival local journalists gave me my first inkling of some of the rumors surrounding Tony Poe. One of them, Lance Woodruff, formerly a reporter on one of Bangkok's two English-language newspapers, said Poe not only hated reporters but also had been known to "do away with people he doesn't like." Woodruff compared Poe to a figure from "Terry and the Pirates" and told me the story of how Poe lined one wall of a house in northern Laos, near the Chinese border, with heads of persons whom he had killed. None of the contacts whom I met in Bangkok had the slightest clue as to Tony's whereabouts— except that he was somewhere "up-country" training tribesmen to fight the communists, possibly in China.

Still unaware that Poe stayed at the Amarin, I drove to a town named Ubon, some 350 miles northeast of Bangkok and 200 miles southeast of Udorn. My hunch, based only on a tip supplied by a former Peace Corps volunteer whom I had met in Saigon, was that Poe was training tribesmen from the Bolovens Plateau in southern Laos to fight against North Vietnamese troops expanding base areas following the South Vietnamese army's assault across the Laotian frontier several months earlier. At Ubon, in hopes of falling into conversations with pilots who might know Tony, I visited the air base, similar to that at Udorn, from which American warplanes fly daily bombing and strafing runs over southern Laos. Newsmen are banned from the base, ostensibly commanded by the Thai government, unless they have special, almost impossible-to-obtain permission from Thai authorities; I got on by flashing a Department of Defense card routinely issued reporters in South Vietnam.

The air base at Ubon was as neat and well-manicured as a suburban American country club. Enlisted airmen strolled casually in Bermuda shorts and sport shirts purchased at the base exchange while off-duty pilots chatted away in the officers' clubs. No one had ever heard of Poe, but an officer in an army special forces unit on the base suggested I talk to one or two American civilian advisers, presumably CIA types operating under the cover of the U.S. Operations Mission. Neither was in when I called, so I hired a taxi and drove some 50 miles to the Laotian frontier. It occurred to me I could learn still more by visiting the town of Pakse, 20 miles beyond the border on the mile-wide Mekong River. Pakse was not only the leading center in southern Laos but also the headquarters for all operations aimed at stanching the North Vietnamese offensive in that region.

It seemed indicative of the government's desire to conceal Poshepny's activities that one of the American refugee advisers, who might himself have been with the CIA, advised me that Tony was "off Florida looking for sunken treasure." None of the other American officials in Pakse volunteered even that much information. The North Vietnamese had just overrun a town some 30 miles to the east, and the wives and families of all Americans in Pakse had been evacuated to the Laotian capital of Vientiane, a sleepy oasis still secure from war.

Since the Americans were in no mood to entertain a reporter, I found a military telephone and called one of the CIA men whose name I had obtained on the air base at Ubon. The spook, named Larry Waters, who had the title of public safety adviser for the Ubon region, told me that Tony had recently been released from a hospital in Bangkok after a grenade had exploded in a training accident, blowing two fingers off his left hand.

It was not until reaching Vientiane, however, that I obtained my first real break on Poe's whereabouts. At the Settha Palace, a graceful colonial-style hotel on a tree-shaded street opposite the Chinese embassy, I met the manager and part-owner, Bob Violet, a balding, one-time administrative officer of the American embassy. Congratulating Violet on the decor of the bar, much improved since my first stay in the hotel in 1966, I asked what had happened to Tony. Violet figured "most of those guys have gone to Thailand."

Among them were three other old Laos hands—Jack Shirley, once stationed at the top-secret American base at Long Cheng, south of the Plaine des Jarres in northern Laos, one Sam Hopler and a man known only as Zeke. All of them were known to hang out at the bars on Patpong Road in Bangkok when not at their desks in the embassy. They often weekended, said Violet, at an island off the town of Huahin in southern Thailand.

Wherever else Poe might be found, he apparently was no longer in Laos, from which he had sent tribesmen on missions as far as 200 miles into the mountains of Yunnan Province in southwestern China. I visited a site for refugees driven from homes on the PDJ 80 miles north of Vientiane, where refugee workers said they hadn't seen him for at least a year. One of them, a male nurse named Jack Thiel, employed by the American aid mission, recalled that Tony periodically visited that site and another at Sam Thong, finally overrun by North Vietnamese troops in March 1970, but then seemed to have vanished.

"He was a tough-looking guy with a red face, a powerful build, about five feet ten inches tall," said Thiel as we sat in the small operating room of the American-run medical facility, the only one in the region for several hundred thousand refugees created by the combination of American bombing and North Vietnamese offensives.

Other refugee workers, even some who had been in Laos for a number of years, were equally vague as to Tony's activities. The reason, of course, was that they would lose their jobs if it were discovered that they had revealed what Tony had done. However, a young American reporter, Michael Morrow of Dispatch News Service, had already "blown Tony's cover"—a factor that accounted in part for Poe's leaving Laos and shifting his operations to Thailand. "Poe is a legendary figure in Laos," wrote Morrow, a radical journalist who later was expelled from South Vietnam for his dealings with pro-communist politicians.* "He is an ex-marine non-commissioned officer, wounded in landing at Iwo Jima, who remained in Asia after World War II. In the '50s he helped organize Tibetan CIA-aided insurgents, escorted them to Colorado for training, and finally went back with them to Tibet."

Morrow, whose article appeared in the *San Francisco Chronicle*, *The Boston Globe* and a number of other papers in September 1970, noted that Poe was "known best for his dislike of journalists, disregard for orders and radio codes, capacity for Lao whiskey, and expertise at clandestine guerrilla operations." The American press attaché in Vientiane, Andy Guzowski, reputedly a Polish navy captain-in-exile in World War II, smilingly showed me a copy of Mike's article—and claimed that Poe had left Laos in July 1970 before it appeared in print. In fact, as I discovered in Vientiane, the article had given the new American ambassador to Laos, a field marshal type with the blueblood name of George McMurtrie "Mac" Godley, the perfect excuse for having Tony removed from Laos to Thailand.

"Tony was acting like the king of his own kingdom," said a vociferous acquaintance of his whom I encountered in one of those Vientiane bars habituated by Air America pilots, marine guards with the U.S. embassy, and others somehow associated with the outsized American community in the lotus-land capital. "He thought he'd been there so long he could defy the ambassador." Godley, a silver-haired patrician who'd previously served as ambassador to the Congo, was, if anything, as hawkish as Poe in his attitude toward communists. He personally had recommended escalation of American bombing of North Vietnamese troop concentrations in 1969 and 1970, a decision that not only created thousands of new refugees but also, as revealed in interviews with some of them, resulted in needless deaths of civilians and destruction of their homes.

Why, then, was Godley eager for an excuse to get rid of Poe, a man who had risked his life on hundreds of occasions while he, Godley, savored the ambassadorial comforts of an air-conditioned office complex, residence, and limousine? The answer may be that Tony was so

---

*Morrow was to distinguish himself as probably the only person kicked out of Vietnam under both old and new orders. Revisiting Vietnam in April 1990 in search of opportunities for building a hotel, he was arrested during lunch in Danang on suspicion of CIA activities, held for three weeks, and expelled. Several Vietnamese whom he contacted were also arrested, including a former NLF fighter who remained under house arrest five years later.

experienced in his work that he viewed Godley as an outside amateur whose orders and advice need not be seriously regarded. Godley, while he respected Tony's ability and courage, was the kind of man who demanded complete loyalty from all his subordinates, and he was enraged by the specter of a CIA person who looked down on him professionally and preferred to operate independently.

Tony, in fact, had just grown too cocky. He was, after all, the senior CIA man in northwestern Laos, near the sensitive tri-border of Burma, Laos, and China, and he had helped to organize an entire army of Meo tribesmen in the early 1960s. This army, although decimated and demoralized by a series of North Vietnamese offensives, provided the last defense for northern Laos—and Vientiane itself.

It was not, however, the North Vietnamese but the Chinese whom Tony really hated the most. It was apparently during his early experience flying with anti-communist guerrillas into Tibet that Poshepny began to focus his hatred almost exclusively on the Chinese regime, whose troops had overrun Tibet shortly after their rise to power in Beijing in 1949. After the United States had officially given up the salvation of Tibet as a lost cause, Poe was a frequent visitor to a camp known as "Little Switzerland" on the Mekong River several miles after it tumbles out of China. Little Switzerland was perhaps the most clandestine, most vital CIA listening post for all of China except for well-known, non-secret facilities in the British colony of Hong Kong and on the island of Formosa, Taiwan, occupied by the American-supported Nationalist Chinese Kuomintang regime. Finally, several years later, Tony succeeded Bill Young, the son of a missionary in northern Laos, in the top CIA post for northwestern Laos.

It was during this period that the legend of Tony Poe began to grow. He was said to dislike all non-CIA Americans, even those working for the government, and to have threatened to kill unwelcome visitors who wandered into his secret headquarters at Nam Yu, the village near the Chinese border from which he sent 15-man teams into China, wrote Morrow, "to tap Chinese telegraph lines, watch roads, and do other types of intelligence-gathering." The tri-border region was also the center of the opium trade, from which both Lao officials and remnants of a division or two of Nationalist Chinese troops, driven from China in 1949, reaped enormous profits.

Although Tony knew all about the opium trade, he preferred to avoid it, to forget it, while pursuing his own ends against the Communist Chinese, who had sent some 10,000 army engineers into northern

Laos to build a road complex stretching from North Vietnam to northern Thailand. Neither Laos nor the United States wanted to risk head-on war with China by destroying the road system, but Tony's tribesmen kept careful watch on what was happening.

So engrossed was Tony in his work that he learned the language of the Yao, the second most important tribe after the Meo (Hmong), so well as to converse fluently in it and not reveal his identity as an American in conversations over the radio with agents deep inside China. The Yao were said to revere him as almost a godlike figure, one of many deities embraced by their animist cult.

Insatiably cruel in battle, Tony was also unbelievably brave. Jumping into combat with his tribal guerrillas, he was wounded a dozen times. There was always, however, more to Tony Poe than blood-and-guts combat, as was revealed in his romance with the daughter of one of the Yao tribal leaders. Although it is not known what she thought of the ears of victims that Tony kept in pickle jars, she lived with him for a number of years in several of his jungle hideaways.

Tony and the girl might have been content with this relationship, but the American embassy in Vientiane strongly urged they get married after local politicians began commenting on the fact that they had brought out-of-wedlock children into the world. "It was a shotgun wedding," confided one of the gossips at the White Rose, a Vientiane bar noted for bargirls who performed impromptu stripteases at a dollar a dance—the dollar bills, in a minor miracle of muscle control, plucked by the girls between their thighs. "But it was still true love," my source insisted, and it also qualified Tony's wife and family for the perquisites and benefits of official American "dependents," including the home at Udorn.

The talk at the Vientiane bars was that Poshepny was connected with air operations at the American air base at Udorn, 40 miles to the south of Vientiane, rather than at Ubon, as I had first supposed. Armed with this tip, I crossed the Mekong back to Thailand and hired a local taxi for the drive to Udorn. Flashing my Department of Defense card to get on this base, also ordinarily closed to newsmen, I went to the airmen's club nearest the entrance to make some phone calls. Since I still didn't know that Tony was covered by Continental, I called Air America and spoke to a man who identified himself as Bill Yarborough. This man said he not only knew Tony Poe but also had seen him a few days ago and suggested I call customer air operations, for which he gave me the phone number.

At air ops a man with a Thai accent answered the phone. "Where's Tony?" I asked. "No here, he no here one week," was the reply, approximately. "Where's he at?" I asked again, attempting to sound like a pilot or young GI. "Up north," answered the Thai, evidently employed as a clerk. "North what?" I asked, since I still wasn't certain whether he was in northern Laos or northern Thailand. "Near Chieng Mai," was the reply. Chieng Mai, it happens, was the leading town of northern Thailand and a cultural center famed for its temples and art.

Sensing that I was getting closer to my goal, I asked the Thai what Tony was doing there. Where, exactly, could I find him? "He at Phitcamp 603," I was told. "What's that?" I asked. "Phitcamp 603," the Thai repeated. Then *he* had a couple of questions. "Why you want to know? Who are you?" I gave my name over the phone—didn't want to be accused of misidentifying myself if an investigation were to ensue. The Thai asked where I was. "At one of the clubs," I replied, over the noise of a jukebox in the background.

The Thai voice then went off the line, and a peculiar buzzing filled the void. My feeling was the phone was being tapped or, at any rate, a tracer was on the call. I hung up, walked off the base and hopped on the night train, one hour later, for Bangkok. No one had yet apprised me of Poe's bond with Continental, but I had discovered what might be of greater importance—the precise code number of the camp in Phitsanulok from which he was then operating.

Although I now had a fair idea of Poe's whereabouts, I still hadn't seen him. After arriving in Bangkok, I checked in again at the Amarin and then went to the Derby King, one of the bars where Tony's friends hung out. The only person at the bar, it happened, was a paunchy, balding American named Stan Griffin, who said he ran a travel agency but seemed to know Tony and Jack and Zeke and Sam, the boys who worked for "the agency"—not Stan's "travel agency," but the CIA.

It turned out that Jack Shirley, Tony's real boss with the American embassy in Bangkok, was weekending by the beach at Huahin in southern Thailand, but Stan told me all about the accident in which Tony had lost two fingers on his left hand a couple of months earlier. It seemed Tony had been teaching some Thai police recruits how to defuse a grenade and it had exploded, killing one of the Thai and wounding Tony. Stan said that Tony had been wounded six times already. "It figures that Tony got out of that scrape," he observed, slowly stirring his drink in the half light of the bar. "He was so damned lucky, he'd get out of anything."

A couple of days later, at Napoleon's, next door to the Derby King, I met Sam—Sam Hopler—a handsome, clean-cut type, straight out of Hollywood, with distinguished-looking grey hair, a pleasant manner, and an open personality. Sam suggested I leave a note for Tony in care of Jack—Jack Shirley, whose offices were on the third floor of the embassy. "Does Tony get down to Bangkok much?" I asked Sam. "He was just here," Sam replied. "He generally stays at the Amarin," where I was also accustomed to staying. It was after returning to the Amarin that afternoon that I discovered that Anthony Poshepny had checked in—and out—while I was looking for him in Laos and northeastern Thailand. Picking up his full Hungarian name and his affiliation with Continental from the registration card, I wrote him a long letter, in care of Jack Shirley, requesting an interview.

"My aim is not to 'expose' your activities," I wrote, "but to chronicle the lifestyle of an individual who has led a fascinating, exciting career on an assignment little known or appreciated by the American public." I left the note with the American embassy marine guard on duty, who immediately called a secretary on the third floor, who came downstairs to get it and deliver it to Shirley.

While awaiting my reply I also spoke to a young foreign service officer assigned to the embassy's counterinsurgency section, technically not run by the CIA but obviously a cover for CIA operations. The official provided me with nonclassified information I already knew about communist guerrilla activities in the northern Thai provinces. He noted that Thai police had some training camps in that region and that the U.S. Operations Mission participated in this program in strictly an advisory capacity. Since it was well known that the CIA in Thailand often shielded its activities behind the USOM police advisory effort, I asked what Tony Poe was doing in Phitsanulok province.

The official said he had never heard of anyone by that name and pleaded ignorance again after I had given him Poe's full, original Hungarian name and the name and number of the training camp where he worked. It was clear from his studied non-reaction that he was entirely familiar with Tony Poe's activities. This realization was underlined by his reply to my comment that it seemed rather fantastic that a wandering American reporter could find all this top-secret information without any kind of security clearance. That, said the official, was "a question that one might well ask" and to which he, too, would like some kind of reply. Still, he insisted he had never heard of Poe and suggested I obtain formal permission from Thai authorities to visit one of the police training camps if I were interested in that particular program.

The Thai, as both of us knew, would keep me away from Phitcamp 603 and send me somewhere else, to some showplace for visitors. When I pointed out this reality to the official, he asked me whether or not I was certain that Poe, "if he exists," was performing any kind of training function on behalf of the Thai. The question helped confirm my suspicion that Poe, since leaving Laos, continued to train mountain tribesmen—for the fighting not in Thailand but in Laos. Since Poe spoke at least one, possibly more, of the tribal languages, it seemed more than likely the CIA would want him to deal with the same people even if he were no longer in Laos. In order to throw me off the search, the official emphasized the point that Poe might have no connection with the training of the Thai police, but his question had quite the opposite effect.

"That's entirely your speculation," he said, rather impatiently, when I told him bluntly that I could tell from what he said that Poe was training tribesmen at a camp in Thailand supposedly set up for training Thai police recruits but actually used for quite another purpose.

The reason for the sensitivity of Americans on this subject was clear. Washington does not want enemy forces, including propagandists, to know the full extent of its role in Laos, already publicized in hearings before Senator Fulbright's Senate subcommittee on foreign relations. The Geneva agreement of 1962 specifically forbids introduction of foreign troops into Laos—a condition flagrantly violated by all participants in the war. Another reason for sensitivity is the reluctance of Thailand to publicize its own role. This reluctance—or embarrassment—accounts for the difficulties encountered by newsmen in obtaining permission to visit Thai air bases, from which U.S. warplanes fly missions over Laos and Cambodia. Thailand welcomes American military assistance but wants to keep an appearance, as much as possible, of independence from overwhelming American influence.

In view of the official desire for secrecy, it seemed unlikely that I would learn much more at the American embassy. Instead, I went to Singapore, the bustling island-nation south of Thailand and Malaysia, to meet two journalists who knew about Poe—Mike Morrow and Sterling Seagrave, son of the famed "Burma Surgeon," glorified in book and movie.* Morrow, who had gone to Singapore after his expulsion from South Vietnam, described Poe as "extremely dangerous." He said that his article about him had resulted in a complete investigation in which Richard Helms, the head of the CIA, had visited Vientiane while on a trip primarily to South Vietnam to find out the source of the leak. Seagrave claimed that Helms had read Poe the riot act for ever letting anyone know about his activities. After Helms' visit, Ambassador Godley, who wanted Poe out of Laos under any circumstances, had no difficulty persuading the CIA to keep him in Thailand.

"It was kind of a blow to Tony," said one of his friends on Patpong Road. "Since the Morrow story appeared, he hates reporters as much as he does communists." It was rather surprising to me, in fact, that Poe even bothered to write a note turning down my request for an interview, but it was awaiting me in a small envelope at the desk of the Amarin when I got back from Singapore. It had no dateline other than "Thailand" in the top right-hand corner and no signature other than "Tony," but I was sure of its authenticity. The handwriting was the same kind of scrawl that I had seen on the registration card. I was sure, after all I had heard about Poe, that he meant what he said—that he would not submit to an interview or even a face-to-face meeting but preferred to remain a faceless legend, even if he could never return to the jungles of Laos and China, where he'd operated in complete secrecy for so many years.

Since Tony's transfer to Thailand, he's suffered even more as a result of the vicissitudes of American foreign policy. President Nixon's decision to attempt to restore some level of relations between Washington and Beijing has forced the United States to curtail, if not entirely cancel, all its secret missions across the Chinese border. Tony's Yao guerrillas must operate exclusively in Laos—and perhaps Burma and Thailand. For old CIA hands, the prospect of rapprochement with China represents the destruction of all their efforts for the past generation. "Nixon's gone soft on communism like all the rest of them,"

---

*Seagrave was to gain recognition in his own right as an author, beginning with *Yellow Rain: A Journey Through the Terror of Chemical Warfare* (New York: M. Evans, 1981), then *The Soong Dynasty* (New York: Harper and Row, 1985), *The Marcos Dynasty* (New York: Fawcett, 1990), *Dragon Lady: The Life and Legend of the Last Empress of China* (New York: Random House, 1992), and *Lords of the Rim: The Invisible Empire of the Overseas Chinese* (New York: G.P. Putnam's Sons, 1995).

observed a grizzled, ruddy type over his beer. "Pretty soon we'll have to clear out of this whole area."

The change in American policy may mean the end of the era that Tony, in secret, came to symbolize. While the United States is softening its outlook toward China, Anthony Poshepny and some of his confreres are quietly looking forward to retirement in homes on the white sandy beaches of southern Thailand, overlooking the Gulf of Siam. "Zeke, Sam, Jack—they're all gone now," said one of the old hands in Vientiane. "But they'll never leave Asia. They'll still be around talking about the good old days when we were fighting the commies like we should, or almost. They were a tough crowd, those boys, the toughest of the tough. They were the side of the war that nobody knew, not even those pinko Senate investigators."

11

A Prince's "Oasis"

Kirivong, Cambodia, April 1970

Their olive fatigues were barely visible against the brown and green jungle foliage beside the deserted road through the Seven Mountains region, about ten miles in from the South Vietnamese border, 20 miles from the southern coast. Our old French Peugeot was almost on top of them before we realized they were carrying Chinese AK47 rifles and Soviet B40 rockets. The rocket grenades pointed from the ends of five-foot-long tubes hefted easily on the shoulders of the young soldiers.

"Who the hell are they?" I asked the team from the Canadian Broadcasting Company, Bill Cunningham and Maurice Embre, with whom I was sharing the car on the drive through the southern Cambodian countryside, reputedly the base area for two or three North Vietnamese regiments. "Let's get out of here," Cunningham responded, but it seemed unwise to turn suddenly in front of the soldiers, standing at 20-foot intervals beside the road.

We drove another 100 feet into the middle of the village and stopped in front of a knot of soldiers and civilians, most of them armed, all of them taut-faced and edgy. A man in blue pajamas walked toward us and waved at the wooden frame of a bed, where he indicated we should all sit down. "These are soldiers of the Sihanouk army," said the man, talking to us through our driver, who spoke Vietnamese

155

and Cambodian as well as French and English. "We fight on Sihanouk's orders to return him to power."

The man, who identified himself as the chief of the village, said the "army" was responding to the call of Prince Norodom Sihanouk, ousted on March 18. Sihanouk, in broadcasts from Peking, had urged Cambodians to rebel against the government of Lon Nol, the prime minister and military commander who now rules the country. "Ninety percent of the army hates Lon Nol," said the village chief. "We are the true representatives of Prince Sihanouk in Cambodia."

While the chief talked, an old man in black pajamas walked around the bed frame, gesturing with a large revolver, pointing it toward us. In the middle of the conversation he handed the chief a small object wrapped in a handkerchief. Cunningham touched it lightly and asked what it was. "A bomb," replied the chief. He did not explain why the man had given it to him. "How about letting us shoot some film," Cunningham suggested, changing the subject. "No pictures," the chief said. He shook his head again when Cunningham asked if cameraman Embre could photograph the chief and the soldiers from behind them without showing faces.

More soldiers, all carrying rifles or rockets, stood in doorways, walked around buildings, or patrolled the road. They spoke in whispers and mutters and ceased talking completely at a wave of the chief's right hand. They carried North Vietnamese army packs and had Chinese-made hand grenades and spare clips of bullets tucked into communist-style belts and webbing. A civilian on the road pulled a Chinese pistol from his pocket. Other "civilians" flashed pistols outside a shop across the road. All the men, numbering perhaps 20 or 30, remained impassive and grim.

The only ones who were smiling were a couple of young girls wearing green shirts and black fatigue pants, standing together under a tree about 60 feet from us. Both girls were armed with AK47 rifles, the butts tucked into their stomachs. "The clergy, the students, the farmers support Prince Sihanouk," the village chief said as a man with a rifle inspected the road maps in our car, which he carefully put back on the seat.

"Any Vietnamese living around here?" I asked the chief. I knew now that the "Sihanouk army" around us was a North Vietnamese or Viet Cong unit, but I tried to indicate I was only curious about whether some of the local inhabitants were Vietnamese. "Yes, some Vietnamese live here," the chief said. "Any Vietnamese fighting with the

Sihanouk army?" I asked. "We are supported by patriotic Vietnamese," the chief replied. The chief and almost all the soldiers and villagers were clearly Vietnamese. Their finely chiseled features contrasted with the soft, rounded facial structures of Cambodians.

Although Cambodian soldiers carry Chinese weapons, Cambodian units also include a mélange of American and French clothing, rifles, jeeps, trucks, and radios. The soldiers around us, however, wore Chinese or North Vietnamese equipment and carried only Chinese-made rifles. Their uniforms bore no Cambodian army insignia. Not a truck or a jeep was in sight.

Why were these "patriots" fighting in defense of Sihanouk? "He led Cambodia to independence from France and then kept the country at peace," said the chief, handing us copies of a crudely printed piece of paper reporting Sihanouk's broadcasts from Peking. "Under the multinational front and the Cambodian Liberation Front I will install another government of the people in Phnom Penh," said a letter written in Cambodian, signed "Sihanouk." "Then we will prosecute the enemies of the people, the servants of the imperialist Americans, for they have cooperated in the plot against me."

It was difficult to think any Cambodian would believe in the letter's authenticity, for the Cambodian script was preceded by a sentence written in Vietnamese. "From the great leader Sihanouk to military officers, soldiers, and civilian officials," said the Vietnamese writing. Our interpreter later said the village chief and soldiers spoke to each other in Vietnamese. The total Vietnamese communist influence over the "Sihanouk army," at least in this district, fit the charges of Cambodian leaders that "Viet Cong" have been responsible for anti-government demonstrations since Sihanouk's ouster.

The village chief was getting increasingly nervous. He toyed with the "bomb" in his hands, then got up to talk to the old man with the revolver. "Let's go," said Cunningham. When we got up, soldiers with AK47s surrounded us. I looked at one of the rifles, some 15 feet away, to see if the safety was on, but it was pointed directly at me. All I could see was the open end of the barrel over the glinting tip of the bayonet.

The chief broke away from his conference with the old man and asked for our identification cards. Cunningham showed a Canadian press card. I kept my American cards in my pocket. "We are all Canadians," said Cunningham. "We came here to cover the Sihanouk army." We shook hands with the chief and the old man and the two nearest soldiers. For the first time they smiled slightly. We got in the car, turned around, and drove—slowly—past the soldiers, waving as we passed. They did not wave back. I looked around and saw the village chief and the old man arguing with each other.

Prasaut, Cambodia, April 1970

"They told us all to run from the camp as soon as they heard the Viet Cong approaching," said one of those who survived. "Then they began shooting us with their machine guns." Cambodian officials claimed the Vietnamese, all civilians, were "caught in a crossfire," but the survivors, huddled in front of an agricultural cooperative, said the Cambodians had deliberately fired on them.

Cambodian troops herded some 200 Vietnamese families into the small camp three days ago. All of them, men, women, and children, were accused of having collaborated with the Vietnamese communists in the fast-expanding war near the South Vietnamese frontier. The killing of about 90 of the refugees was the worst incident of the fighting triggered by the downfall on March 18 of the leftist Prince Norodom Sihanouk. Cambodian troops near the end of last month fired into pro-Sihanouk crowds in several towns, killing 27 in one incident and 65 in another.

Cambodian officials here were convinced the local Vietnamese community was responsible for the success of the North Vietnamese and Viet Cong in cutting off roads and blocking most towns within five or ten miles of the border to government troops. Authorities rounded up some 1,000 local Vietnamese civilians and registered names of several thousand more to keep them from aiding the communists. "Viet Cong," officials say, have forced government troops into defensive positions as far as the provincial capital of Svay Rieng, eight miles to the west.

Vietnamese refugees were still lying and sitting near the bodies of their relatives when I visited the camp. Old men and women were murmuring to each other in undertones while most of the others remained sullen and silent. At first they did not talk about the incident, but then some of them said no Vietnamese communist troops had been around at the time of the shooting. There were no bullet holes in the buildings behind them, indicating all the shots had been aimed deliberately at them rather than at nearby positions occupied by Cambodian army troops.

Several of the bodies lay on the ground in the back of the building, where some of the refugees had been running to escape the barrage. Most of the bodies were lying beside one of the fences. Some of the survivors still lay among the bodies of their loved ones, clasping their hands and moaning. Another 20 or 30 people were wounded, some of them wrapped in blankets, others lying as they had been hit.

Cambodian officers did not deny the Vietnamese refugees had been shot at by Cambodian troops but attempted to prove they had been caught between opposing forces. They said hundreds of "Viet Cong" had attacked from all directions. One Cambodian officer showed me the bodies of four dead Vietnamese as well as spent bullet and rocket rounds.

"The main force of the attack was here," said the officer, Major Noup Pramoun, but the small number of empty bullet and rocket rounds indicated the enemy had not fought long before Cambodian soldiers forced them to retreat from around the refugees. Another sign of the weakness of the attack was that only six or seven Cambodians were wounded.

The Vietnamese communists also hit the center of the town, nearly knocking out the Cambodian command post with a single rocket round fired from the second floor of a Chinese-owned shop. The round fell 20 feet short of the command post, slightly wounding two officers. Cambodian troops replied with machine gun and cannon fire, destroying the shop and some other stores where they said "Viet Cong" had holed up.

The next day, Cambodian troops patrolled all the shops, forcing Chinese merchants and their families to leave with their hands over their heads. The Cambodians then systematically looted an entire street of shops, emerging with bottles of whiskey, rugs, canned foods, agricultural equipment, and other merchandise.

Cambodian officers said they planned to hold this town at all costs and defend the highway. It was highly uncertain, though, whether they could achieve this goal. Local officials said "Viet Cong" were "only five miles away," "a mile away"—perhaps closer. Villagers said they were broadcasting Sihanouk propaganda over loudspeakers and forcing Cambodians to support them. "VC," according to reports picked up here and elsewhere on the highway, were claiming to represent the "army of the king"—Sihanouk.

Neak Luong, Cambodia, August 1973

The stench still hangs over the row of concrete houses smashed to bits of rubble and ashes by the bombs. "We've taken out all the bodies," says a shopkeeper, "but there's still the smell of death."

He points at the fallen balconies, the crumpled walls, the piles of boards and concrete. "We counted 58 craters," he says, but a Cambodian soldier standing near him interrupts and says there were more than that. "We understand it was a mistake," the shopkeeper goes on as a small knot of men and children gather around us. "But we're not only sad about the deaths, we are angry. We do not know what to do."

The faces of the people in this Mekong River ferry crossing town 40 miles southeast of Phnom Penh are contorted in lines of rage and agony over the American bombing error in which 137 people were killed and 268 wounded. Old women stare silently from the flimsy wooden marketplace in the center of town a few feet from the worst craters. Chinese traders on the tree-shaded main street look derisively, turn and snap sarcastic comments as a couple of foreigners walk by them.

In front of the blasted-out military headquarters of the fourth brigade of the Cambodian army, a colonel briefs officials on what happened. "Six people were killed here," says the colonel, standing in front of piles of ammunition crating. "They were all soldiers working in brigade headquarters. I was sleeping next door. Many of my men died in the bombing."

The tall trees on the main street escaped with only shrapnel marks, but a shopkeeper warns not all the bombs have exploded. He points at a hole that one of them has gouged into the pavement without exploding. "We are afraid it will go off at any time. There will be more dead." Near another crater stands a sign in Khmer, "Beware unexploded bomb." The shopkeeper and a soldier discuss how the bombing occurred and dispute the Pentagon report that only one B52 was responsible. "I saw two airplanes," says the soldier. "If there had been one more, everyone in the town would have been killed." Most of the victims were soldiers and their families.

Flying up the Mekong from here, one can see how a computer error could have misdirected a mission. Neat rows of brown craters, the result of B52 strikes, "arclights" in military parlance, dot the green fields beside the riverbank. At least two of the rows of craters cut across roads, and one series runs through a village.

A cluster of houses lies smashed and empty near the riverbank on the opposite side. Smoke puffs up from still another strike. Orange flame flashes through the brush nearby. "Who knows why they fell," says a Cambodian soldier. "At first we thought they were enemy rockets, and then we heard the explosions and saw the planes. We do not know why. It makes no difference why."

Phnom Penh, May 1985

When we got to Prey Veng, old ladies were selling rice and meat and vegetables in the dim shacks of the marketplace on the main street. An occasional Soviet-built jeep carrying provincial officials roared down the potholed streets. Otherwise the town was a picture of backwater calm, much as I remembered from 15 years before.

The last time I had been through, the war was spreading rapidly over vast stretches of surrounding rice paddies and forests through which the North Vietnamese had been shipping arms down the Ho Chi Minh trail into South Vietnam around the parrot's beak. It was like old times—an eerie tranquillity that made you forget the realities of killing and disease, torture and starvation that were as much a part of the daily lives of these placid people as the glistening river and the hot dust swirling from the road.

It wasn't until we'd dumped off our bags in the spacious rooms of the governor's guest house that our hosts abruptly reminded us of the slaughter they had survived before Vietnamese troops invaded on Christmas Day 1978.

Packing us into a small convoy of Land Rovers and jeeps, they led us to a grassy square surrounded by shabby yellow buildings, legacies of the French colonial era. A small crowd gathered curiously around a couple of holes in which two men were digging furiously with shovels. Children looked eagerly into the depths, where white chips of bone and pieces of old clothing gradually emerged from the dirt. Occasionally one of the diggers plucked out a skull, a shard of a leg or pelvic bone, a blouse blackened with damp grime, and flung it into a small heap. Flesh and hair still clung to some of the skulls. Most of them were broken—grim evidence that the Khmer Rouge killers had clubbed the victims to death as they knelt before the graves.

One of the diggers, a provincial official named Ok Ear, looked up as we focused our cameras on him. "We have just found this mass grave. We were digging out a trench for the foundation for an office for provincial authorities, and we hit some bone." Almost all the local populace had vanished during the Khmer Rouge's bloody reign—either to work camps and eventual execution or across the Vietnamese border 20 miles to the east. Those few who had lived in the area said the Khmer Rouge had tied their victims together and led them by ropes to the center of town. They assumed they'd been executed but weren't sure exactly where.

Ok Ear tugged occasionally at frayed pieces of rope hanging loosely around bones, hair, and clothes. So far, he said, he'd found the remains of more than 10 people—and guessed about 30 to 50 were in each hole. That was the number the Khmer Rouge usually buried in a single grave.

The discovery of the grave must have been the reason I had gotten to go to Prey Veng in the first place. Yos Son, the director of the press department of the foreign ministry, hadn't given us much choice. The temple complex of Angkor Wat, the Bayon, Angkor Thom, and other wonders of a bygone civilization was open only to groups willing to charter their own aircraft to get there—if local authorities approved. And the authorities in Battambang in the northwest and Kompong Som, née Sihanoukville, on the southern coast, were "too busy" to receive us. What he didn't say was that the Khmer Rouge, with about 40,000 Chinese-armed guerrillas, still lurked in camps along the Thai border despite repeated dry-season offensives to dislodge them. They regularly ambushed Vietnamese and Cambodian forces in the western and southern provinces.

Along the broad boulevards of Phnom Penh, in the few restaurants that had reopened to foreigners since the Vietnamese had installed their own Khmer allies here, the fear of a second coming of the Khmer Rouge was as pervasive as the national hatred of the Vietnamese. Outside the Monorom Hotel—where I had stayed during my many reporting trips to Cambodia before 1975—an aging cyclo driver recognized me from the old days and babbled about his escape from the Khmer Rouge as he drove me through the city. His uncle, son, and wife had all died, he said. He alone had made it. The only way out was a trek across country to Vietnam. Life there was tough, too. The Vietnamese didn't kill Cambodians, but they looked on them with contempt. He had driven a cyclo in Saigon for a while and then returned home behind advancing Vietnamese forces.

Vietnamese troops were everywhere—not in large units but in twos and threes, in speeding jeeps, in dark, high-ceilinged ministry offices, and in a couple of old buildings across the street from the Monorom. Sometimes the officers wore their insignia, but more often than not they preferred to hide within anonymous, unmarked fatigues or in civilian clothing—even though Cambodians could easily recognize them as Vietnamese by their faces.

The low profile was needed not only to avoid offending the Cambodians but also to promote overall policy. Vietnamese leaders in Hanoi persisted in the view that the government of Heng Samrin, a onetime Khmer Rouge officer who had rebelled against his leaders, was really independent. The Vietnamese foreign minister, Nguyen Co Thach, in a conversation with me and other journalists, had promised that Vietnam would withdraw its troops whenever the Khmer Rouge and the noncommunist rebel coalitions no longer presented a threat to the present regime.

In any case, Cambodians were still too terrified of the Khmer Rouge to think of rebelling against the regime here, let alone contesting the Vietnamese. Nightly, crowds gathered outside the railroad station, awaiting the train from Battambang. No one was ever quite certain it would arrive. The Khmer Rouge ambushed it occasionally—and had long since cut off the country's other railroad to the southern coast.

Passengers spread rumors in furtive conversations with hawkers selling drinks in plastic bags. The guerrillas had hit a Vietnamese unit, knocking out a tank. The guerrillas had overrun a Vietnamese outpost. Vietnam was sending more troops toward the Thai frontier.

Vietnam had about 160,000 troops in the country—four times the number of Khmer Rouge and about four times the size of the Heng Samrin army that Hanoi keeps claiming is waging the war largely on its own. Despite the reassuring rhetoric, however, the real reason reporters couldn't go west, north, or south was obvious. There was no security.

The government was eager, though, to prove that its strength was growing. One morning we watched a couple of battalions of officer trainees, decked out in broad-brimmed trainee-style hats, marching and shouting in unison at a training school on the main road south to the airport. They were "all volunteers," said Mao Sivath, one of the training officers. "They joined the revolution against the Khmer Rouge. Some of them had families killed by the Khmer Rouge. They kept their anger since then. They will be company commanders."

Some of the trainees leaped behind Soviet anti-aircraft weapons, poised near a signboard listing "design of enemy aircraft"—a galaxy of U.S., British, French, and Chinese planes along with the flags of all the potential "enemy" countries. Behind the board, in a garage, were a couple of Soviet tanks. Hiding discreetly in the shadows was a Vietnamese officer, trim in fatigues showing his rank as major. A couple of pens, also signs of rank and power, protruded conspicuously from his breast pocket. Clasped tightly in his left hand was a clipboard—another symbol of authority.

"We still need Vietnamese assistance in training," said Mao Sivath, admitting the presence of five Vietnamese advisers at the school but maintaining, "You have seen improvement of the army in a short period." The Vietnamese presence makes Phnom Penh a sanctuary just as the U.S. bombing had guaranteed the safety of the capital and outlying towns until it stopped in the summer of 1973. In those days the Cambodian elite, buoyed by U.S. aid, reaped fortunes from bribes and shakedowns, and the black markets flourished with stolen goodies from the U.S. post exchange system in Vietnam.

That all soon changed. When the Khmer Rouge swept into town fewer than two years later, they drove out and then killed most of the local people. Now, 80 percent of the residents of Phnom Penh are refugees from the countryside. Many of them live and cook in markets set up helter-skelter on the streets. They crowd into French-built apartment blocks, sleeping in corridors, ripping out plumbing, tearing up walls and furniture. They are not revolutionaries or radicals. They know nothing of city life. They see it only as a haven where they can sleep free of ambushes and killings, hunger and poverty in a land still often barren of crops and the irrigation systems to water them.

As in the old days, however, the new Phnom Penh has risen as a center of capitalist enterprise and corruption. One market several miles from the center of the city teems with everything from modern medicines and tape recorders to washing machines and clothing from Hong Kong, Singapore, Japan—even the United States and Europe. The goods are smuggled in from Thailand over jungle trails and roads or simply shipped from Hong Kong and Singapore, up the Mekong or through Kompong Som, past the greased palms of Vietnamese officials.

The market is a labyrinth of counters and sheds spread under a vast array of cloth and plastic and wooden coverings. There are no taxes—and no police. Young Soviets, members of a 3,000-person advisory force housed in a huge complex on the southern fringe of the city, wander in search of bargains. Looking like Americans in sport shirts and jeans, they pause to haggle while *nouveau riche* officials drive by in black limousines and Mercedes-Benz sedans.

Underneath it all, the memory of suffering and torture intrudes upon the sense of revival. One afternoon, a thin man with silver-speckled hair waved and shouted from the entrance of a garage as my cyclo driver stopped at the corner. The thin man hobbled out, telling me he knew me from the early 1970s. He'd driven me in his taxi down the main roads from Phnom Penh on stories. I wondered how he had survived the Khmer Rouge. He rolled up a pants leg and showed off the scars from the shackles that finally left him lame. "My family died. I don't know why they left me. I got away when the Vietnamese came. Now I can't drive any more. I have no money, no car. I can only help in the garage."

Why some lived and some died is a question that people here are just beginning to ask themselves. The nightmares, the sudden screams in the night, the long mourning are wounds only now healing. "I knew it would be barbarous so I did what I was ordered to do," recalled Ban Sang, a teacher who hid his 'elitist' background when he was sent to Prey Veng in a work brigade of farmers. "Seven teachers were with me. They all were killed. Two of my children died. One was killed after refusing to work and claiming the work was too hard. The other died of disease."

Cheam Yeap, chairman of the Prey Veng provincial committee—equivalent to a governor—told of the terror in his area. "We estimate 485,000 people were killed in this province out of a population of more than 1 million. We suffered more than any other province. We have discovered 1,467 mass graves, including the one you saw today."

Later, over glasses of Vietnamese beer in a French gazebo, Cheam Yeap told us his own story of escape and survival. He'd been strung up from a tree by his Khmer Rouge inquisitors. He'd been dunked into pots of water. He'd been held in leg irons for 15 months. He should have died during those dark days, but he didn't.

"I was on my way to be killed one afternoon, and while they walked me blindfolded to the graveyard I fought with the soldiers and escaped with four others." They got away, he said, when two of their guards left them for a drink of water. His blindfold was slightly loose, and he saw only a young boy was guarding them. "We threw him into the water and ran," said Yeap. "We walked three days without food to Vietnam." Ever since, Cheam had been allied with Heng Samrin in fighting the Khmer Rouge after the Vietnamese decided in mid-1978 to invade Cambodia.

Cheam's story is a microcosm of the suffering in his country. No foreign visitor leaves Phnom Penh today without seeing two sights raised to the level of national memorials. The first is the "killing field" in Kandal province, down a potholed road about six miles south of here. There, in a placid setting of grass and trees, is a wooden enclosure heaped high with hundreds of skulls and bones dug up from 86 gaping holes in the surrounding field. While birds twitter happily in the branches above, workmen dig haphazardly in search of more skulls still buried in 34 more holes.

A local official pointed at a small pile of bones and pieces of clothing at the top of one of the holes. "This is the last tomb that we've dug up," he said, handing me a pen to sign a "guest book" in which visitors write down their impressions. The pages were full of lengthy discourses about "man's inhumanity to man," human evil, etc. I spent a long time thinking about it, wrote, "Seeing is believing," got in my waiting van, and left. My escort, repeating the words, seemed pleased.

The other memorial is at Tuol Sleng. Once a prestigious high school in a pleasant residential district, Tuol Sleng was turned into a prison for those perceived as the worst foes of the regime. Guides now show visitors the crude equipment for torture, the cells, the photographs of those imprisoned, tortured, and killed. Most of them were slaughtered as "spies" for the CIA or KGB or "intellectuals"—engineers, teachers, craftsmen, whatever.

In the end only 14 or so escaped as the Vietnamese swarmed over the city. They fled with their jailers—and then disappeared as the shells exploded around them. Six of them showed up later to tell the story of Tuol Sleng. Curiously, three of them were artists—spared because the prison directors needed their talents to make busts of the Khmer Rouge leader, Pol Pot, as part of a grand plan for eventually building a huge statue of the man.

Tuol Sleng today embodies the worst horror stories of Khmer Rouge rule. As testimony to the atrocities there are paintings by survivors of Khmer Rouge soldiers dragging women and children, beating them with poles. There is a group photograph of the Khmer Rouge jailers—tough, smirking men, big-boned and ham-handed—and the Khmer Rouge women, blank-faced, staring dully after cooking the pots of watery soup needed to keep the victims alive until their executions. And there, in cells near the entrance, are photographs of bloodied bodies found chained to metal bunks when the Vietnamese arrived—their stomachs slit open by their captors in the minutes before they fled.

The fanaticism of the Khmer Rouge extended into every walk of life, every corner of the country. The overwhelming drive of the Khmer Rouge hordes, mostly village boys driven by cadre, was to rid society of any sign of foreign influence. In outlying towns, schools and hospitals were turned into warehouses and stockrooms, pagodas were burned, and statues of Buddha destroyed. Portions of paved roads were ripped up, and banana trees were planted in the potholes. Valuable rubber trees from the Chup plantation, stretching east of the Mekong to Vietnam, were sawed down for kindling wood—or merely neglected. As the Vietnamese approached Prey Veng, the fleeing Khmer Rouge blew up power generators and dams for channeling water into rice paddies.

Most extraordinary of all, even while attempting to "rebuild" through vast projects requiring thousands of workers, they ignored the most practical precepts, ordering construction of dams and ditches going the wrong way and executing anyone who questioned their wisdom. "Dams and dikes were broken by the American bombing, but the real damage was caused by Pol Pot," said Sim Man, an agricultural official in Prey Veng. "Under Pol Pot they built the dams in the wrong place and destroyed rice fields." The result: starvation, malnutrition, and disease that accounted for more than half the death toll of 1 million to 3 million of the country's 8 million people.

In the rebuilding process, authorities are torn between the desire for revenge and the need to suppress hatred for national unity. "You do not know Cambodia anymore," mused my old cyclo driver as I urged him to drive me down back alleys near one of the black markets. "It is not like before when you were here. Police are everywhere. Be careful." The prime minister, Hun Sen, claimed in an interview, however, that forgiveness was the government's policy. "We have no camps like the ones under Pol Pot," said Hun Sen, a former Khmer Rouge officer like his boss, Heng Samrin. "More than 160,000 people who abandoned Pol Pot are now useful citizens."

Even the hard-core cadres are treated leniently—many are in prison but will not be executed. Theoretically only Pol Pot, who supposedly "retired" as Khmer Rouge leader in September 1985, and Ieng Sary, his main ally, face death sentences in the unlikely event that they're captured. "At first the people were very angry and in some places had to take care of these bad people themselves," said Hun Sen. "But we are educating people about clemency and national unity while fighting to clear the last of the Khmer Rouge guerrillas out of the jungle."

With the Chinese pouring arms into the rebel camps through Thailand, the war can only worsen. Obliquely, Hun Sen admitted the truth of the rumors whispered by cyclo drivers and station vendors—the Khmer Rouge might strike again in the capital. The threat of an ongoing Khmer Rouge presence is not enough to deter his people, said Hun Sen. "We continue our struggle because of the crimes and barbarism of Pol Pot. He is the obstacle to freedom."

Phnom Penh, November 1991

The markets overflow with canned food and medicines, blue jeans and spare parts—an outburst of capitalism that reminds a visitor of the old days before the downfall of the U.S.-backed Lon Nol regime and the rise of the dreaded Khmer Rouge in 1975. Then the U.S. military post exchange system in Vietnam was the source of much of the loot. Now the goodies come from Thailand, through jungles menaced if not controlled by the Khmer Rouge, or from Vietnam, the power behind the regime here ever since the Vietnamese drove the Khmer Rouge from the capital at the end of 1978.

The image of black market prosperity provides a fitting background to the onset of what may be a peace of sorts in the region's most bloodied land. Probably the greatest proof that peace may really be at hand, though, is not a paper signed in Paris but the return this month of Sihanouk in his latest role as president of the nation's Supreme National Council. No other apparition could inspire such a burst of preparations—authorities have rebuilt the airport, banished trucks and bicycles from the main avenues coursing the still graceful capital, and ordered an emergency renovation of the gilt-roofed palace complex.

The timing seems fortuitous—amid a three-day water festival, the most lavish holiday of the year here, at the confluence of the Tonle Sap and Mekong rivers. It is then that Cambodians, according to an official guide, "thank the water, the earth, for their gifts and to excuse that men had to defile and soil them." What could augur better fortune than the sight of the prince walking up a newly constructed landing from a refurbished royal barge while pirogues, manned by 30 to 40 men each, skim the waters and showboats display brightly lit panoramas of ancient Cambodian history?

Sihanouk, by extraordinary irony, may turn out to be the last hope for reuniting the country, even though he has not been in his native land since the Vietnamese invasion at the end of 1978. It was only then that the Khmer Rouge authorized him to leave the palace and fly on to China and the United Nations in quest of international sympathy. The mission did nothing for the Khmer Rouge, responsible for killing at least 1 million of their countrymen, including five of Sihanouk's relatives, but immeasurably enhanced his own prestige as he flew about the world drumming up sympathy—for himself.

For all the euphoria surrounding Sihanouk's return, some observers here wonder if the future will be all that smooth. "The younger people don't take Sihanouk seriously," notes Gre Cornelius, in charge of a team from World Vision, one of the largest of the 50 to 60 voluntary private groups dispensing aid and advice here. With Sihanouk ensconced as titular leader, though, the government could at least gain the UN seat still held by the Khmer Rouge. On that basis, the regime could anticipate a windfall of foreign aid—even if it had to endure the presence of a gaggle of onetime Khmer Rouge killers back in the capital. As it is, businessmen arrive daily in quest of contracts, at least three new hotels are under construction, and the Cambodiana, a luxury lodging envisioned by Sihanouk before his overthrow in the 1970 coup that elevated Lon Nol to power, is full.

Relaxing in a restaurant on the banks of the Tonle Sap, Philip Brown, a former New Jersey schoolteacher working for Food for the

Hungry, observes that "things are quieter." A few months ago, he says, "There was fighting along the main road" south to the coast, but now it's open to traffic. A British worker, Steve Penny, with Christian Outreach, senses the longings. "Older Khmer remember that era," he says, when the prince could travel freely through the land calling his kingdom "an oasis of peace."

12

La Guerre Populaire

Disillusionment among anti-communist forces in Indochina was universal by the early 1970s, but there were variations. The Cambodians had their own special approach to the conflict. When it all began in Cambodia, after the overthrow of Prince Norodom Sihanouk on March 18, 1970, while he was visiting Moscow en route to Beijing, Cambodians responded as if they were going to a party or maybe a crusade. They patriotically rallied, climbed on Pepsi-Cola trucks and a mélange of other conveyances, and went down the roads in search of the enemy—at first largely Vietnamese communist forces, then, somewhat later, the Khmer Rouge, possibly less effective but far more cruel. The frivolity, the fatal gaiety of the Cambodian approach was embedded in my consciousness when I joined a Cambodian general on *la guerre populaire*, an upper-class effort to inspire the peasantry with a sense of loyalty.

The general, as the real war worsened, was rewarded for his easygoing incompetence, his cunning, and his corruption by a promotion and reassignment to Phnom Penh as commander-in-chief of the entire Cambodian army. The peasants, whose loyalty the government never won, were either forced to side with the Khmer Rouge or fled to the relative safety of Phnom Penh as the war spread over the countryside and the Americans bombed in support of Cambodian troops. The students and bureaucrats, anti-Sihanoukist at the outset, displayed varying degrees of lethargy or nostalgia for the Sihanouk era while the government in Phnom Penh bumbled through incessant political and military crises.

The Cambodian soldiers in the field never learned to learn to fight the war no matter how much time they spent at it. Whenever I saw them, more than two years after my excursion with the general, they were sleeping or cooking when they should have been advancing. They rarely prepared more than porous barbed-wire defenses, and they clung to the main roads and villages while the Khmer Rouge swept around them, set up ambushes, and infiltrated government-controlled areas. The basic image of the Cambodian army, as I witnessed it in 1971, remained constant despite massive infusions of American aid, air strikes, and training. As the corrupt general, imitating the French, might have said, "*Plus ça change, plus c'est la méme chose,*" the more it changes, the more it stays the same.

Phnom Penh, April 1971

The high command in the yellow building on one of the capital's widest French-designed boulevards had mounted what it dubbed *la guerre populaire*. With my interpreter, a student of ancient Khmer inscriptions, I dutifully drove out of Phnom Penh in a Mercedes-Benz taxi, past the charred remains of military structures near the airport, and on to a town named Kompong Speu, some 40 miles down the highway. Skeletal frames of old buildings reminded us of a series of battles for the town some months ago, but the war today was off the main road. Jumping into a Russian-built military truck, we rode down a dirt track from which tiny particles of red dust billowed furiously behind the wheels of dilapidated buses, Land Rovers, and new American-supplied jeeps.

Ten miles south of Kompong Speu we met the regional commander, Brigadier General Sosthene Fernandez, sitting under a green canvas tent labeled, "Relief Supplies from the Government of New Zealand." General Fernandez, a short, compact man with a crewcut, deprecating smile, and deep-set, almost pleading eyes, waved us to seats across an improvised table made of boards and crates. Beside him were his senior subalterns, Colonel Ung Than, the provincial governor, a rotund civilian who confessed he only wore his military reserve uniform *pour l'opération*, and Colonel Norodom Chantarangsey, a brigade commander and wealthy member of one of Cambodia's two principal royal families.

"Our life is happy because we can share equally," said General Fernandez, pointing toward bottles of cognac and whiskey and steaming plates of fish, pork, beef, and rice, surrounded by side dishes of vegetables and sauces. *La guerre populaire*, it was clear from first glance around the general's "forward headquarters," set at the base of a couple of knolls on which soldiers were mounting small outposts, was a grand picnic in which all members of the general's following in Kompong Speu were deployed on a two-day holiday before returning to more humdrum chores. "This is the first time we make such popular war with villagers, monks, military, civilian, young, and old," Fernandez explained, offering succulent pieces of sausage to his guests. "Those who have no rifles, who are not military, can come with canes and knives because we are one-minded against the enemy."

La guerre populaire, as waged during our excursion with General Fernandez's troops south of Kompong Speu, typified the Cambodian military operations I witnessed in a month of travels around the country. There was the momentary flush of enthusiasm of students and teachers, freed for two days from classes in town to propagandize among the peasantry. There was the military ineptitude of the troops, who rarely patrolled far beyond main roads, did little more than guard stationary outposts at night, and were powerless to provide real protection against roving bands of Viet Cong or North Vietnamese troops supported by more indigenous Cambodian guerrillas than officers in Phnom Penh cared to admit. Finally, there was the overpowering sense of privilege, of condescension mingled with cynicism exuded by senior Cambodian officers, few of whom had really had to fight seriously before the overthrow of Prince Sihanouk in March of last year.

"It's remarkable how much this army has improved," runs the cliché of diplomats and military attachés assigned to the burgeoning American embassy, expanded from a dozen to nearly a hundred men in the past twelve months. The main improvements, however, are quantitative rather than qualitative. The army, operating with a steady flow of American arms and ammunition ferried up the Mekong or flown aboard American or South Vietnamese cargo planes from South Vietnam, still controls little more than a third of the country, mainly the heartland around the capital of Phnom Penh. North Vietnamese seized most of the northern and northeastern provinces shortly after Sihanouk's fall and also range virtually unopposed, except by American air strikes, across the mountains south of the capital. South

Vietnamese troops, whom most Cambodians regard with the same hatred with which they view the Vietnamese communists, have secured
some of the border regions and may well insist on holding them even if
the Cambodian government asks them to leave.

After more than a year of warfare, the hold of the government over
even the center of the country is so tenuous that American officers
admit the communists "could overrun Phnom Penh anytime they want."
North Vietnamese sappers dramatized this point by a raid on the airport
in which they adroitly knocked out more than 30 planes and helicopters,
burned military barracks and hangars, and damaged meteorological and
radar equipment before Cambodian guards could begin to respond. Intelligence experts estimate at least 1,000 communist "troops"—including saboteurs, spies, and propagandists—are permanently in the capital,
defended by 45,000 men, roughly a quarter of the government's army.
Phnom Penh's best defense, however, probably lies in the reality that
North Vietnam does not seem to want the city while attempting to
solidify positions in the countryside.

"The communist strategy is to try to restrict the government pretty
much to the environs of the city but not to take it over," observed an
experienced diplomat here. "The North Vietnamese would find Phnom
Penh much too difficult to govern if they actually held it. They'd have
to set up an entire satellite regime. They might bring Sihanouk back
from Peking, but it's doubtful if he could ever appear in public after all
the propaganda and political support he has given the Vietnamese
communists against Cambodians."

North Vietnam's strategy has worked so well that foreign analysts
jokingly described General Lon Nol's powers as similar to those of a
glorified "mayor of Phnom Penh." Now the communists can exploit
Cambodia's pervasive political and military weakness even more successfully in view of incurable difficulties in forming a viable, lasting
cabinet under Lon Nol, who suffered a heart attack in February, was
flown to Hawaii aboard an American air force jet for treatment, and
returned in April, this time on a U.S. navy propeller-driven DC6.

"Nobody is loved by all the people," summarized Lon Nol's loyal
"special assistant," his youngest brother, Lieutenant Colonel Lon Non,
explaining away the rumors of discontent among senior officers allied
with Sisowath Sirik Matak, the deputy prime minister to whom Lon
Nol turned over power during his absence in Hawaii. "Even my
brother is not loved by all," remarked Colonel Lon Non with a smile of

broad-minded tolerance that scarcely concealed his own role in mustering much of the opposition to Sirik Matak and persuading Lon Nol to remain in power with a new cabinet.

The result of the machinations of Lon Non and other influential politicians and officers was a state of semiparalysis, always fraught with the danger of a civil war within the greater war for national survival against the Vietnamese communists. The real significance of the crisis was that it illustrated the fundamental ineptitude, lack of understanding, and weakness among national leaders—far more accustomed to bickering and conniving among themselves than to battling the enemy. The North Vietnamese, in the meantime, found it much more expedient to watch the government disintegrate over political differences than to intimidate it into unity by posing a direct threat to Phnom Penh.

The spirit of *la guerre populaire*, as I observed it toward the end of March, indicated the malaise afflicting Cambodia's intriguing politicians, generals, and colonels. "We are glad to come and meet our people here," said Fernandez, now speaking Cambodian, as he arrived with his entourage at a village a few miles down the road from his camp.

The general, who dared move through the countryside only in a military convoy, addressed a crowd of a hundred or so peasants under a banyan tree in front of a monastery. The peasants, who had waited for six hours while soldiers forbade them to return to their homes and fields, listened impassively. Few of them bothered to smile, even politely. *La guerre populaire*, as they had experienced it while Fernandez and his staff had been drinking and dining, had not been pleasant. The Viet Cong, apparently informed in advance of the army's plans, had attacked the village and monastery, which were guarded by two battalions for the official visitation.

Cambodian soldiers, far outnumbering the communist attackers, had repelled them—for the moment. The bodies of two of the enemy, one a Vietnamese wearing Ho Chi Minh sandals made from a truck tire, the other a Cambodian, lay just beyond the bamboo fence surrounding the monastery. Curious Cambodian soldiers stared at them, but the villagers furtively walked by without looking. They paused and cringed, however, when several farmers arrived carrying two poles from which dangled bloodied slings made of multi-colored cotton material used for sarongs.

Inside the slings were the unconscious forms of two farmers, severely wounded by exploding shrapnel from artillery shells fired by Cambodian soldiers. Half a dozen student nurses, members of the propaganda team sent to the village for the day of *la guerre populaire,* dressed the wounds and put the men in an ambulance for the bumpy ride to Kompong Speu. The wife of one of the wounded insisted on sitting beside him. She was nursing an eight-month-old baby whose right arm bore the marks of a bruise suffered in a fall in a bunker during the shelling.

The specter of the wounded and the enemy dead outside the fence accounted in part for the numb reaction accorded Fernandez and his staff. Another reason, perhaps, was inbred suspicion of the general's pledges. "We will search for the enemy in the mountains and the forests," said Fernandez, talking into a microphone set up by the propaganda team. "We come not to destroy but to defend." Fernandez, a Catholic whose paternal grandfather had migrated from the Philippines to perform in the royal orchestra, played upon the Buddhist beliefs of the populace. "We come with monks from this monastery. We will protect the monastery chief. We will leave a colonel here with a battalion."

The general then introduced the chief of the monastery, the Venerable Reth Sam An, who had sat behind him with three other orange-robed monks throughout the speech. The venerable, gaunt and bony-faced, still limping from a beating inflicted by Viet Cong troops, shouted anti-communist denunciations. Fernandez and officers smiled among themselves when he suggested the army drive the communists "as far as Hong Kong." Finally, the monk, who had fled the monastery for the relative safety of town several months earlier, led the crowd in a singsong prayer for peace. Dismissed, the villagers filed slowly, silently as before, outside the monastery. They did not carry the leaflets handed out by students and teachers. "We cannot read," a woman told a soldier.

If *la guerre populaire* was over for the people of the village, it was still in full swing for Fernandez and his officers. As soon as the peasantry had left, he invited us to another multi-course meal, accompanied by the usual libations. Boxes of canned tomato juice, supposedly for the villagers, held up the table boards. Bandages, always in short supply, served as napkins. The governor's Land Rover arrived with freshly roasted beef and chicken, still on the sticks on which his men had cooked them. Some monks looked on from a respectful distance, but otherwise none of the local inhabitants could watch, even from the monastery gates. The general and his staff were convulsed for most of the meal by a nonstop series of jokes. "I wish I could have had my wedding banquet without the wedding," was a particularly well-received sidesplitter that my interpreter translated for me.

The feast lasted nearly two hours, twice as long as the speech-making and propagandizing. Then, packed into their convoy of trucks, buses, Land Rovers, and jeeps, Fernandez, his colonels, and two companies of guards began the drive to town. Ahead of them, walking along the road, were the students, the low-echelon government workers, the teachers, some of them still carrying the leaflets they were supposed to have distributed among the peasants. Students and soldiers alike spoke disparagingly of the villagers, whom they looked on as social inferiors and suspected of collaborating with the enemy. "Don't trust the stars, don't trust the skies, don't trust in women, don't trust your mother who says she has no debt," said an army officer, quoting an ancient Khmer maxim, explaining why so many troops had to accompany his superiors on their trips to the field.

Judging from the attitude of Cambodian officers, however, one had to conclude the aphorism applied better to themselves than to the villagers whom they feared and despised. While General Fernandez, responsible militarily for all the provinces south of Phnom Penh to the Gulf of Thailand, was reveling amid *la guerre populaire*, the Vietnamese communists carefully prepared a series of ambushes on the vital road link from the capital to the coast. Several days later communist soldiers, whom Cambodian and South Vietnamese troops had driven from the highway in a combined operation in January, fired on a convoy, destroying or damaging some 15 vehicles. The battalion promised the village during Fernandez's visit was eventually withdrawn to answer a call for reinforcements.

"How can the villagers cooperate with the soldiers when they realize the communists will come back as soon as they leave?" asked a teacher participating in *la guerre populaire*. We already knew that local agents recruited by the North Vietnamese had visited most of the villages in the region. "They left behind their informers who will tell them everything about our visit," said the teacher, a self-assured French-speaking graduate of a lycée in Phnom Penh. The intimidating presence of informants among the populace illustrated the government's failure to penetrate, much less govern, the countryside. Since Sihanouk's overthrow, the Cambodian army had swollen from roughly 32,000 men to perhaps 180,000, but still was as helpless as it had ever been against a Vietnamese communist force that probably never exceeded more than 10,000 regular troops actively engaged against Cambodians.

"When they started expanding in April of last year, they had in mind an army of 500,000 men," said Fred Ladd, the political-military counselor of the American embassy, sent here a year ago in 1970 to coordinate the first shipments of American equipment since 1963, the year Sihanouk renounced all American aid. "They have learned that such an army is out of the question. They know every volunteer won't become a Sergeant York tomorrow. I guess they'll never go over 200,000." Ladd, a retired army colonel who once commanded all American special forces, "green berets," in Vietnam, nonetheless defended the Cambodian army in relative terms. "I don't think they even *had* a real army before 1970. Sihanouk ordered the soldiers to build roads or perform garrison duties. Now they're getting training and equipment."

Few observers, Cambodian or American, could dispute Ladd's contention that the army had certainly improved. Sihanouk, crowned as king by the French in 1941 at the age of 18, deliberately permitted the armed forces to stagnate after Cambodia gained independence—by diplomatic rather than military means—in 1953. He wanted a force strong enough to fend off encroachments against his power from within but feared the rise of a military elite that might ultimately overthrow him. His relationship with Lon Nol, defense minister in all his cabinets from 1956 to 1966, revealed his basic attitude toward the armed forces. On the one hand, the prince—he abdicated as king in 1955 so he could participate more actively in politics—realized that he had to give Lon Nol enough power to suppress local leftists after a revolt in 1967 in the rice-growing western province of Battambang. On the other hand, Sihanouk deliberately played Lon Nol against leftist politicians in order to hold the general's ambitions in check.

Lon Nol himself was as skillful in the game of Cambodian military politics as was Sihanouk. A conservative politically, he opposed Sihanouk's decision to rely on North Vietnam and other communist countries for aid and friendship and addressed a series of reports to the prince in 1968 and 1969 on the dangers of communist sanctuaries in Cambodian border regions. At the same time, the general, an enigmatic man of few words, sensed the futility of refusing to obey Sihanouk's orders. The prince was not only immensely popular—a god-king to the peasantry outside Phnom Penh—but had too many political allies in the capital. Nor surprisingly, among Sihanouk's closest friends was General Fernandez, who, like most other Cambodian officers, had spent several years in training in France and emulated Sihanouk's own French-influenced social mannerisms.

As secretary of state for national security for the last three years of Sihanouk's rule, Fernandez was one of two or three principal figures in the movement of Chinese and Soviet arms and ammunition from southern Cambodian ports to Vietnamese communist base areas and storage points. He had access to the palace whenever he wanted it, and he was on close terms with Sihanouk's beautiful wife, Princess Monique, and her half brother, Colonel Oum Manorine, secretary of state for national defense, with whom he coordinated details of the arms traffic. Oum Manorine was jailed for attempting a counter-coup, but Fernandez was totally absolved after the National Assembly voted him out of office two days before Sihanouk's overthrow.

"I was not for the Viet Cong," Fernandez shouted in an interview at his headquarters compound in Kompong Speu, explaining his renaissance from disgrace at the hands of the Assembly to command of an entire military region. "When I was in charge of national security I made reports in duplicate on Viet Cong activities. One was for Sihanouk and the other was for Lon Nol."

For all these protestations, however, Fernandez excelled as the kind of artful compromiser who flattered the prince while appeasing opponents. The resurgence of Fernandez illustrated the desire among Cambodia's top leaders, particularly Lon Nol, to forgive and forget the former activities of those who claimed they were only following Sihanouk's orders in shipping arms or otherwise aiding the communists. The majority of Cambodian officers, if not Lon Nol himself, did not object to Cambodia's *de facto* alliance with the Vietnamese communists so long as the country remained stable politically and economically.

While literally all Cambodian officers today denounce Sihanouk and the communists, the presence of Sihanoukists in the military structure has severely weakened its power. If some of Sihanouk's former cronies and allies are not exactly conspiring for his return from Beijing, where he leads a government-in-exile, they still lack the will to offer much more than *pro forma* resistance to the enemy. Many of them, moreover, wallow in such hopeless corruption that no one knows precisely how many troops are now in the army.

The sudden expansion of armed forces in the year after Sihanouk's fall provided the perfect opportunity for commanders to report the number of men in their units as far higher than they really were and to keep for themselves the payrolls of those who did not exist. This practice, common to all armies in Southeast Asia, might have gone unnoticed had American officials in Phnom Penh not demanded figures on real manpower strength so they could distribute weapons and other equipment.

"Cambodian authorities are investigating discrepancies," a senior American diplomat solemnly informed me. "They've sent special teams into the field to ascertain the size of each unit." For all these assurances, however, officers outside Phnom Penh said they had never heard of such an inquiry. The investigation, if it occurred, was apparently limited to rather cursory scrutiny of payroll lists in Phnom Penh. Far from eradicating corruption, it had the negative effect of arousing hostility among officers against Sirik Matak. "As long as Lon Nol survives there will be no difficulty," said General Fernandez, "but if he goes away, then there will be trouble." The general denied firmly that he opposed Sirik Matak but said "two or three" others were against him—a bold revelation in view of the government's claims of complete unity against the enemy.

The politics of Phnom Penh in some respects might resemble, as a young Frenchman who had lived here for several years remarked to me, that of "any small provincial town in France."

The comparison was doubtless apt, but the difference is that Cambodia's political and military difficulties may ultimately tip the balance in the contest for the Indochinese peninsula. If the government cannot very quickly settle its internal feuds, in the opinion of worried American officials, then North Vietnam, always operating through local Cambodian fronts set up in Sihanouk's name, may permanently rule regions now beyond Phnom Penh's authority.

Intelligence analysts in Saigon believe North Vietnam views complete restoration of infiltration routes and sanctuaries in these regions as prerequisites to defeating South Vietnam's army, at least as long as the United States supports the latter with aid and air strikes. The key to much of Hanoi's strength in South Vietnam before Sihanouk's fall lay, after all, in Cambodia's willingness not only to let the communist countries ship arms for North Vietnamese troops through Cambodian ports but also to grant them sanctuary in vast border bases. The Vietnamese communists, logically, did not resort to military means until diplomacy vis-à-vis the Cambodian government had failed them—in terms of long-range aims not in Cambodia but in South Vietnam.

Probably the most aggressively anti-communist Cambodian leader is Sirik Matak, who easily impressed Americans by seizing upon the concept of *la guerre populaire* and urging continued offensives against the enemy, particularly while Lon Nol was recuperating in Hawaii. Primary responsibility for conduct of the war, however, rested not with Sirik Matak but with a council of perhaps half a dozen generals in charge of a general headquarters within the ministry of defense.

The question is whether Cambodia's generals are at all better qualified militarily than Sirik Matak, by profession a diplomat who served as ambassador to China, Japan, and the Philippines before Sihanouk temporarily "retired" him in 1968. Most senior Cambodian officers were trained by French officers in conventional infantry tactics that bear little relationship to the peculiar brand of hit-and-run warfare waged by communist troops along all major roads leading toward Phnom Penh.

Lon Nol himself, after having attended Saigon's fashionable Lycée Chasseloup-Laubat ten years ahead of Sihanouk, began his career as a civilian magistrate under French colonial authorities in 1936. He did not enter military service until 1952, when he was appointed commander of Battambang province, and had no formal training until 1955, when he studied for several months at the French-advised Royal Khmer Military Academy.

Unlike Lon Nol, many of Cambodia's officers spent several years in France—or else, before 1963, studied in the United States under the old military assistance and advisory program. General Fernandez, for instance, has been to France three times: first in 1951 at infantry school, again in 1953 at staff school, and, finally, from 1959 to 1961 at the Advanced School of Warfare, the equivalent of the various war colleges for potential top officers in the States. Often, however, the experience of training in France was more valued socially than professionally. Sihanouk himself was raised speaking French—and far preferred to discuss political and military problems in French than in Cambodian. General Fernandez, like other onetime Sihanouk lieutenants, reflects his French background and close associations with the prince. "Poof," he said, pursing his lips and turning up his palms in a typically French gesture of frustration, when asked if he knew whether or not any officers were still selling arms to the communists.

If an education in France was an asset in the milieu of Sihanoukist Cambodia, however, it proved almost useless when the fighting began in earnest a week or two after Sihanouk's demise. Cambodian troops were quite capable of dispersing peasant mobs shouting pro-Sihanoukist slogans by firing into them, but they were almost powerless against Vietnamese communist attacks on towns and villages along the frontiers. It was then, in April 1970, that the army began commandeering multi-colored commercial buses in which to rush what were known optimistically as "mobile forces" in response to pleas for aid from besieged and beleaguered outposts on all sides of Phnom Penh. Untrained, ill-equipped, and unwieldy, these units proved woefully incapable of defending all but the immediate environs of the capital, particularly since the communists widened their campaign in pursuit of new base areas and supply routes after the cross-border incursions by American and South Vietnamese troops.

"Nobody dares say we support the new government or the old one," the wife of a village chief told me at the beginning of April 1970 after a company of communist troops had blared propaganda for several hours on behalf of Sihanouk's United National Front of Kampuchea, the ancient name for Cambodia.

The woman, wearing traditional sarong and blouse, was standing beside her husband beneath the home on stilts where they lived with their eight children. Some 50 villagers gathered around as she recounted the incident in trembling tones. "The Viet Cong came into the village at eight last night. They had a loudspeaker and shouted 'Long Live Prince Sihanouk' in Cambodian. They made us put up pictures of Sihanouk by the doors. They burned down the police station and the village office." The villagers, said the woman, "did not care about Sihanouk"—or, for that matter, Lon Nol. Their only concern was security.

Almost immediately, the government revealed it could not defend them against more raids and threats. A battalion of troops, packed into trucks and jeeps, roared by bewildered villagers the morning after the raid but did not pause en route to an embattled district town some 15 miles to the north. The battalion was stymied near the village at a bridge blown up by sappers. Commanders deemed it too risky to go ahead by foot—or even to send patrols into surrounding countryside, studded with trees and stones behind which guerrillas could easily lie in ambush. A French-speaking major, in command of the convoy, explained that his troops, hefting Chinese, French, American, and Russian weapons, were "well equipped" but might run out of ammunition if the war expanded along the frontiers.

For all their equipment, the major's troops would have been powerless if the Vietnamese communists had chosen to ambush the convoy, running almost bumper-to-bumper down the road. There was no artillery support and, at that stage in the widening war, no liaison with American or South Vietnamese airplanes. The major explained that his men had little time to worry about fine points of tactics or defense. The government was sending them from one trouble spot to another with no advance planning or even warning. "We have to defend all places at once," he said, climbing into his jeep and leading the convoy whence it came so his troops would be secure in their quarters before dusk.

The weakness of government forces in the spring of 1970 was un-understandable, but army officers could present no such excuses for the failure of a vaunted "counteroffensive" up route six, a critical highway north of Phnom Penh, the following September. For the first time in the war, according to Lieutenant Colonel Am Rong, the Cambodian army spokesman in Phnom Penh, Cambodian forces were "seizing the initiative" and beginning to drive the North Vietnamese from strongholds they had held since the previous spring and summer. Along with other reporters and photographers, I clambered into a Mercedes-Benz, the standard conveyance for reaching any of the fronts in this elusive, multi-fronted war, and hurried to the scene of the latest fighting, 60 miles to the north.

The aim of the offensive was to open up route six as far as the town of Kompong Thom, a major government enclave some 80 miles north of the capital, but it was questionable if the special "task force" spearheading the drive could even get into the village of Taing Kauk, into which communist troops had dug a complex network of trenches and bunkers. The weakness of the task force was all the more humiliating in view of the American role in the operation. Cambodia and the United States had solidified an unwritten agreement under which Washington was providing full air support—described as "interdiction of North Vietnamese supply routes" by Defense Secretary Melvin

Laird—as well as new weapons, ammunition, and even training for Cambodian troops in South Vietnam. At least 1,000 of the 5,000 men poured into the offensive had just completed a three-week refresher course in South Vietnam after American transport planes had evacuated them from unstable positions in the sparsely populated, jungly northeastern provinces.

Two American planes, a slow-moving C119 gunship laden with machine guns and an F4 phantom jet on a photo-reconnaissance mission, were wheeling and diving overhead when I reached the tail of the task force near a blown-out bridge outside of Taing Kauk. Cambodian soldiers were lolling in hammocks slung between mud-spattered buses and French armored cars on which they had driven from Phnom Penh, and a work crew was attempting to rebuild the bridge with a new orange-colored steel girder, supplied by the Americans. I walked across the girder, past soldiers fishing and swimming in a canal by a rice paddy, to the "front," several hundred yards up the road.

Bullets cracked and twanged, occasionally kicking up geysers of water in the rice paddies. French-trained junior officers shouted, "*Avancez!*" Their charges, bunched together in defiance of common-sense rules of safety under fire, fought from trenches cut into the road by North Vietnamese saboteurs. A squad of Cambodians moved slowly toward the cement framework of an old schoolhouse. They poked through ashes and gaping holes in the walls, already bombarded by American planes. Automatic-rifle fire crackled from the shadows.

Major Hang Yieu, battalion commander, barked orders in Cambodian from one of the trenches. More soldiers inched forward along a wall beside the schoolhouse. In a moment the rifle fire died down, and the American planes faded in the distance. Standing beside the major, I saw the bodies of three Cambodian soldiers lying next to an entrance to the school grounds. "It is normal for an offensive," Hang Yieu remarked, neither sadly nor callously, as some of his soldiers stared at the bodies. Up ahead 50 feet lay the bodies of two North Vietnamese, their hands still clutching a long pole on which had hung a sack of rice. Across from them was the body of one more Cambodian soldier, his white sneakers shining in the midday sun.

"It will be a long time before we reach Kompong Thom," said Hang Yieu as some of his troops fired a few final perfunctory shots into the schoolhouse, now apparently deserted by the last enemy snipers. As if to prove the major's point, most of his men slouched under some trees in the shade of abandoned village homes. Others foraged for pigs and chickens or drank water from a well. "We are waiting for our support," the major explained. A mile behind him, some of the "support" slowly lumbered forward—a few buses, armored cars, and hospital trucks identifiable by their red crosses.

"We think maybe 2,000 or 3,000 communist troops are ahead of us," Hang Yieu said, but his estimate seemed grossly exaggerated. A mere 20 or 30 snipers could easily have held up the entire column. The fighting on the fringes of Taing Kauk dramatized the pattern of the operation, if not of the entire war. The enemy's main purpose was to harass, delay, and pin down Cambodian forces while opening new supply and infiltration routes through eastern and central Cambodia to South Vietnam.

"Cambodian troops are advancing slowly but steadily," announced Colonel Am Rong (whose name, it was often noted, seemed peculiarly appropriate) the morning after I returned to Phnom Penh. The North Vietnamese, sneaking around Cambodian positions, soon cut the road in several places behind them and threatened to surround them. It was all the Cambodians, supported by American air strikes, could do to fight their way into Taing Kauk, set up a more or less permanent base in the shelled, strafed, and bombed-out town, and hold the North Vietnamese at arm's length with occasional sporadic patrols into the treelines.

On my next visit to Taing Kauk, at the beginning of March 1971, I discovered the commander of the task force, Colonel Um Savuth, stripped to the waist, sitting at a table in front of a Buddhist temple, guzzling glass after glass of American Black Label beer, purchased on the local "free market."

"I have not yet started to fight against the enemy base areas ahead of us, I am organizing local popular troops," explained Colonel Um Savuth, who Americans later assured me was "better drunk than most Cambodian officers sober." The colonel claimed he commanded some 12,000 Cambodian troops, but this figure seemed high to observers who had driven the 20-mile stretch between Taing Kauk and Skoun, another bombed-out town at a junction on the way to Phnom Penh. Soldiers at small bunkered outposts along the road said they rarely, if ever, patrolled more than a mile or two in the daytime, and none of them had ventured more than a few hundred yards beyond the last guard post on the other side of Taing Kauk.

Nor did it seem that Colonel Um Savuth had spent much time organizing popular forces, since most of the residents had fled the region. The ruins of Taing Kauk and Skoun were inhabited largely by families of the soldiers, who evidently believed they would remain where they were for quite some time.

If Colonel Um Savuth had failed to prove himself an aggressive commander, however, he had at least impressed upon his men one standing order: behead any North Vietnamese soldier killed or captured in battle. "We never keep prisoners," said one of the colonel's subordinates, also drinking beer outside the Buddhist temple. "After we have finished questioning a prisoner, we kill him." As a case in point, the officer said some of his men had interrogated a Vietnamese several days before my arrival and chopped his head off with a bayonet.

At the forward post on the edge of town, one of the soldiers told me he personally delivered to Colonel Um Savuth the heads of North Vietnamese killed while attacking his position. Otherwise, said the soldier, "the spirit of the dead man could rise again in another body and attack us"—a belief that reflects deep-seated animist superstitions among Cambodians as well as the Buddhist backgrounds of most Cambodians and Vietnamese.

Soldiers admitted, however, they had relatively few opportunities even to attempt to carry out the colonel's special order. "A few nights ago a Viet Cong came on bicycle, got off, and crawled to our position," said one of the guards at Taing Kauk, describing a typical skirmish. "Our men fired, but he escaped. It was very dark at night. We did not go and search for him. We were afraid of the iron nails"— spikes implanted in front of the post for protection.

The only Cambodian troops who impressed me as particularly aggressive or well led were the Khmer Kampuchea Krom, Cambodians from the Mekong River delta region of South Vietnam, trained into elite units by American special forces before Sihanouk's fall and sent across the border as units of the Cambodian army in the spring and summer of 1970. None of the KKK, as they are generally known, were on the route six offensive, but I found them at other critical points defending the northern approaches to Phnom Penh against repeated attempts by the communists to isolate the capital entirely from the countryside.

Some ten miles north of Phnom Penh I met a wiry major named Kim Chi, born of Cambodian parents in South Vietnam's Vinh Binh province. Major Kim Chi, at 42 a veteran of some 20 years in KKK units, had just led his battalion against North Vietnamese troops entrenched in a village named Kompong Popil, reached after a circuitous journey by sampan, motor scooter, military truck, and, finally, foot.

"I spread my soldiers on either side of the stream," said Major Kim Chi, walking across a bamboo suspension foot-bridge that bounced up and down like a spring beneath our steps. "Then I called in aircraft, but the planes couldn't see where to bomb and didn't drop anything. We went from house to house through the village driving the Viet Cong from their bunkers." Major Kim Chi's men also sank a camouflaged sampan in which the communists had stored arms and food. And "we are still finding rifles in the bunkers."

While Kim Chi was talking, some of the villagers tentatively peered from behind shuttered windows and half-closed doors. Most of them had fled, but those who remained seemed to welcome the presence of the KKK, at least in comparison with the Vietnamese who had occupied their village for the past few months. "Both North and South Vietnamese soldiers have been here," said Yu Nguon, an elderly shopkeeper who ground axes and knives for his village. "The North Vietnamese taxed us and stole our animals. They said we had to stay here and dig holes in case of bombing. The South Vietnamese also robbed us and violated women. Then the South Vietnamese left and the North Vietnamese came back and set up committees to rule us. We are glad Cambodian soldiers can now defend us." Realistically, however, Yu Nguon sensed the KKK would soon leave and fight elsewhere. "We need weapons and permanent protection. Otherwise we cannot live here. We must escape."

The KKK, totaling only ten or a dozen battalions of several hundred men apiece, were most needed around the town of Kompong Cham, a provincial capital on the Mekong some 45 miles northeast of Phnom Penh. "Every night we see trucks moving through the rubber plantations across the river," said a young KKK captain, Thuon Savan, in charge of an encampment ten miles upstream from Kompong Cham. "We called them by radio, and they said they were friendly troops, but they refused to give their unit number. We think they are North Vietnamese."

Intelligence analysts confirmed that elements of three communist divisions—the fifth, seventh, and ninth—were based in the rubber plantations, periodically invaded by South Vietnamese troops attempting to protect the approaches to Kompong Cham and Phnom Penh. The KKK formed, in effect, the first indigenous Cambodian defense after the South Vietnamese. And KKK officers believed the North Vietnamese would cross the river in sampans and attack them as soon as the South Vietnamese had departed.

The question, then, was why the KKK were not capable of pursuing the North Vietnamese on their own—or at least of defending Kompong Cham and the road to Phnom Penh. The answer again seemed to lie partly in the form of leadership, in this case provided by Brigadier General In Tam, a career politician who, as president of the National Assembly, had helped to overthrow Sihanouk and then had assumed command of the entire region north of the capital.

Like Colonel Am Rong, General In Tam explained that his troops were moving "slowly but surely" when asked why they spent agonizing hours, if not days, waiting for orders to advance down roads harassed only occasionally by snipers. Several hundred North Vietnamese, dug into a series of villages south of Kompong Cham, blocked a brigade of In Tam's troops for a month despite American and South Vietnamese air strikes. Accompanied by a squad of In Tam's soldiers in an armored car, my interpreter and I drove eight miles down the road to the last outpost at a village named Rokor Koy. Villagers were just beginning to return to their homes—or what was left of them after Allied bombing and shelling.

"We must finish building our camp," said the local commander, Major Ben Sawn, looking over fresh mounds of dirt and bamboo fences surrounding the outpost. "At least 200 of the enemy are only two kilometers away. If we advance too quickly, they will try to encircle us and attack us from our rear." The major's explanation may have seemed sensible, but he and his battalion were still at Rokor Koy when I visited them again three weeks later. "Now the communists are spreading rumors. They're telling the villagers they intend to attack Kompong Cham again," said General In Tam. "The troops here won't advance again until we've built our defenses behind us. We're also waiting for all the villagers to return so we can defend them and they can help us." If nothing else, In Tam's remarks showed how tenuous and fragile was the hold of his troops over the relatively small swath of territory that had supposedly been cleared, at untold cost of life and property, over the past two months.

Unlike other senior Cambodian officers whom I had met, however, In Tam impressed me as a personally sensitive man, alive to the suffering and fear of the people among whom he lived. He seemed to owe this sensitivity in part to a factor that may also have accounted for his military weakness: he was not essentially a soldier but a civilian administrator who had assumed rank and command for want of any other qualified officials.

In my travels with him, In Tam displayed his political, if not military, expertise. "Don't drink so much," he good-naturedly abjured a garrulous villager at a peasant wedding ceremony before handing him a 500-riel (about five-dollar) note as a gift. "Don't discourage your husbands and make them afraid," he asked cringing wives of local village defensemen, whom we met at a small outpost by the river. One of the men, wearing new military fatigues, clasped his hands together and bowed before In Tam in the manner of adoration and reverence reserved for political or religious, rather than military, figures.

In Tam's concern for his people was perhaps best displayed at a meeting with commanders in his residence. "Don't let your soldiers steal chickens, don't kill animals," he warned. "Obey the good Buddhist doctrines. Your soldiers should be famous in war so the villagers will trust them." In Tam also advised the KKK not to set up their camps in villages. "People are afraid the enemy will shoot them when they shoot at the camp. It's better to go far away to spare their houses." The commanders smiled knowingly at each other, then jumped in their jeeps to join their units. The KKK had advanced a mile or two to a stream, where they had killed one civilian, a farmer out fishing, whom they claimed to have mistaken for an enemy soldier.

If In Tam was not so harsh as career officers, he was as eager as any Cambodian for more and better American equipment. "I am requesting American rifles for all my soldiers," he said, standing near the new bunker complex in which he both sleeps and works. "If I have enough, then I will send my troops farther."

All the KKK battalions carry American weapons, including M16 rifles, with which they were supplied while in Vietnam, but many of the other soldiers still rely entirely on Chinese AK47s and Soviet SKS semiautomatics or old American carbines. "It is very difficult obtaining enough ammunition and spare parts with so many different kinds of weapons," said In Tam, echoing one of the primary complaints of both Cambodian commanders and American officers sent here to expedite American arms shipments. The United States has begun to compensate somewhat for this problem by equipping Cambodian battalions trained in Vietnam with M16s, but Cambodian officials still said they needed much more than allotted under the present military aid program, $185 million for this year alone.

"One of the problems is to get first-class weapons out of the hands of those on static defense around government offices and into the hands of those who need them for fighting," said Fred Ladd, the American who probably knows the most about the Cambodian military establishment. "If you or I drive down the road, we can find a battalion with as many as nine different kinds of weapons." Fairly soon, Ladd anticipated, the Cambodian military, armed entirely under Sihanouk with AK47s, "would have to standardize toward both the M16 and the AK47." For the first time in the Indochinese conflict, the United States is supplying ammunition for a communist-made weapon—AK47 bullets produced since September in a factory near Washington, D.C.

American officials recognize, however, the futility of even attempting to reform Cambodian units in the image of their American or even South Vietnamese counterparts. "Anybody who talks about Cambodia in terms of American standards is immediately frustrated," said Ladd. "They wouldn't know what to do with all the equipment in an ordinary American brigade or battalion even if we gave it to them." The most pressing need, according to specialists here, is to train the Cambodians to use the equipment they have. Americans are never really certain of the competence of Cambodian soldiers since the United States does not keep advisers with units in the field. Another problem, on a higher level, is that Cambodian commanders lack the managerial skills and experience needed to channel and coordinate the arrival and deployment of matériel throughout the country.

In the final analysis, if there is any reason for hope, it is in the lingering spirit not of the army's Frenchified, stultified leaders but of the average soldiers, who seem either unaware of or unfazed by the defeats and humiliations suffered by the army for more than a year. Shortly after communist sapper attacks on the main airport at Phnom Penh and the oil refinery at the port of Kompong Som, formerly Sihanoukville, I drove to a bombed-out town named Saang, some 20 miles south of the capital on the Bassac, paralleling the Mekong. Vietnamese communist and Cambodian troops had fought back and forth through Saang at least half a dozen times since June. The communists had last overrun the town toward the end of January at the same time they attacked the airport. Cambodians recaptured Saang at the beginning of February and now were manning a bunker line beyond the last houses.

"My soldiers weren't well trained at first," said Eang Nim, a sergeant who had joined the Vichy French forces as a paratrooper in 1942. "We had time to show the new recruits how to load their rifles and then sent them to fight after three days of training." Like most Cambodians, Eang Nim had never really expected a war. "The Viet Cong were our friends. They helped us clean our weapons sometimes when we met them. Then, after Sihanouk's fall, our government asked them to leave and they refused. They attacked and drove us back from the border." Eang Nim's soldiers insisted, however, the Viet Cong were now afraid of them. "Yesterday some VC saw our troops and ran away," said a young corporal in charge of firing a mortar. "We want the VC to fight so we can kill them."

Some of the soldiers pointed to a cluster of stones in a gully emptying into the Bassac. "The Viet Cong came ten meters from where we are," said a man in a bunker. "We fired at them before they could throw grenades at us. We found two of their bodies. You can still see the bloodstains." The soldiers claimed they didn't like their stationary positions and had asked to go on patrols. "Formerly the enemy looked for us," said a 24-year-old corporal, Keo Sarath. "Now we should search for them. We should not stop here. If we have the chance, we will keep on fighting." Another corporal, Heng Ngan, was almost as critical of the South Vietnamese as he was of the Vietnamese communists. "Both Vietnamese are alike. They have the same faces. The villagers are afraid of all Vietnamese. They want us to protect them."

The soldiers at Saang, looking toward a no-man's-land of deserted houses and impassable roads, were evincing perhaps the oldest sentiment of Cambodia's traditional quarrel with the Vietnamese, bitter enemies for centuries before the arrival of the French colonialists more than a hundred years ago. In the absence of any real leadership, however, it was highly questionable whether even this kind of spirit, reflected among almost all the troops to whom I spoke, would really suffice. "We are not afraid, we are not afraid," the soldiers at Saang kept telling me, repeating the refrain as if they were trying to convince themselves. "If the Americans give us enough arms, some new weapons and uniforms, we will win."

While they were talking, literally on the last line of defense of the town, their battalion commander was returning from Phnom Penh in a Land Rover, followed by a platoon of his men in a convoy of three vehicles, laden with food and drink for his staff. "We don't know anything about our government," said one of the soldiers, looking toward the commander's headquarters in a former schoolhouse in the center of town. "We only fight for our country."

13

"Now the VC Can Go Anywhere"

The war for Vietnam, as American officials were reluctantly recognizing, had to be a Vietnamese struggle. One of the greatest mysteries of the changing conflict was how well the South Vietnamese would perform on their own after years of American infantry, armored, and air support. You couldn't quite tell from the initial losses suffered by the ARVN in the 1972 Easter Offensive. The South Vietnamese often had their own way of regrouping and waiting it out—surviving without winning.

One place to go to try to assess the feelings of the South Vietnamese was a region under pressure but still held by the ARVN. The Queson Valley offered a microcosmic view of the entire conflict as it had surged back and forth over the years. No other phase of the war could have better demonstrated the futility of a struggle that had really proven nothing except, possibly, the depths of man's cruelty to man. No one will ever count how many thousands of Americans and Vietnamese died in the Queson, but it was the scene of some of the worst, underreported fighting of the Indochinese conflict. American advisers, as they were leaving the valley for the last time, were no more sanguine about the prospects for real peace, much less victory, than was a youngish Vietnamese battalion commander with whom I went on a rather aimless patrol from an old American firebase named Ross.

The Americans, at least, were going home; the Vietnamese had to stay. Three months after I visited the Queson the North Vietnamese overran Ross and the nearby district town. A glib Vietnamese regimental commander, a colonel whom I had interviewed on the base, ordered a premature, needless retreat while reinforcements were already on the way in helicopters. The battalion commander, a major who had never shared his colonel's false optimism, nor his cowardice, was severely wounded—blinded in one eye. On my last visit to the region I heard the colonel had a comfortable desk job in Danang while the major was serving unhappily in regimental headquarters near route one, pleading for another chance to rejoin his men in the field.

Queson Valley, May 1972

It has been a long war for the American adviser on Landing Zone Ross, a patch of dirt and cement large enough for a dozen 105- and 155-millimeter cannon and a couple of companies of infantry. He returned here eight months ago and found the war had come almost full circle from the time of his first tour with the same South Vietnamese regiment, in the same valley, in 1965 and 1966.

"Oh, things were a little different," says the adviser, a lieutenant colonel whose main job, then as now, is to call in American air strikes for the South Vietnamese. "It was very dangerous to drive up the road, and the ARVN didn't patrol much in the valley." Just about the time the adviser was going home from his first tour, the American marines were settling in here. LZ Ross, says the adviser, a West Pointer with silvering hair, was named for a marine colonel. You still see the names of marines painted on some of the big boulders near the top of the base, where the commander of the fifth regiment of the second ARVN division keeps his command post.

Then the marines pulled out of much of the Queson—rolling farmland sinking into forbidding, jungly hills on either side—and troops from the army's old Americal division began sweeping the valley. The soldiers left their imprint on Ross, half a mile or so up a rutted road from the market town of Queson, itself some 20 miles from the lowland highway leading to Danang, 50 miles up the coast. Black peace signs, considerably more popular among army soldiers than marines, are splashed on some of the rocks. The initials "FTA" for "Fuck the Army" appear on one boulder just below the newly painted symbol of the fifth regiment, a medallion showing three mountain peaks over a dragon emerging from the sea with the slogan, *"VUON LEN,"* "Rise up, Overcome."

The Americal, for all the recalcitrance of some of its soldiers, may have fought harder and longer for the Queson than did the marines. The names of the onetime Americal firebases, scraped off lonely hilltops, still dot the situation map in the sandbagged briefing room in the fifth regiment headquarters. There they are, red and black grease-pencil marks on the grid lines, sobriquets embedded in the memories of the GIs who defended them but otherwise largely forgotten: "Kala," "Irene," "Mimosa," "Melon," "Judy," "Grant," "O'Connor," "Pleasantville," "Marge," "Mary Ann," "Mildred," "Young," "Barrier," "Center." Among them perhaps only Mary Ann achieved much fame—or notoriety. Before dawn on March 28 of last year, North Vietnamese sappers pierced its flimsy defenses, overrunning most of the base and killing 33 GIs—the highest number of American dead in a single ground attack in the history of the second Indochinese war.

If the Americans never defeated the North Vietnamese, they at least drove most of them out of the valley. "We opened the road in the middle of 1968," says a Vietnamese officer in the town of Queson, a district center still bustling with betel-chewing women selling rice and meat in open stalls in the central market and crafty shopkeepers peddling cloth and hardware to farmers from outlying hamlets. In fact, before the last Americal soldiers went home several months ago, it was safe to drive eight miles farther up the valley to another, smaller district center named Hiep Duc, on the other side of a steep, rock-strewn slope known as "Lion Hill" to the Americans, "Hon Chieu" to the Vietnamese. Among the hills beyond Hiep Duc, in jungle sparsely populated even in moments of peace, American soldiers until the end could expect to encounter regular North Vietnamese troops lodged in almost impenetrable caves and cement-lined bunkers bound by tunnels and trenches.

In the populated regions of the valley, however, security was such that South Vietnamese troops did not immediately replace the Americans after their withdrawal. It was not until early April, several days after a new North Vietnamese division, the 711th, had launched a series of attacks around Hiep Duc, that the fifth regiment was rushed in a convoy from the southern lowlands, reopened Landing Zone Ross, and reoccupied a string of old hilltop firebases and outposts. "Now the VC can go anywhere. We don't have enough troops," says Major Nguyen Thai Buu, sitting on one of the new sandbag piles thrown up on Ross a few weeks ago. "My soldiers are very tired. They have been walking every day for the past six weeks. We have to keep the VC away from Queson. If the fifth regiment leaves Ross, they will go all the way to the lowlands."

As it is, says Buu, who has fought at one time or another among almost all the hills and valleys in the Queson region since graduating from the military academy at Dalat seven years ago, the ARVN has abandoned the valley beyond Hon Chieu, rising three miles to our west. "We began fighting around Hiep Duc on April 11," says Buu, commander of the fifth regiment's fourth battalion. "We left there on April 14 to keep the VC from moving closer to Ross." Major Buu, who rose with the regiment from platoon leader to company commander to battalion executive officer before his appointment as battalion commander a year ago, does not appear humiliated or even slightly embarrassed by the retreat. "We attacked the VC at Hiep Duc for three days. They attacked us for one day. We killed 51 of them and captured 16 weapons."

It might be unfair to interpret the withdrawal of Major Buu's battalion as a defeat in itself or even as an adverse reflection on its performance. It was just that the 711th division included two fresh regiments, besides an old one bloodied by the Americans, and South Vietnamese commanders rightly anticipated the possibility of the sudden loss of the entire valley. At the same time, two provinces to the south, in Binh Dinh, North Vietnamese troops plunged all the way to the lowlands, driving the South Vietnamese from a series of small towns and villages and cutting route one, the main north–south highway. Three provinces to the north, the enemy had poured across the demilitarized zone, driven the ARVN from a string of firebases once held by U.S. marines and army soldiers, and were on their way to surrounding the provincial capital of Quang Tri, finally overrun at the beginning of May after the collapse of the third division.

Nor was Hiep Duc immediately abandoned after Major Buu's retreat. "As our battalion moved back," says Buu, a slender, broad-chested son of a small landowner from Quang Ngai, "the VC surrounded Hiep Duc and attacked the regional force troops left inside the town every day and every night for several days." Finally, the district chief, responsible for both the civilian populace and local territorial troops, ordered the town's evacuation and *de facto* surrender. "On the way from Hiep Duc to Queson, the RF lost an entire company, and the district chief himself was killed." For Major Buu, accustomed to roaming the hills and lowlands ever since he was a small boy riding his father's water buffalo, the flight from Hiep Duc was the beginning of a series of tactical withdrawals, none of them necessarily defeats as such, all characterized by heavy losses on both sides.

"We had to move back to keep the VC from moving to the east. As we moved back, we attacked them three times. One time we contacted two battalions and requested air strikes, but they arrived too late. A day later we searched the area and found 20 bodies of VC. Everywhere we go, the VC mortar our battalion." Major Buu says the VC—a term he uses indiscriminately to include both Viet Cong guerrillas from South Vietnam and regular North Vietnamese troops—had overrun a couple of old American firebases by May and are still lodged on one of them. "Air strikes hit the top of one hill and the side but missed the enemy bunkers. When our battalion moved close to the firebase, the enemy shelled it with mortars. They don't care about their own casualties."

Major Buu talks easily, softly in the final glow of daylight. Looking over the valley, he sounds almost academic as he tries to explain why the North Vietnamese seem more determined than his own soldiers, why his battalion has had to retreat time and again just to keep from falling apart and to protect Ross and the rest of the valley. At 32, younger than average for a battalion commander, he does not seem to have lost confidence or faith in his army. There is, one gathers, a rational explanation for almost everything, ranging from the defeat at Quang Tri to the corruption of some if not most of the country's leaders. Major Buu's long bony fingers, his jut jaw, and a scar around his left eye all seem to give him the appearance of an experienced jungle fighter, a commander who would be an asset to any army, and yet he is a man marked prematurely by a curious sense of resignation.

Major Buu has just returned from a patrol some four miles west across the valley from Ross. "Almost every day we have some contact with the enemy. Today we find three of them and kill one. The other two run away." Somewhat deprecatingly, he unfurls a newly sewn National Liberation Front flag, red and green with a yellow star in the middle, found in the pack of the dead soldier, and offers me an NLF medal showing a pith-helmeted guerrilla hurling a grenade at a tank with the initials "US" on it.* "The enemy now uses the tactics of close contact. They set up strong points: two men with AK47 rifles and one with a B40 rocket launcher. With these they can hold a company or a battalion for a couple of days. We have to destroy the strong points in order to get through the area." One question the major asks is whether it is wiser to request air and artillery strikes, often inaccurate, or to risk high casualties among his own men by storming enemy concentrations on the ground.

"We don't want to fight like the VC," says Major Buu, who attributes the scar around his eye to a childhood rock fight but has twice been wounded in earlier campaigns. "We try to save our men. Any time we have close contact, we call in air and artillery." Sometimes, however, highly disciplined enemy troops respond by fighting harder rather than falling back. "The VC are very smart. When they see tac air, they just move forward toward our men. Now they are determined to hold their strong points. They stay until death, and it is very difficult for us to recapture any place once it falls into their hands." Buu also notes the adverse effect of airpower on the South Vietnamese. "If you do not depend on it, you fight better. If you depend too much on airpower and artillery, you know you just do nothing. In the end, in battle, you cannot depend on anyone. You have to fight for yourself."

Buu admits, however, that without American airpower the enemy would probably have overrun Ross and Queson in the first few weeks of the offensive. "At the present, airpower holds the enemy," he says, shrugging. "We don't want to lose our men. Perhaps we save them for the long run." That afternoon, while he is on patrol with half his battalion, American jets and helicopter gunships are blasting away as usual at the sides of Hon Chieu with 500-pound bombs and rockets. "Outstanding," shouts the regimental commander, Colonel Nguyen Huu Luu, when the commander of the third battalion, holding the top of Hon Chieu, reports by radio that half a dozen enemy soldiers have died within 50 feet of his bunkers.

---

*Ken Englade, then with UPI, gleefully noted in a review of the first edition of this book that red and blue, not green, with yellow star, were the proper colors. He conceded, though, that the VC "grandmother" who had sewn it might not have had blue cloth when I protested that I had seen dark green and was not colorblind.

"The communists will be killed, all of them," Colonel Luu announces to his American adviser, calling in the strikes, but his triumphant smile vanishes as the battalion commander radios that he and several of his men have just been wounded by enemy mortar fire.

"The NVA are attacking right now," Luu rasps. "We need more gunships." His adviser patiently calls in more strikes while a South Vietnamese medevac chopper whirls in to pick up the casualties. "For the last three days Ross has received 82-mortar and 75-recoilless rifle fire," says the colonel in a lull in the fighting for Hon Chieu, overrun two days before by the NVA and recaptured the next day by the ARVN. "The reason they shell us—they do not want our artillery to support our troops in the field." If the enemy overruns and holds Hon Chieu, "they can fire at us more easily from better positions."

Luu, who spent 18 years with the first division somewhat to the north before coming to the fifth regiment a year and a half ago, appears to have resolved not to yield any more territory—for tactical or any other reasons. "We must hold what we have," he says that evening over dinner with his officers in a tent behind his command bunker. "We must fight to the last man."

That night the North Vietnamese renew their attack on Hon Chieu. The colonel, in white shorts and T-shirt, again shouts at the American adviser for more air support. "Please keep one gunship on station all night," he demands. The next morning he is even more impatient to wipe out the enemy mortars, apparently firing from abandoned rice paddies around the base of Hon Chieu. "We must know exactly where they are," he admonishes an intelligence officer, who has been pointing rather vaguely at some tiny black dots on the situation map.

As soon as the briefing is over the colonel orders Major Buu to patrol the road and rice paddies around Hon Chieu in search of the mortar men, probably no more than a squad. A few hundred yards from Ross, in a tin-roofed village named Son Lanh, nine armored personnel carriers and a couple of tanks line up in front of soda stands that once peddled PX Cokes in cans to GIs. A company of Major Buu's infantry, 110 men of his battalion of 320, lounge by the road or haunt the food stalls, purchasing tea and pork rinds, fish and vegetables for their day in the field. It is an hour later, almost nine, before the infantry, followed by the armored, is ready to push through a crowd of curious children toward the barbed-wire gate, opened by a toothless old man wearing faded, threadbare olive-green fatigues and rubber sandals.

While the APCs and tanks flounder through a rice paddy that is just yielding a new crop, the infantry vanish into the trees in front of us. Major Buu, riding on an APC bristling with antennae that link him both to Ross and to his own officers on the ground, stands up and yells at stragglers to spread apart. Passing the cement opening of an enemy bunker, our column slows down and forms an arc in front of a dark, silent treeline. "We are going slowly because this area is very dangerous," Buu explains as more of his men disappear into the trees. "On our left are many more bunkers and tunnels. We must search around here very carefully."

A minute later, after the infantry has finished checking the treeline, the column again begins to rumble, this time across overgrown fields probably not farmed for several years. Some of the soldiers on Major Buu's APC yell and point. We are passing under a tree laden with ripe pineapplelike fruit. The APC stops while the soldiers knock them down with their rifle butts.

It is almost lunchtime. While the infantry checks another treeline, Major Buu orders the armored to halt. A couple of soldiers produce blackened pots from their packs and boil water on a small fire at the base of a tree that provides just enough shade to shield us from the noonday sun. One of the soldiers passes out little soup dishes, chipped and cracked chinaware with blue-enameled designs, filled with rice. Another offers meat soup, which we pour over the rice, and glasses of hot tea. While eating, the major keeps talking on the radio. "We've intercepted a VC message. They are planning to shoot B40 rockets at our APCs. Some of our soldiers have seen the VC in front of us. They are hiding under camouflage, perhaps a company of them." Buu orders a couple of APCs to "recon by fire"—spray the bushes with their machine guns—and calls in artillery from Ross.

"We will wait for the artillery," he says, as shells from Ross whistle overhead, slamming into the brush a few hundred yards away. "It is difficult to attack the VC in their underground tunnels and bunkers." One of the tanks begins firing with its single big gun, igniting a small blaze in the dry grass. A lieutenant on our APC listens for a moment to a call on the radio. "Now the VC are moving to another area, toward the hills," he reports. Again, Major Buu orders the infantry and armored to resume their advance across the paddies and scrub. "When the VC shoot, the distance is very close," says Buu, accounting for why his soldiers have not been fired on. "Maybe ten or fifteen meters." We stop again, this time shielded from view by overhanging branches, near the foundation of an old house blasted away in some bygone campaign.

Some of the soldiers in front of us are chattering excitedly. Three old women, chewing betel nuts, wearing conical hats, followed by two little girls and a small boy, emerge slowly from behind the bushes. Soldiers hover over them while Buu questions the boy—not impatiently but in matter-of-fact, carefully monotonous tones. The boy looks more nervous than scared, as if he were reciting a lesson for a teacher but not quite giving the right answers.

After a minute or so Buu turns to me, his mouth twisted in a somewhat cynical smirk. "Yesterday they see a company of VC with 82-mortar. This afternoon the VC have a squad here, but they run away when we fire the artillery, and they don't see where they run." There is no way of telling, really, how much the villagers know. "They always say, 'no see, no hear.' Now we have to search this village carefully." Buu orders his soldiers to poke into half a dozen or so thatched-roof huts, invisible among the trees—all that remain of the hamlet.

While the soldiers are searching, Buu again discusses enemy tactics. "Whenever they go away, they leave men to attack our flank, to observe and control our activities, but if they decide to attack us, they never run. At the present time, we operate very slowly and carefully because we have to defend our rear, because we don't know where the VC are." Again Buu reflects on the limitations of artillery and air strikes. "It is hard to judge them effectively. If we are firing on only one strong point, no sweat, but if they have two or three or four, it is very difficult. While we are firing on one, the others will fire on us. They support each other." Buu also notes the contrast between rear-echelon training and battlefield realities. "When we study, we keep one platoon in the front, one in the rear, but here we send in three- to five-man groups. If they have no contact, a platoon or company follows them to search the area."

The enemy, having decided this time not to fight, has totally eluded Buu's men. After checking by radio with two of his company commanders, Buu orders the column to turn around. Several soldiers prod the women and children, who get up and begin walking with the infantry. "We will question them further at headquarters," says Buu. The

APCs are thundering back through empty fields when an explosion kicks up a cloud of dust and smoke a quarter of a mile to our left. It is the parting shot of the 82-mortar squad, a blast that reminds our nine APCs, two tanks, and 110 men of our failure to find them. The APCs stop while a soldier on one of them fires in the general direction of the impacts with a .50-caliber machine gun. "We don't know where they are," says Buu. "No sweat." He grins as he uses the American expression and orders the column to keep on rolling.

It is 5 P.M. of a sleepy, sun-splashed afternoon, the end of an eight-hour day as our patrol clanks to a final halt on the dusty road in the middle of Son Lanh village. Old women display bottles of beer and soda, and soldiers hastily drink them down or wash themselves with water from the village well. Major Buu and two or three of his officers settle into a little shop and purchase Ba Muoi Ba—"33" beer—poured solicitously by a young girl into large ice-filled glasses. "The regional forces are setting up an ambush, and they will return to the village by sundown," says the major. "When it is dark, the VC may come back. We will stay on Ross at night to defend the perimeter."

In a war characterized by more watching and waiting than real fighting, it has been a fairly typical day. After seven years of it, Major Buu betrays neither optimism nor much disillusionment. "There are bad people in government," he says. "You only find all good people in heaven." He offers three reasons for the collapse of the third division in Quang Tri. First, it faced superior forces—approximately three divisions. Second, it was a new division, staffed with the worst officers from other units. And then, he adds with just a trace of bitterness, "The United States is not eager to help South Vietnam." Otherwise, why would the Americans have waited until after the offensive began to offer the latest M48 tanks and other new equipment to the ARVN? "They knew the north would invade South Vietnam, but they do nothing until afterward. It was the same when they gave us good weapons in 1968 after the Tet offensive."

Buu's remarks on American aid epitomize the response of a broad range of South Vietnamese officers and civilian officials, convinced that Washington has somehow sold them short again. Yet Buu does not think his army will completely fall apart. "American withdrawal is not too much of a problem. We have enough manpower and capability. All we need are the arms and the airpower." Nor does he think the 711th division can threaten the Queson Valley forever. "They are only waging a campaign. If we can stand it for two or three more years without defeat, they will go away. The difficulty is the government must use its troops to protect an entire territory while the enemy can hit a certain place and run. Sometimes it looks as if they are everywhere. We must follow a policy of flexible endurance."

The question, then, is what motivates the major to keep enduring, if not always fighting. "I do it for my living, my family, my country," says Buu, who is paid 24,000 piastres—60 dollars—a month to support his wife and two little girls in Quang Ngai. "My country is the most important," Buu insists as we walk back up the road from the village to the base. "I do not agree that most Vietnamese fight only for their families." It is difficult to say whether religion might also be a factor in his outlook. "I believe deep in my heart in Buddhism," he says, but so do some of Saigon's most outspoken anti-government politicians, who favor compromise and reconciliation with the enemy. Unlike many of his soldiers, Buu disdains the wearing of a Buddhist good-luck charm around his neck: "It brings neither good nor bad luck."

Buu's loyalty to the army if not the Saigon government probably lies embedded in early childhood indoctrination by his petit bourgeois family, including stories of Viet Minh persecution of his merchant uncles. "My family was against the policies of the Viet Minh because we owned our own land," says Buu, raised in Duc Pho district, 35 miles south of the provincial capital of Quang Ngai and 80 miles south of Queson. "The Viet Minh jailed those who they thought were too rich or were landlords. They accused them of corruption and killed or executed them. They were very cruel." Buu's father died of natural causes in 1952, but the Viet Minh the next year picked up an uncle in Duc Pho and tried him in public. "They said he was guilty of using the blood and sweat of the people, and they imprisoned him for two years. Then he died."

Buu denies that his family owned much land, "just a couple of hectares," but in a class war he inevitably identifies by birth and up-bringing with the elite. Sent through primary and high school in Quang Ngai, he then studied in Saigon for a year before taking the entrance examination for the military academy at Dalat. His younger brother now studies law in Saigon while his three brothers-in-law are all junior officers, one in the air force, two in the army. It might never be possible to fathom the family and communal relationships responsible for Buu's early rise to a battalion command, but it seems probable he has certain influential friends and relatives. "I believe in President Thieu. I don't believe in any party but the army. We don't like to fight, but it is our responsibility to fight against the communists to the last blood."

It is not surprising, in view of such sentiments, that Buu speaks with contempt of General Duong Van "Big" Minh, who is associated politically with peace-minded Buddhists in Saigon, and dismisses negotiations in Paris as a "waste of time."*

The sun is again setting over the Queson, and Major Buu gets up to check the outer defenses of Landing Zone Ross, criticized by the Americans as too thin on barbed wire and sandbags. One of the advisers radios an American gunship—a twin-tailed, twin-propellered C119 known as "Stinger"—to fire on an "enemy concentration" on a hilltop to the west. Colonel Luu enthusiastically suggests a combined "American-Vietnamese marine invasion of North Vietnam" and then discusses the merits of "napalm" versus "powdered tear gas" in "denying areas to the enemy." The adviser, patient as always, explains that napalm "breaks apart and burns out vegetation" while tear gas powder just "settles in and stirs up when you walk through it." The colonel has decided the simplest way to get the mortar men around Hon Chieu may be to "defoliate all the ground around it."

The next morning, after the briefing, Major Buu gives me the names and address of his wife and mother in Quang Ngai. The American adviser warns me the road from Queson to the lowlands isn't as secure as it once was; I drive down the valley in a jeep with a young lieutenant on his way to see his father-in-law. Regional force troops are walking slowly along the potholed macadam with mine detectors, and a pair of charred trucks lie in a ditch where they were tossed by explosions a couple of weeks before. In the next district south of the Queson, North Vietnamese forces already have penetrated as far as the abandoned north–south railroad, paralleling route one along the coast.

It is still reasonably safe, however, to drive down route one to Quang Ngai, a town of small shops and old homes now crowded with refugees from nearby districts terrorized of late by local guerrillas. Major Buu's wife, a schoolteacher, lives in a sturdy two-story cement building crowded with relatives, half of them, it seems, below the age of ten.

---

*Major Buu's fears about "Big" Minh were borne out when General Minh, named president for the last two days of the Saigon regime, on the morning of April 30, 1975, called on South Vietnamese forces to lay down their arms. Minh, whose brother was a general in the North Vietnamese army, now lives in France.

A tiny woman, expecting her third child in several months, Madame Buu has not seen her husband since the offensive began in early April. Even before that, he rarely was home more than one night a month. "He is a soldier. He must be far away, for many days and years. Two years ago he was wounded in the leg and had to spend a year at home. Since then the longest we've been together is a few days during Tet." Madame Buu, eight years younger than her husband, married him five years ago at the age of 19. She opens an album of photographs showing her and her husband strolling by a lake at Dalat, attending a party of officers, sitting in a garden. They both had gone to the same schools in Quang Ngai. Their families had known each other for years. Above her, on a whitewashed wall, hang tinted photographs of Buu's parents, his father looking somberly through large-rimmed glasses.

"He chose the military life when he was very young," says Madame Buu. "He will continue as long as the war lasts. He will be a soldier forever." A friend translates the lines beneath his picture in the 1965 military academy yearbook: "I grew up in war, I was a farmer, a cowman. I chose the military life because my country suffers. I want to see my country at peace and happy again." Major Buu's mother, considerably heavier now than when she posed for the photograph on the wall, says she prays for peace, prays that her son will return, prays the war will end, in fact, "in two more months." She is not counting, however, on any immediate answer to her prayers. Beneath a table are packages full of belongings hustled from relatives' homes in Duc Pho before the road south of Quang Ngai was cut in mid-April. A next-door neighbor is filling sandbags outside.

"I am afraid the communists will return and put many people in prison," the elder Madame Buu is saying. "Then we must go to Saigon or Danang, to a place that is free of communists." Buu's wife, holding one of her little girls, also prays for peace but seems more hopeful. "I always think my husband will defeat the VC. Then he will come back in a few more weeks or a month. The war will end and peace will come to Vietnam and the world, and the American and Vietnamese soldiers will not die any more. The VC will not occupy Quang Ngai. The soldiers of South Vietnam will not be defeated. President Thieu will bring peace to Vietnam."

Her mother-in-law, perhaps recalling the Viet Minh era of the early 1950s, smiles indulgently from across the room.

14

"Just Observers"

After the Paris Peace came the peace-keepers. One could never tell what the Poles, Hungarians, and Indonesians really thought about it all, and the few remaining American officers, many of them members of the Four-Party Joint Military Commission, set up under the intricate terms of the Paris agreement, were forbidden to talk to reporters. In any case, they were embittered by the way the press had covered the war and were hardly prone to speak frankly even when coaxed into background or off-the-record briefings. The presence of the Canadians was refreshing because they spoke so frankly—and didn't hesitate to talk to anyone who asked. For them it was great just getting a Vietnam tour on their records even if it all turned sour as the peace degenerated and they realized they were accomplishing little or nothing.

The sense of futility among Canadians was beginning to set in when I visited some of them at a town named Phan Thiet on the coast six weeks after they had gotten there. They were still hopeful, but they chafed under restrictions and obstructions. They did not think their government would want Canada to remain on the peace-keeping team much longer. Within another six weeks Canada would decide to withdraw the entire contingent at the end of July, rounding off six months of interesting if wearisome, largely useless, service.

Ironically, I had my most dangerous experience in Vietnam two weeks after the ceasefire. It seemed all the more ironic that the violators, in my case, were not the North Vietnamese, whom the Canadians blamed for most of their problems, but a pair of South Vietnamese air force pilots. The terror of exposure to bombing gave me some idea of what the war had been like for millions caught unwittingly in the midst of indiscriminate use of air power. You can talk endlessly to survivors and victims, but you can never imagine it until you've lived it. Or, as GIs used to paint on their helmets, "You haven't really lived until you've nearly died."

Binh Phu, February 1973

A row of thatched-roof hootches strung along a rice paddy here marks the shadow borderline between the "liberated zone" of the Viet Cong's Provisional Revolutionary Government and the territory controlled by the national police and army of the South Vietnamese government in Saigon. From the nervous, almost frightened expressions on the faces of the old men and women crowded into their homes at the close of a sunny, seemingly placid morning, you sense you are walking in a limbo between two sides. They cast inquisitive, not unfriendly glances as a couple of foreigners, Don Tate of Scripps-Howard newspapers and I, walk by them after a stroll through rice paddies and bush quite firmly held by young Viet Cong soldiers carrying both Chinese AK47 rifles and American M16s.*

One old man shakes his head when I point across the rice paddy toward a Viet Cong flag fluttering from the end of a bamboo pole near a single hootch. He shakes his head just as emphatically when I point down the row of rice paddies toward a cluster of tree-shaded homes flying South Vietnamese flags. None of the hootches on this particular dike between paddies flies any flags at all—in clear contradiction of the "rules" of the new Vietnamese war in which flag-flying is required as a minimal symbol of loyalty to one side or another.

"VC, VC," a couple of kids inform us, gesturing toward the hootch near the VC flag. "No VC," they say as they wave down the dike on which we are standing. It is not necessary to let us know of the presence of the VC across the rice paddy. We have just been on a guided

---

*Don Tate 13 years later produced one of the best, if underacclaimed, novels of the war—*Bravo Burning* (New York: Charles Scribner's Sons, 1986), reflecting his experiences at Dak To.

tour of the area led by one Le Minh Hoang, an 18-year-old Viet Cong trooper who slung an AK over his shoulder and escorted us across the paddies, oblivious to the presence of South Vietnamese APCs on route four only a mile or so away—well within range of their .50-caliber machine guns.

We are partly responsible for the apprehension of the peasants around us since a spotter plane and helicopter have both swung low over the paddies while we were with some Viet Cong soldiers in a hootch. Since South Vietnamese police on the road through the village tried to keep us from entering the "liberated zone," we conclude the spotter and the chopper were dispatched in part just to see what we're doing.

Shortly after they buzzed away, South Vietnamese artillery opened up from near the road. Our AK-hefting guide seemed unfazed as the rounds whistled overhead and landed amid some bushes several hundred yards ahead of us. It was the same kind of show of government force that a stream of other newsmen in the same area had witnessed over the past few days. For Le Minh Hoang, the sound of the artillery was a matter of small concern. "No," he said, grinning, as Tate and I crouched beside an old burial monument under the trees. Hoang seemed certain from the sound that the rounds were well above us.

Government soldiers did not appear to have seriously attempted to dislodge the VC from portions of this village beyond the main road. "Bombing," said Hoang, as we passed a couple of hootches blasted away by artillery or bombs, but most of the buildings remained intact—and there was no sign of any attempt by government soldiers to intrude on the ground between the paddies. "Welcome peace, welcome agreement," said the Vietnamese lettering in the hootch where we met Hoang and two other soldiers at the beginning of our tour.

Copies of the newspaper *Ap Bac*, named for the village near Saigon where VC forces had scored one of their most significant early victories nearly a decade ago, were pinned on the wall. "Peace is coming. Everybody can do their daily work in the rice paddy," communist cadre told the people of Binh Phu. "The National Liberation Front will not harm anyone in the village. The war has ended." As if to underline this point, women and children crowded around us as we entered the hootch where we met Hoang and another rifle-bearing soldier, Nguyen Minh Hung, who scrawled his name and his age, 19, in my notebook.

If the "liberated zone" of this divided village some 60 miles southwest of Saigon is beyond the military power of the Saigon regime, it is almost deceptively easy for a civilian to come here. After slipping down a tiny path off route four, the main road through the Mekong River delta, one walks along narrow footpaths across a network of tiny canals. Although government flags fly from all the buildings near the road, we had no compunctions about informing the local citizenry of our desire to get to the portion of the village controlled by the NLF. We just drew pictures of the NLF flag—two stripes with a star in the middle—on the palms of our hands, and villagers cheerfully pointed the way.

Our main concern was to avoid the South Vietnamese police, whom we had left behind on the road after indicating we were returning to Saigon. They did not attempt to follow us after noting our empty car by the road—largely because they could not be sure of their own security. On both sides of the conflict, however, villagers evince an underlying desire for "peace" as opposed to clear-cut support for one side or the other.

A couple of old women in a sampan offered us a lift down a narrow canal to a clearing where an old man in a pith helmet pointed at a couple of NLF flags and then at the bombed-out remains of what once was a large thatched-roof home. He delegated two small boys to lead us deeper into the "liberated zone" after we indicated we wanted to meet some VC with rifles. The soldiers themselves emerged from no-where after we arrived at their hootch. They volunteered to pose for photographs as if they were actors in a set-piece scene. Grinning all the while, they pulled little VC flags from their pockets, raised them on bamboo poles, and adjusted their rifles in classic guerrilla poses.

More VC soldiers emerged from a much larger wooden structure another mile or so across the paddies. Among them were civilians, old men as well as women. Amid the whine of occasional artillery shells, they pointed to bunkers and gestured down another path leading us back to government-held territory. One of the VC asked us for ciga-rettes and warned us against the government police back on the road. The VC vanished again into the shadows.

It was not until we were alone on the dike, on the way back, that we noticed the absence of men and women in the paddy—and the scared looks of those who seemed to fall on neither side of the invisible line between opposing forces.

The struggle for Binh Phu illustrates the delicate nature of the peace signed in Paris on January 27. Although the Viet Cong still control much of this village, peasants report that South Vietnamese soldiers have driven the VC from many hamlets nearer the main road over the past few days. "They tore down VC flags and put up their own," says a teenage boy in the central market after we return to the road. "Two days ago the Viet Cong were almost on the road." Despite a post-ceasefire offensive, however, Saigon soldiers clearly lack the strength, in terms of manpower or local support, to annihilate the VC.

At one village, shopkeepers report that residents of a VC hamlet freely come and go on shopping expeditions every morning from eight to ten. "No one stops them," says a woman selling cakes beside the road, "but the police discourage them later in the morning." While we are talking, two national policemen with radios show up and order us into their jeep for a ride to the district headquarters two miles to the east. Such cursory efforts by Saigon officials to discourage contact with the VC technically violate the provision of the accords permitting free movement between "zones" under government and communist control, but artillery and small-arms fire represent much more serious threats to the peace.

Members of the International Commission for Control and Supervision of the ceasefire remain optimistic about instilling some measure of real peace and security in the region. "It's a challenge," says Colonel Robert Screaton, commanding Canadian members of the team at the nearby center of Mytho. "I'm not frustrated yet." Screaton confesses, however, that he and other team members are powerless to act on their own. "It's up to the Four-Party Joint Military Commission to decide who controls what ground. We're here to help them do what we hope they want to do."

It seems unlikely that the JMC—composed of representatives of the United States, South Vietnam, North Vietnam, and the Viet Cong's Provisional Revolutionary Government—will function with much if any equanimity. For many of the villagers on route four between Binh Phu village and Mytho, it is already too late. "The communists raised their flags so the government soldiers shell into my hamlet," charges a high school student named Le Van Lam. "They've been shelling since the day the ceasefire was signed."

While we are talking on a path beside the rice paddy, a girl screams uncontrollably. Two other women beside her are sobbing. "The soldiers grabbed my mother as she ran away from the hamlet," screams the girl, named Nguyen Thi Lahn. "They made her pull up one of the flags. A grenade wired to the flag exploded and killed her."

The fighting reflects the cynicism of both sides in the war as they attempt to claim as much territory as they can before the ICCS delineates areas held by one side or the other. "The VC came into the hamlet, dug bunkers, and raised their flag the night before the ceasefire," says Lahn. "They said the peace would come at eight on Sunday morning, and then they left." While we are talking, three more VC flags appear over the trees. The South Vietnamese troops, under fire from VC soldiers up and down the treeline, are powerless to drive them out.

"Please intervene with the field commanders to stop the shooting," an old woman urges us in the belief we are members of the ICCS. South Vietnamese A1 Skyraiders and F5 Freedom Fighters dive down on the treeline. The explosions send shock waves over the rice paddies. Across the road, South Vietnamese troops fan out toward another treeline over which hang several more VC flags. "My home is destroyed. Ten people in my hamlet have been killed," says the woman. "Peace, peace, they promised us peace. We had everything we needed—cows, pigs, food. Now they're all gone."

Phan Thiet, April 1973

The young Canadian staff officer for once was excited. "Get in my jeep," he offered. "I'm going out a little way. I want to find out what's happening." With some embarrassment, as we were driving on a dirt road inland from this coastal fishing town, the officer explained that his investigation was entirely unauthorized. That is, his own commander on the Canadian delegation of the ICCS knew where he was, but representatives of the other countries on the ICCS had not endorsed the expedition and would doubtless have frowned on it had they been aware of what he was doing.

We bounced down the road for two or three miles while the major, a Czech-born, British-educated career officer named John Hasek, quickly sketched the scene. "They've been fighting for a hamlet named Ap Tan Binh two kilometers away. It's abandoned, blown away, but the people still come out from here to work the fields. The ARVN are well established where we're going. They send out patrols at night to Ap Tan Binh. And the PRG [the Viet Cong's Provisional Revolutionary Government] also come in at night. That's where the clashes occur."

It was an almost classic example of low-level confrontation in Vietnam, but it was the prospect of peace-keeping rather than fighting that aroused Major Hasek's interest. "Both sides are requesting an investigation through the Joint Military Commission," said the major, a veteran of the UN peace-keeping force on Cyprus. "We're hoping the JMC will ask the ICCS to carry out its own investigation. It would be the first real chance we've had since coming here. So I just want to get out here and take a look before all the ICCS people begin falling all over each other."

The momentary enthusiasm of Major Hasek epitomized that of most of the 250 or so members of the Canadian delegation of the ICCS. Highly trained, with previous experience on any of a dozen other Canadian peace-keeping teams from Kashmir to New Guinea to Yemen, they came to Vietnam after the signing of the truce on January 27 exuding much the same verve and camaraderie as American combat officers in the early years of the war.

Strolling along the streets of Saigon in their dark green bermuda shorts and green berets, the Canadians were novelties in the jaded eyes of taxi drivers and bargirls lamenting the loss of the American GIs. (The berets, it was revealed, were not new at all. They were made by the same Canadian manufacturer that turned out headgear for the American army's special forces, the "green berets.") Specifically ordered by their own commanders to explain their role to anyone who asked, the Canadians were wont to pause for a chat or lengthy interview on street corners, on the terrace of the Continental Hotel, in the dark recesses of tattered GI bars, or anywhere else they happened to lurk in their few off-duty hours.

"The point about the mission," a major from Calgary explained to me when I accosted him on the steps of the Continental, "is that its supervisory capability lies in the terms of the agreement." Technically, the Canadians and the other members of the ICCS weren't peace-keepers at all, "just observers," he said. In contrast to real peace-keepers, who were armed on Cyprus to shoot to kill if necessary to keep order, ICCS representatives in the field could only carry sidearms for self-defense in case of extreme emergency. "At no time will we become involved in armed conflict," said the Canadian, who had served six months in the Suez during the 1967 war. "We report infractions if requested by the JMC. We observe, but we have no power to change a situation."

For all these limitations, however, the Canadians were relentlessly optimistic. "We think the ceasefire will eventually come," said the major, who was awaiting orders to go to one of seven regional ICCS headquarters at critical points from Hue and Danang in the northern provinces to Cantho in the Mekong River delta. "We're ready to go in the bush, all of us," he added with gung-ho aggressiveness. "We know what we're going to do."

It was two months after that conversation, in late March, that I drove some 100 miles east of Saigon to visit the regional headquarters here and encountered Major Hasek in his jeep outside the old American military advisory compound, now used by the JMC. Wiry, athletic, Major Hasek kept himself trim by running two or three miles each afternoon around the small air base beyond a cemetery on the edge of town where the ICCS maintained its regional offices. He was friendly with local South Vietnamese officials and the Americans at the new Area Resettlement and Reconstruction Office, successor to the old CORDS (Civil Operations and Revolutionary Development Support) team operated by the departing U.S. Military Assistance Command Vietnam.

Major Hasek and his ICCS colleagues lived in a small hotel near the market and dined quite often at either of two leisurely Chinese restaurants tucked into a row of shops and coffee stands. It was not, if you thought about it, a bad way to spend a hardship tour. It was clear, however, that the major was not only extremely bored but damned impatient for action.

"Now, if an investigation gets launched, both sides are going to try to get possession of the village," Hasek noted with the terseness of a field commander reviewing his latest situation reports. At the outpost nearest the abandoned village a South Vietnamese officer saluted the major as he climbed out of the jeep and explained what was happening. The major wanted to venture closer to the village, but the South Vietnamese dissuaded him. "There's no security out there, and anyway I'm not supposed to be here at all," Hasek agreed. "There'd be hell to pay if anything happened to me. I'm supposed to be back at the ICCS headquarters twiddling my thumbs and looking at reports."

The South Vietnamese, of course, were just as much to blame for the lack of security in the village as were the VC. "They've been throwing in mortar rounds and artillery all morning," said the major. "No idea where they're landing. We're liable to get hit if we go out there without ARVN troops. They think the PRG are massing to attack."

It was one of the lesser ironies of the skirmish that it actually worsened as a result of the immediate possibility of an investigation. Both the South Vietnamese and PRG members of the JMC, which also included Americans and North Vietnamese for the first 60 days after the signing of the Paris Peace, had indicated they would ask the ICCS to look into the matter—but for entirely different reasons. The PRG was protesting incessant artillery and air strikes by the ARVN, while the RVN—South Vietnam—charged the PRG with ambushing a patrol early one morning near an old French fort built in the Viet Minh era. The battle was petty, in the overall context of the post-ceasefire fighting, but Major Hasek relished it as an excuse to get out of town and possibly launch the first ICCS investigation requested by both sides in the war.

The greatest irony, however, was the sheer inability of the ICCS to do anything about it even though it was happening within binocular range of the ICCS regional compound, perched on a gently rising bluff overlooking the lowland plains as far as a range of blue-green hills in the haze some 20 miles to the west. "It's our resident battle," Hasek remarked somewhat wearily as we turned back from our excursion into the field and drove up to the compound. "It's kind of like the oldest established permanent floating crap game."

Absentmindedly, Hasek handed me the binoculars through which I could see a South Vietnamese L19 spotter plane turning lazy circles over dusty rice paddies. Shells occasionally boomed in the distance, smoke gusted where they hit, and the sounds of the explosions reverberated seconds later. "That way every day," said Hasek, before changing for his afternoon run around the base. "The ARVN have combed all over there. We've seen a dozen air strikes at least. It's a real Mexican standoff."

But what was to keep the ICCS from initiating its own investigation before receiving self-interested requests from members of the JMC? Nothing, technically. In fact, however, the leaders of each of the ICCS delegations here seemed to while away much of their time in endless debates inside a shack built by GIs several years ago and remodeled as the ICCS meeting room. The pattern of debate was fairly typical. "We have no difficulty getting the other members of the commission to report unfavorably on RVN violations," observed Ambassador Michael Gauvin, the chief Canadian delegate to the ICCS, "but we can never get the Poles and Hungarians to agree on a negative report concerning the PRG." Indeed, Canadian regional team leaders had difficulty just persuading the Poles and Hungarians that the roads were safe enough for them to travel.

"That's not the first problem," said the leader of the Canadian regional delegation, Colonel Frank Campbell, standing beside Major Hasek and me as we gazed at our "resident battle" through the binoculars. "The two most responsible parties, the South Vietnamese and the PRG, both have to guarantee security or the Poles and Hungarians won't go anywhere." Colonel Campbell, tall, greying, cautious, rule-bound, did not quite share Hasek's impetuous desire to get to the fighting without the approval of the other delegations.

Rather, as the officer in charge of half a dozen Canadians based here, the Canadian colonel preferred to engage in gentle persuasion, careful review of the terms of the agreement, and exposition of the facts. Still, for all his patience, he could not help but reflect the exasperation of the entire Canadian contingent. "My feeling is we must get into a much more active observer role," he suggested. "We shouldn't be waiting for complaints. We should just pile into our jeeps and make our presence known. There's nothing in the Paris agreement to keep us from initiating our own investigation if all four members approve."

As it was, however, Campbell was not entirely unhappy with the record of investigations in the first 60 days since the signing of the agreement. He noted with real pride that the ICCS at Phan Thiet had just produced one of the first unanimous reports in all Vietnam on quite a serious incident in which six persons had been killed and 13 wounded by a mortar round fired into the central market of the town. Yet his description of the investigation did more to illustrate the basic weakness of the ICCS than to prove its long-range potential.

"First thing we did when we got the complaint from the South Vietnamese late one evening, we agreed we would get a copy to the JMC first thing in the morning," said the colonel. "We argued we must put on a time limit for the JMC to reply or the PRG would delay the investigation, but it still took another day for them to say anything. Then the PRG refused to support the investigation." At this point the Canadian delegation might have abandoned the quest, but the Poles and Hungarians for once could not plead that the road to the scene was insecure. "We were in luck because it happened right in town," said Major Hasek. "It gave us a chance for a test case. The Poles and

Hungarians had to go along. The mortar landed only a few blocks from where we live."

The Poles and Hungarians had yet another excuse, however, for delaying the investigation. The leader of the Indonesian delegation, rotating that week as chairman of the regional center here, could not reach the ICCS chairman in Saigon by telephone to request his formal approval. "You can't go anywhere these days without written authorization from Saigon," said Campbell. "Three days later we finally got approval from the Hungarian ambassador, who was serving that week as ICCS chairman."

Was it just by chance that the line to the Hungarian chairman was perpetually out of order? Or was the Hungarian, as Canadian ICCS members argued, deliberately attempting to sabotage an investigation that might reflect badly on the PRG? For that matter, why did a regional ICCS need the approval of the ICCS in Saigon at all? The agreement does not require any such time-consuming bureaucratic procedure, and Canadian officers strongly opposed it while blaming the Poles and Hungarians for conjuring such a wasteful regulation. By the time the investigation was really launched, five days after the mortar round was fired, much of the evidence of the blast had disappeared.

All the delays probably had little substantive effect, however, for the most the Poles and Hungarians would have conceded under any circumstances was that a mortar round had indeed been fired. The Canadians were still happy because enough people happened to have been standing around the marketplace to verify conclusively that the round had landed and exploded, and the Poles and Hungarians had no choice but to sign a report alleging just that much. The happiest observers of the entire proceeding, though, were the PRG and North Vietnamese members of the JMC, whose own regional delegations were confined to barbed-wire compounds across the airstrip from the ICCS. The report, after all, stated that the investigating team "could not conclude that a ceasefire violation had occurred"—a blanket vindication of the Viet Cong guerrillas who had almost certainly fired the round.

"So we may say that the ICCS had a very objective opinion and has come to a very right and reasonable conclusion," said a North Vietnamese major, Phan Huynh, whom I met in the conference room of his compound shortly before the departure for Hanoi of all the North Vietnamese JMC delegates at the end of the 60-day post-ceasefire period. "So maybe the shell exploded by itself. We think nobody fired it," reasoned Major Huynh, smiling as he offered me banana candy and poured a glass of vodka distilled in Hanoi from a bottle with Russian Cyrillic lettering.

The North Vietnamese major's tone hardened and his smile tightened into a glare, however, as he accused the United States and South Vietnam of conspiring to frame the PRG. "I want to know for what purpose the U.S. and RVN delegations on the JMC have fabricated the circumstances of such an incident," he asked, looking at me quite sternly beneath a portrait of Ho Chi Minh and a large North Vietnamese flag, yellow star on red field, hanging on the otherwise bare wall. "It is correct to say they have brought up such an incident in order to hide their own violations," he charged. "While they launched many 'nipping operations' against the liberated zones, they also trumpet about what they have done in order to gain the sympathy of the people, in order to say that the truth belongs to them."

So pleased were the North Vietnamese with the ICCS verdict in the mortar case that the leader of the delegation sent a formal letter thanking the commission for its "thorough, impartial investigation"—a gesture that did more to diminish rather than increase the Canadians' satisfaction. "Sure," admitted Colonel Campbell, showing me a copy of the North Vietnamese letter, "the investigation proved nothing in itself." As a next faltering step, he still hoped to induce the Poles and Hungarians to cooperate on real investigations into incidents of a much more serious nature.

It was a sign of the fundamental lack of rapport between the delegations that the Canadians rarely met with the Poles and Hungarians outside the conference room even though they lived in the same hotels in town and occupied offices within 50 feet of each other on the base. The Canadians were often more successful in dealing with the Indonesians, an indication of the common attitude of both delegations toward the entire peace-keeping mission. The Indonesians, reflecting the anti-communist policy of their government, tended to follow the Canadians' lead while opposing the Poles and Hungarians.

A conversation with the head of the Polish delegation at Phan Thiet left me with a sense of bafflement and disappointment. I first saw Colonel Marian Kozlowski in the old American compound watching a Steve McQueen movie about car racing. Officers from the other ICCS delegations were also there, banded together in their own national cliques, identifiable by their uniforms among the American civilian officials and contractors who had dropped by to watch the movie.

Like the Canadians, Colonel Kozlowski was personally courteous when buttonholed after the movie but entirely uninformative on the subject of the mortar incident. "It is an honor to perform this duty despite the heavy task," said the colonel, speaking to me through a bright young civilian interpreter who the Canadians were convinced was an intelligence or political agent—and possibly the real leader of the Polish team.

But why did the investigation take so long to begin? "Perhaps Saigon is too full of complaints," the colonel from Poland replied blandly, "and besides there is trouble with the telephone." Why didn't the ICCS investigate the real fighting outside town rather than piddle away its time on a stray mortar round? "We are prepared for all kinds of incidents," said the colonel, an air force officer trained as a navigator on Soviet-built transports. "If the JMC asks us, we will do it."

But the JMC never asked. Whenever the PRG wanted an investigation, the South Vietnamese opposed it. When the South Vietnamese wanted an investigation, the PRG opposed. The only question that mattered for either side was who controlled what territory. If PRG forces were in the village and the South Vietnamese were shelling, then naturally the PRG welcomed the prospect of an ICCS inquiry. If South Vietnamese troops were patrolling territory in their hands and Viet Cong guerrillas ambushed them, the South Vietnamese righteously demanded the aid of objective observers—that is, if South Vietnamese troops still held the territory after the ambush.

There was also the secondary question of which specific phase of Phan Thiet's "resident battle" really mattered to which side. Talking to members of the PRG delegation in a cement-block building beside that of the North Vietnamese at the airstrip, I couldn't be quite certain we were referring to the same places. A PRG liaison officer conceded, however, that "RVN forces now occupy one strategic hamlet," presumably near the outpost to which Major Hasek and I had driven the previous day. The PRG, of course, held the rest of the area—even though "the people were forced to leave by the RVN."

In the end Major Hasek had to concede defeat—or, more properly, another frustration. "Doesn't look as if anything will come of it," he told me as we sat drinking cups of thick black coffee in a snack stand across the road from the JMC conference room, a white clapboard building once used as an American army chapel. "They're still talking over procedure." The major sank back psychologically into the lethargy of the assignment. But "we're not giving up," he said in the pursed-lip style of a field officer stubbornly clinging to a position that he knew was untenable.

The sense of depression, of futility among Canadian officers here was symptomatic of the weary bitterness of Canadian officials at all levels. In the Mekong River delta, a strong-minded young diplomat named Manfred Von Nostitz, in charge of the Canadian delegation at Cantho, denounced the unanimous ICCS reports as "meaningless" and said the Canadians and Indonesians would submit separate reports fixing the blame when necessary on the PRG or the North Vietnamese. "There's no ceasefire," he told me not long after my visit to Phan Thiet. "The North Vietnamese are rolling across the Cambodian border. There are four North Vietnamese regiments in Chuong Thien province south of here. Three of them arrived since the signing of the ceasefire."

At Cantho, Canadian officers serving under Von Nostitz, one of the few civilians leading a regional delegation, claimed the Poles and Hungarians had delayed communications with Saigon by fiddling with the radio equipment. They said the Poles and Hungarians, if induced to visit the scene of a ceasefire violation, would listen respectfully to statements implicating the Viet Cong and then deny having heard them on returning to headquarters.

In one case, the killing of 15 persons by a grenade thrown into a Buddhist pagoda, the Canadians and Indonesians signed their own independent report after the Poles and Hungarians discounted the word of a monk that VC agents had threatened to blow up the pagoda several days beforehand. "We were told by our briefers that it has been estimated that there have been some 7,000 incidents since the ceasefire came into effect," said the Canadian secretary of state for external affairs, Mitchell Sharp, after a swing through Indochina in March. "Out of these have emerged only 31 requests for investigations by the ICCS. . . . From these requests just two Commission reports have emerged"—one of them presumably on the mortaring in Phan Thiet.

The Canadians, notably Sharp, had been skeptical about the efficacy of the ICCS from the time that American diplomats had pressured them to participate before the signing of the Paris Peace. As evidence, they could cite the unpleasant precedent of the original International

Control Commission, formed under the 1954 Geneva agreement on Indochina with delegations from Canada, Poland, and India. "Bitter, frustrating experience with the ICC . . . conditioned the Government's wary approach to any new involvement in Vietnam," said an official Canadian press release, explaining why Canada originally limited its membership in the new ICCS to an initial trial period of 60 days.

Sharp lengthened the trial until the end of June after his visit, but his skepticism turned into outrage with the shooting down over PRG territory on April 7 of an Air America helicopter flying nine people, including one Canadian captain, one Indonesian officer, two Hungarian officers, and two PRG liaison officials, to an ICCS team site near the Laotian frontier. "The general situation has not improved; in fact it has deteriorated," said Sharp in a speech to the Canadian House of Commons. "If it does not improve very substantially, it will be clear that by continuing to serve in the ICCS, we would be staying on to observe not a peace, not a ceasefire, but a continuing war."

It was just that, a continuing war, that Major Hasek could glimpse every day through his binoculars from the ICCS regional center by the airstrip at Phan Thiet. "Last Saturday an ARVN patrol got ambushed in the area of an old abandoned French fort. Obviously, they'd been doing the same thing with the Viet Minh 20 years ago. There's an old American firebase out there, too, Firebase Sherry. They've been fighting this time for the past six weeks. It just goes back and forth."

The sense of history somehow forced a pause in our conversation. The pattern of a generation of warfare would not change, and Major Hasek knew it. "We're actors in a charade," said one of the Canadians. "There's nothing we can do but watch while the real war goes on all around us. That's what makes it so hard."

Along Route 13, February 1973

It is the middle of a lazy Sunday afternoon, and my driver and I are sitting on bamboo fences in a small hut beside the road talking to a young North Vietnamese army lieutenant. The conversation is dragging somewhat because we are awaiting the arrival of the colonel who commands all the communist troops on a five-mile stretch between the towns of Lai Khe and Chon Thanh, some 40 miles north of Saigon. "Big guns shoot here," says the lieutenant, named Tran Kim, and we all turn and look dutifully at a cloud billowing on the horizon two or three miles away.

In any case, I am not overly impressed. Obviously the North Vietnamese are putting on a slight propaganda show for us. I have driven up from Saigon to see how far the road is open in the new era of "peace" in Vietnam, and I would rather find out what's really happening than accept the honeyed words of a skilled communist political officer. I drove this road for the first time on April 6, 1972, several days after three divisions of North Vietnamese troops poured across the border from Cambodia, knifed south through the flatlands and rubber plantations, and surrounded the provincial capital of An Loc, ten miles north of Chon Thanh, 50 miles north of Saigon, in what the Americans came to call the "Easter Offensive." It is route 13, the old rubber road, built by the French to move the rubber from the plantations to Saigon, then rebuilt by U.S. army engineers before they withdrew in 1970.

It is a dull black ribbon through the tinder-dry yellowing bush. It is the kind of road you would never remember, never care to drive again, unless you had to, for business or for war. I drove up the road many times in April and May 1972, always thinking the South Vietnamese would punch through to An Loc, but they were always stopped by small-arms fire, rockets, and ambushes at a critical point by the shelled fragments of an old watchtower several miles north of Chon Thanh. Now Chon Thanh itself is surrounded, and the South Vietnamese have abandoned the struggle to reopen the road. They have left it to the North Vietnamese, remnants of three divisions scattered and scarred but never defeated by incessant American air strikes that ended only on the day the ceasefire was actually signed in Paris, January 27, 1973.

It is several months since I last drove up route 13, detouring on a dirt road bypassing the South Vietnamese base at Lai Khe, then back on the main highway. We—my driver and I—have left our car at the last South Vietnamese outpost, two or three miles north of the base. South Vietnamese guarding the outpost only stared idly as we parked the big 1960s-era Chevy by some rolls of concertina wire stretched across the road.

A couple of miles ahead of us, shimmering in the sun, looking deceptively near, we could see a white banner strung across the blacktop. The South Vietnamese guards did not object as we picked our way through the wire and began walking up the highway. There is, after all, a ceasefire. The Paris agreement specifically states that anyone can move freely from one zone to another. Although the fighting has raged along route 13 for months, we are relaxed, unconcerned. It is a new era in the Indochinese conflict.

"Hoa Binh Roi Cong Ca Nha," reads the first line of the sign, actually white letters on a red field rather than entirely white, as we thought when we first saw it from the South Vietnamese outpost. "Hoc Tap Chung Huong Hoa Binh," says the second line. "When peace comes, all members of the family will have jobs," is the English translation. "Study together about peace." Beside the sign are two flags of the Viet Cong's Provisional Revolutionary Government, red and blue stripes with gold stars in the middle. A North Vietnamese soldier, wearing a green shirt and black trousers, looking almost as weary as the South Vietnamese down the road, has casually waved us over to the bamboo hut. He is 21, and he comes from a town near Hanoi—my driver quickly gleans these details. He says he cannot really talk to us though, until his superiors have arrived.

Lieutenant Tran Kim, when he appears a few minutes later, announces that he is "the chief of the gate" and has been fighting around here for two years. He carries a Chinese pistol on his American army belt, a pair of sunglasses in the pocket of his green shirt, and two American- or Japanese-made pens. "Every day, they bomb and rocket this area," says the lieutenant, as my driver interprets for me, but it is hard to imagine any real bombing on this particular afternoon. I keep asking questions, and he orders the soldier who first met us to cross the road and find the commander, who, he assures me, can tell us "everything."

"The Saigon soldiers can come here to talk, too," says the lieutenant, smiling genially, "but they must leave their weapons behind." As if to underline the propaganda mission of the men at the gate, he looks up at the leaflets and calendars with photographs of Ho Chi Minh that are hanging from the thatched ceiling. It is so hot and I am getting so bored with this conversation that I am beginning to fall asleep when we hear the crump of a bomb a mile or so away. It is so commonplace, this sound of exploding bombs, that none of us even turns to look, though it does vaguely occur to me that these bombs are not "friendly" anymore or, if they are still friendly, that I am definitely in unfriendly territory.

That passing thought evaporates as the colonel, the top commander, finally emerges from the bush accompanied by a young soldier who speaks English. "I studied the language for three years in Hanoi," explains the soldier, named Do The Vinh. "I was a cargo surveyor in Haiphong harbor." It is a matter of more than passing interest to me that Vinh admits he is from North Vietnam, since Hanoi officially refuses to concede the presence of any of its soldiers in South Vietnam. Only true southerners, native-born guerrillas fighting for the National Liberation Front, have risen up against the Saigon regime and the American imperialists, if one is to believe the propaganda. I am still more excited, however, by the prospect of a long discussion on "life on the other side," and I am vaguely wondering how to open the interview when we hear the thud of more explosions a mile or so away.

"Don't fear—far away," says Vinh, and we get on with the interview. "The commander's name is Truong Minh Sanh," Vinh writes carefully in my notebook—the whole sentence, not just the name. I am about to begin the interview with the colonel when a rocket lands 100 feet or so beyond us. It is fired from a spotter plane still some distance away, perhaps as much as half a mile, circling almost invisibly against the bright rays of the sun.

All of us turn and look toward the nearest shelter, a typical bamboo-lined fighting hole, but Vinh, the colonel, and I keep talking. It is hard to analyze why. Either we are difficult to scare, or all of us—the North Vietnamese, my driver, and I—fail to comprehend the danger. "I do every work, as the commander tells me," says Vinh when I ask him rather off-handedly how he's been whiling away the time since coming south three years ago. The commander, who looks somewhat like the driver, only thinner, smiles ingratiatingly and hands me a letter to deliver in Lai Khe.

A rather odd request, I am thinking, but I smile back and accept the letter—a handwritten appeal to South Vietnamese officers and soldiers to "cease shelling and bombing in our liberated areas," to "exchange letters when necessary," and to "visit our side without weapons."

The first bomb targeted for us lands a couple hundred feet away as I am putting the letter in my pocket. Hastily I scribble my last notes—that the colonel is wearing an unlikely outfit of green shirt, blue fatigue pants, and black Ho Chi Minh sandals—as he and the rest of us spring up and wait just a moment in indecision. Then the colonel and the lieutenant jump into the nearest fighting hole. Another soldier runs across the road. Vinh waves for me to follow, but my driver shouts for us to begin walking back to the car. Neither of us wants to get caught on the North Vietnamese side in a battle. Besides, we cannot quite believe the bombing will go on since the South Vietnamese at the last outpost know we are here.

We are on the road, walking under the banner, when we hear the distant jet scream of the next bombing run. At the graceful long whistle of a 500-pound bomb we hit the ditch by the shoulder, then are up and running a second after it explodes in a cloud of black and grey smoke 50 or so feet away. We cannot run back to the North Vietnamese fighting holes because we do not know where they are anymore. We must keep on the road or the pilots will see movement in the bush, assume we are enemy, and fire on us with their 20-millimeter cannon.

We hit it again at the sound of the next whistle, again across the road, but we know we cannot run for two miles. We walk and hit, walk and hit with each scream of the jets. We must get away, away from the North Vietnamese outpost. I am hoping the South Vietnamese know we are civilians, the driver's shirt is white, mine is yellow, but pilots of jet aircraft cannot always make such fine distinctions. And even if they could, they could probably not sight the bombs with such accuracy as to land on the North Vietnamese positions while avoiding the two people walking away from them.

I am sure the pilots have mistaken us for the North Vietnamese when one of the bombs lands 100 feet ahead of us on our side of the road. We do not have the shoulder to protect us this time, and the dirt and shrapnel spout up in a black geyser, flying by us, over us. We are unhurt and force ourselves to get up and walk—toward the spot where the bomb would have killed us had we been there just seconds before.

It is the moment between strikes when the fear claws at you, and you wonder why you are here and if you will get out alive, and you are sure you will not but you have to keep moving. The fear mounts as you hit the dirt and crests into a sense of calm at just that instant when you are flat in the brush and you hear the long crescendo of the bomb and you wonder if you will get up again or if you will get it on route 13 the way thousands of others got it when you were covering the campaign from April through June.

You think dimly, subconsciously, for the duration of a fleeting image, perhaps, of the others whom you knew who died on route 13. There was Lieutenant Colonel Burr Willey, a soft-talking south-erner who was advising a South Vietnamese regiment at Chon Thanh when you first met him in his sandbagged bunker in May. It was just as hot then as it is now, and the colonel was fretting because the South Vietnamese, as always, were refusing to move swiftly against just a handful of North Vietnamese troops dug into old bunkers near the road.

"It's payday," Willey, desperately feigning patience and understanding, had tried to explain. "It takes them all day to hand out the pay and get resupplied." The regiment from the 21st division was supposed to have started moving at seven in the morning, but it was already two in the afternoon. "They have their excuses. No, they're not as motivated as we would like them to be."

There was always the feeling back then, in just the second month of the North Vietnamese "Easter Offensive," that sooner or later the South Vietnamese would break through to relieve An Loc—not just by air, as finally happened at the end of June, but also by road. "They don't push, they figure it'll eventually get done so why take chances," rationalized Colonel Willey, who'd done a previous combat tour in Vietnam with the special forces. "It's pretty much a Vietnamese syndrome."

Then there were always those tantalizingly encouraging intelligence estimates. "We hear rumors the enemy command structure is falling apart," Willey reported, but he himself didn't seem to buy such easy talk. "We still haven't got word that any of the enemy soldiers have begun moving out. We assume parts of three enemy divisions are still in the area around An Loc. . . . We also have rumors that an enemy battalion is cutting the road between our regiments."

Colonel Willey was a rarity in the Vietnam war, an American adviser who wasn't afraid to level with reporters, who refused to accept the corporate optimism of the top command, who deserved and won respect. I saw him almost every day for a while. Then one day in June I got tired of covering the static, stagnating battle for route 13. That day, back in Saigon, I heard that Colonel Willey had been killed by an enemy rocket as he reconnoitered up the road in his jeep. He died near the skeletal watchtower north of Chon Thanh at just the spot where the forward line of South Vietnamese troops was hopelessly dug in, entrenched and immobile, against the North Vietnamese several hundred yards away.

Nobody knows for sure how many thousands have died for route 13—perhaps 6,000 South Vietnamese soldiers and twice as many

North Vietnamese and thousands of civilians trapped in An Loc as communist gunners pummeled it with mortar, rocket, and artillery fire day and night at the height of the fighting. Colonel Willey was just one of the dead, one whom I'd known only slightly but couldn't help remembering with a twinge. Sadness, fear, panic, identification with another American? You can never sort out the senses of loss.

There are other memories, too. Phantom, fragmented mental pictures of refugees arriving at a schoolyard in Chon Thanh after walking out of An Loc. At first I thought they were happy, overjoyed at escaping after weeks of living in bunkers and holes in the shadows of shelled-out walls, but then I saw they were weeping and moaning. Some of their clothes were soaked in blood. The communists had fired half a dozen mortar rounds into the group as they trudged down the road midway between An Loc and Chon Thanh. The uninjured had carried the victims to the first South Vietnamese outpost at Chon Thanh.

"We had just passed the stream when they began firing at us," said a grey-haired man holding the almost lifeless form of his five-year-old son. "The North Vietnamese did not stop shooting until the airplanes flew overhead. Then we began running away." A little girl and a middle-aged man scrambled from the back of one vehicle with a gap-toothed old lady in their arms. "She is my mother," said the man, weeping profusely beside his daughter, who was five or six. "She was shot in three places."

Then there was the last American killed before the Paris Peace. His name was William Nolde, like Willey a lieutenant colonel, and he didn't begin to participate in the fighting until it was almost over. The many different "fronts" had stabilized, the South Vietnamese had given up the struggle for the road, and the North Vietnamese had almost ceased the shelling of An Loc when Nolde was assigned as senior adviser of Binh Long province, of which An Loc is the capital. Since the North Vietnamese held the entire province except for An Loc and Chon Thanh, Nolde could do little more than concern himself with advising some of the regional forces on perimeter defense and worry about the refugees jammed into camps in the next province south.

"It's eased off an awful lot," Nolde, a tall man with a sensitive, slightly swarthy face, had told me when I met him at the end of November. "The big problem is, there's so much lost. The civilians want to go back, but what are the terms of the ceasefire? That's a big question mark." Nolde lived long enough to read the fine type of the Paris agreement in *Stars and Stripes* but was killed by a communist shell that struck his bunker in An Loc on the evening of January 26, eleven hours before the ceasefire began.

The faces and memories flash before you like random, disjointed shots in a movie, and you hear the long whistle of the bomb and lie waiting for life or death. And it crashes across the road, and you are alive, and you can't understand how it could explode so close and not blast your body into strips of ugly red flesh to rot under the Sunday sun or send the little single sliver of shrapnel through your brain or heart, and you are walking again as the jets gracefully curl away into the blue, and you wonder, can they do this again?

They must have expended their bombs by now, but they are a pair, two jet fighters with six bombs apiece underneath their chunky swept-back wings,* and they are diving one at a time, not together, and they are determined to get you, and they keep returning, dropping one at a time.

We hit it again and get up, and this one has fallen particularly close, just across the narrow blacktop. Engulfed in black, billowing smoke, we are choking, unable to breathe for a second, then swallowing and inhaling the smoke, and we know if the next one hits in just the same place it has to get us, and we run through the smoke and into the open daylight as one of the planes again rolls in, and we hit it again.

Then we hear the crackle of the North Vietnamese AK47 rifles behind us, and the edge of relief hovers, almost invisible, but still there, over the fear. In four years of covering the war, it is the first and only time I have heard the staccato of the AKs and been glad. The planes now know the North Vietnamese positions, and maybe they will attack them and not us.

The next time the bomb falls it is at least 200 feet behind us, and we hear the sound of their twin 20-millimeter cannon cutting across the road. I wave my hands as I walk because the pilot now has another target, and I want to convince him I am unarmed. The planes have unloaded all their bombs, and they are coming in only for strafing. We keep flinching at the sound of the diving jets, but we are no longer

---

*In my initial report on this incident, I identified the planes as F5 Freedom Fighters. In fact, they were probably A37s, also a mainstay of the VNAF.

hitting the dirt—cannon are much more personal, they will kill you just as well lying down as standing.

Each time the planes dive the sound of the cannon is somewhat fainter. They are apparently strafing the brush on either side far behind us. We keep walking, without jumping now at the screams of the diving jets, and then we see the dots of South Vietnamese soldiers down the road and a tower over the last South Vietnamese outpost, and the fear begins to lift.

We are safe when we cross the first strip of barbed wire across the road, but I raise my feet unnecessarily high over a single strand linked to a mine. Half a dozen South Vietnamese soldiers watch as we stumble back to our car, lungs still clogged with bomb smoke, half-breathing, and flop into the seats. One of them offers a drink from his canteen, and we swig and spit out, but we are too tired to shake hands or even say thank you. Besides, we suspect that some South Vietnamese commander deliberately called in the strikes on top of us to keep reporters from meeting the North Vietnamese, particularly since the window of our car displays a sign saying *bao chi* for reporter.

The South Vietnamese, since the ceasefire began, have been battling correspondents constantly to keep them from visiting Viet Cong villages or talking with communist members of the Joint Military Commission. Policemen arrest reporters entering VC "liberated zones" and demand special passes, often impossible to obtain, at the gates of compounds occupied by JMC members. It is probably a bureaucratic error that soldiers at the last outpost on route 13 were not ordered to stop us. Possibly no one in Saigon believed that anyone would cross a no-man's-land still littered with the debris of months of fighting—rusted hulks of rocketed trucks, shell casings, helmets.

If the South Vietnamese are not brave enough to fight for the road on the ground, however, they are glad to have any excuse for bombing at will—in violation of the agreement. They can always say we were caught in a crossfire and cite our case as a warning to other correspondents wandering into "insecure areas." Our survival may demonstrate what many analysts of the war have been saying for years, that airpower alone is not always an effective weapon.

It might be appropriate to end this story as we peer back, John Wayne-style, brows furrowed, scanning the road to see the North Vietnamese banner still flying above the road on the horizon, but we do not look back, we do not ask questions. We just drive and do not talk until reaching a soft drink stand 15 miles to the south. We get out and gulp down our colas, swallowing hard over the dust in our throats, and my driver notices his watch is gone—lost in one of those dives in the dirt. "You buy me new watch," he says with a grin, and we are alive and we laugh. The fighting for route 13 may sputter on for years, but for us the war is over.

15

"Back in the World"

There was still a war to fight "back in the world." For the first time in American history the returning GIs were not greeted as combat heroes. Nor did they particularly *feel* like heroes as they formed pressure groups such as Vietnam Veterans Against the War, staged demonstrations, and demanded better breaks from Congress and the Veterans Administration, attuned to veterans from a different era, with different attitudes. The mood of the GIs reflected not only their experience in Vietnam but also the outlook of an entire society fed up with overseas adventurism.

Like the GIs after their year at war, I returned to the States in late 1971 with a sense of chagrin over the response of Americans to the Vietnam experience. For me, the sense may have been deeper than it was for many GIs, since I had not been home in more than four years, most of that time in Vietnam.

It was not the opposition to the war that bothered you so much as the apathy, the misunderstanding of the nature of the war, the lack of concern. "Did you see anyone get killed in Vietnam?" trilled a young society matron in Chicago during a small interlude in a cocktail-party conversation before turning to other, more interesting topics. "Did you hear bullets?" asked a Chicago police reporter, apparently influenced by World War II novels. Beneath that level, you discovered, there was not much real interest in whatever had happened to us in Vietnam.

You had only to talk to Vietnam veterans to confirm that the war had indeed had a deep impact on them and, in some indefinable way, on our entire society as well. Interviewing veterans in New York, Washington, Philadelphia, Chicago, and a number of points in between for a series in the *Chicago Tribune*, I found a common thread of depression and bitterness.

It was, perhaps, the best time in the war to conduct such interviews. We were still fighting in Vietnam, but we knew by then the hopelessness of the cause, and the veterans were at a high point of both organized and individual discontent. Somehow it seemed a fitting way to conclude my own impressions of the war, though I was back in Vietnam by the end of the year for the *Tribune* and wound up covering some of the major battles of 1972.

Later, as they merged into the rest of our society, the veterans began to lose some of the edge of their anger. "You can't get anyone organized anymore," complained a former army captain, wounded twice in Vietnam, whom I met in late 1973. "The movement has lost its force." The question remained, however, in what way the veterans, sinking again into the mainstream of American life, would affect those around them, turning their experience in Vietnam into a personal legacy for all of us to bear.

Chicago, South Side, October 1971

Chicken Unlimited sells four- to twelve-bit dinners at prices ranging from $1.49 to $4.75 at its gaudy white-tiled outlet on South State Street and Garfield Boulevard, but the biggest operator around the corner may be an afro-haired hustler with a deceptively engaging manner and the soul name of Brother Rap, the same sobriquet, as it happened, of another "brother" whom I had met several months earlier on Soul Alley in Saigon.

"You just need somethin'," says Brother Rap, letting the words slide between almost pursed lips in a low undertone, "you see me." As long as he's convinced you're not a cop or an informer, you can "score skag" with him for "a nickel or dime"—five to ten dollars or even a bargain-basement three dollars for a small capsule. "Good enough to keep you goin' for a little while, anyway."

Brother Rap swears he can answer a junkie's needs "for not too much," but he admits he'll never hustle skag for the low-low rates he used to charge at the army's big logistics base at Long Binh, 15 miles northeast of Saigon. "I got so used to hustlin' in 'Nam, I kind of dug it," says Brother Rap, talking to me in the relative sanctuary of the lobby of the Veterans Administration Assistance Center on West Taylor Street. "We got it for a couple dollars a vial and sold it for five. It was 95 percent pure around there. Here we have to cut it way down."

Brother Rap, who refuses to give his real name for obvious reasons, says he was "puttin' skag myself" for a little while but claims he's off it now. "Oh, I snort maybe once or twice a week. I was shootin' over in 'Nam."

Brother Rap smiles nostalgically at the memory of injecting heroin into his arm. "I Jonesed on the plane coming back. Throwin' up and aching all over. The Jones is something else." He shudders at the memory of a typical physical response to coming off heroin. Brother Rap now wants a job—he's visiting the VA Assistance Center for advice on finding one—but he's not at all certain he can adapt to humdrum routine and regular hours. "I haven't been working for ten months, ever since I got out of the army. I didn't even want to work. I was a little screwed up. I think I still am."

Brother Rap's plight is typical of that of untold thousands of veterans, white and black, who got hooked in Vietnam. "It's impossible to tell the exact effects of the war on the drug problem," says Dr. Edward Senay, director of the Illinois Drug Abuse Program, "but I would estimate that 1,000 of 30,000 addicts in Cook County are Vietnam veterans."

The depth of the drug problem, exacerbated by the wide-open availability of heroin outside literally all U.S. military installations in Vietnam, defies precise analysis in part because most of the victims are not seeking assistance in organized drug programs. "There's so many junkies around here, they all got the habit in Vietnam," says Brother Rap. "They might kick it for a while but then start all over again. Drug programs don't do no good. Man goes there for an overdose. He straightens out for a while. Then he's shootin' up again."

Psychologists and doctors might accuse Rap of a certain hyperbole, but basically they agree with his view of the difficulties as reflected among Vietnam vets. "There tends to be a lag period between the time a person gets strung out initially and the time he comes for treatment," says Dr. John Chappel, clinical psychiatrist with the Illinois Drug Abuse Program. That's why relatively few Vietnam vets have approached the program for treatment even though they are given priority above others. "Initially, the individual feels, 'Well, I can kick it myself.'"

Another complication, cited by Dr. Bernard Rappaport, chief of psychiatry at the West Side Veterans Administration Hospital, is the sense of disillusionment shared by most Vietnam veterans, particularly those on drugs. "They don't want to talk about Vietnam," says Dr. Rappaport, who has organized the hospital's drug clinic, the only one operated by the VA in Illinois. "It's difficult for them to discuss their experiences."

The result: almost no Vietnam veterans requested treatment at the clinic, capable of caring for 30 bedridden patients and another 200 on an outpatient basis, when it opened in August 1971. "Most of our patients are hard-core addicts, people who've been on drugs for ten or 15 years. The Vietnam people are just beginning to come as word of our program spreads."

In a conference room off the drug ward, a onetime marine lance corporal, wounded by shrapnel at Khe Sanh in 1968, tells why he happened to get into the program. "I was shootin' all day before getting into the service," says the ex-marine, in the presence of a couple of young rehabilitation coordinators who forbade him to give his name. "I stopped in basic training, but then I went back in Vietnam. I was high when I went on my first operation."

Mingling braggadocio with guilt, the ex-marine recounts his success in "ripping off" military post exchanges in both Vietnam and the States, then in looting stores and homes in Chicago after his discharge. "It was costing me $150 a day to keep up the habit. I was mixing heroin with cocaine and shooting it." He might not have abandoned this life of petty crime had he not been sent to the VA hospital for treatment for serum hepatitis, spread by shooting with unsterilized hypodermic needles.

"We get all the referrals for hepatitis," interjects one of the rehabilitation coordinators, Joel Laskin, who is studying for his Ph.D. in clinical psychology at Loyola. "We informed him we had a program and asked if he was interested. He was. He's been in the clinic for two months now."

The ex-marine, in a real sense, is among the fortunate few—fortunate to have had to go to the hospital with hepatitis before he was finally arrested or hurt in a holdup, fortunate to have been at a hospital with a new drug clinic, fortunate to have encountered doctors and rehabilitation coordinators personally interested in helping him. His case, judging from interviews with a number of veterans, is a rare exception.

"We admit the drug problem caught us by surprise," says a VA official in Washington, noting that the first VA drug clinic was not opened until late 1970. "We're still geared to alcoholics from World War II and Korea. We already have 41 alcohol treatment centers and only 32 for drugs. We're planning 28 more drug centers and 21 new alcohol treatment centers."

So far behind was the VA on the drug problem, according to some psychiatrists, that certain of its top administrators opposed extensive treatment for drug addiction. "They're still reluctant to develop an outpatient program," says a Chicago drug expert, requesting anonymity. "That's ridiculous, since the majority of cases don't require bed care."

As for Brother Rap talking about the sale of drugs on South State Street, he may subconsciously reflect another legacy of Vietnam: its effect upon the attitudes of black GIs after they return to the States.

While drug problems cut across racial lines, blacks seem to suffer more and to share a deeper sense of resentment than do whites over the effects of the war on their total lives. Whatever their response may have been in individual predicaments in the field, black veterans say the war has united them against whites, has taught them how to fight whites, has steeled their determination to defeat the white majority in some climactic, if vaguely defined, revolutionary conflagration.

"The military did one thing for me," says a brawny freshman at Malcolm X College, toying with a black power bracelet made of shoelaces from his old army boots. "It showed me how screwed up this country really is. Here, people are indoctrinated to the policies of the U.S. In Vietnam you know reality—death. The war made me understand how the system is run, why the white men make wars, what it's like to be in wars. I regret having gone to Vietnam for fighting," he concludes, biting off his words, "but it showed me the true way of life. I now want to work for the black veterans movement, so we can better ourselves against the white man."

If black and white veterans sometimes seem to share a similar sense of guilt and futility, they differ sharply in both the degree and direction of their anger. The former tend to express resentment against *all* white society, while the latter focus on the leaders responsible for sending them to Vietnam or, at most, on government bureaucracy in general.

"Vietnam was a racist war," says Brother Maurice, another Malcolm X student, a machine gunner with the 25th division who was court-martialed, but not convicted, in Vietnam for refusing to go to the field—and discharged as "undesirable" after returning to the States. "They called us 'nigger' and gave us the worst jobs. The black dudes looked after each other's backs in the field. We was pretty heavy with each other."

Brother Maurice's charge of racial discrimination in the army may not be entirely accurate, but there is no doubt the Vietnam experience has added both cohesion and strength to black movements in America. Black GIs generally shared quarters with each other, hung together in the field, formed Black Panther and other organizations at bases, and, at some installations in rear areas, fomented riots against white authority. One obvious symbol of black unity in Vietnam is the DAP, the elaborate handshake ritual by which black GIs greet each other. Now the DAP—for "Dignity for Afro Peoples"—is spreading to the States as black veterans teach their younger soul brothers how to do it.

"The black GIs were like one happy family," says Brother Maurice. "We called the handshake 'the blessing.'" Brother Maurice insists that vets at Malcolm X do not force students who haven't served in the army to learn the DAP, but the fad is spreading quickly around campus, as proven by the sight of students engaging in the ritual between classes, in the cafeteria, in the halls.

The search for racial identity among black veterans extends from the symbol of the DAP to the reality of black commando groups, made up of men who were trained by the army to kill and sensitized by the Vietnam experience to hate "white oppressors." A factor in the rage of black commandos, some of them Black Panthers but many affiliated with underground, unpublicized organizations, is the inability to find jobs in a period of economic recession.

"We have some of the world's best commandos right here in the ghetto," observes Samuel Campbell, a 23-year-old former army sergeant who served in both Vietnam and Thailand and now works full-time for the Committee of Concerned Veterans, an organization formed here to help black GIs look for jobs. "These men might not all have salable skills, but they're experts at firing weapons."

What's more, says Campbell, some of them are hoarding weapons for the time when they can use them. "They may have no other choice." If the threat appears exaggerated, Campbell points out that hundreds, maybe thousands, of blacks in the ghetto received less than honorable discharges as a result of perpetual conflicts with military authorities, "the system," in Vietnam. They not only are ineligible for VA benefits, including hospitalization and education allowances and job advice, but also are *persona non grata* at virtually all employment offices.

"They can always say they have honorable discharges," says Campbell, "Sometimes employers will check. Anyway, there aren't many jobs available." As a case in point, he notes that his office once had a request for a dozen housemen to work at a convention and received 36 applications within a few hours after spreading the word. Inside the office of the Committee of Concerned Veterans, on the far South Side, several blacks with undesirable or bad conduct discharges talk about their problems. "An undesirable stigmatizes you for life," says a man recently laid off from a job on a garbage truck. "You're enslaved. You can't do anything or get anywhere. A man getting out of prison has a better chance of getting a job."

One of the Vietnam veterans boasts that he sent a letter to President Nixon threatening to "blow up the White House with you inside." He shows the calling card of a Secret Service agent who knocked on the door one day to ask what he meant and to advise him of the illegality of such threats against the president. "I told him I didn't care what he said, I didn't have a job, and I *would* blow up the White House if that's what I had to do to survive," he says, angrily pounding a tabletop, glaring at me. "I have a family. I have to eat. I'll do anything."

The desperation of some of the ghetto-dwellers, including war veterans, often discourages them from participating in essentially white anti-war protests staged by such groups as the Vietnam Veterans Against the War, a nationwide organization. "Our people don't care about the war one way or another," says Campbell. "It's not our war. It takes money to march around in peace groups. We haven't got the time. Why march for peace in Vietnam when you haven't got peace here?"

Chicago Circle, October 1971

Blacks, however, are not alone in their distaste for demonstrations and such. A block west of the modernesque towers and walkways of the University of Illinois at Chicago Circle, a rundown shack reverberates with the sound of stereo music mingled with occasional shouts and laughter.

The paint on the walls and roof of the shack is chipped and peeling, and the only external visual sign of life inside is a crudely written placard advising visitors to enter by the rear door. The occupants of the shack once adorned it with a banner saying "Veterans' Club," but they had to tear it down after longtime residents of the old Italian neighborhood charged that regulations forbade such "commercial advertising," as if the veterans and the war represented nothing more than an aesthetically displeasing business venture.

"We just set it up as a place where a guy can come here, relax, and try to get away from the sterile atmosphere of the campus," says James R. Janicki, who served a year at the army's logistics center at Long Binh and now is studying for a degree in business administration. "Guys sit around and tell war stories, but we don't talk about gruesome experiences. It's kind of a mixed-up thing."

The small talk at the clubhouse may illustrate the problems and attitudes, the revolt and confusion, among today's veterans, anxious to forget but unable to rid themselves of the memory of their year at war. Open to all 1,200 veterans on the Circle campus, the club, almost entirely white, is typical of hundreds of veterans' social groups at colleges and universities throughout the country. "If anybody comes in here and boasts about how many men he's killed, there's usually a very bad response," says Charles Buccholz, an ex-marine who once went on special reconnaissance missions in the northern provinces of South Vietnam and sometimes strayed across the borders into enemy strongholds in southern Laos and North Vietnam.

Sitting on a stool in front of the long wooden bar in the dimly lit clubroom, Buccholz denounces the war as a "waste" but admits he can't stop talking about it—not the encounters with an omnipresent enemy but "the girls you met, the camps you've seen, the old sergeants, leave in Bangkok, stuff like that."

The fact that Buccholz, like other members of the club, not only opposes the war but refuses to brag about his exploits indicates the mood of Vietnam veterans, who scorn and often loathe the "old men" from World War II and Korea. "The guys in the Veterans of Foreign Wars and the American Legion look at the war from a different point of view," says Wayne Olenick, a lieutenant with the military police in Saigon during the 1968 Tet offensive, in which 37 MPs were killed.

"They fought their wars to win, but there's no way we're going to win this war."

If the members of the Veterans' Club do not identify with their counterparts in the old, established veterans' organizations, however, they still relate to each other and their own war—a phenomenon of possibly far-reaching consequences if the United States ever enters another armed conflict. Almost instinctively the veterans cling to some of the customs formed in Vietnam. The decor of the club, for instance, resembles that of officers' or NCO clubs at small installations throughout Vietnam. The cheap soft lighting, the beer signs, and the American flag behind the bar all contribute to the effect.

Nor are the veterans anti-military as such. "I still can't really knock the marine corps," says Buccholz, who left the service as a sergeant and hopes to go to law school. "I just don't believe the marines should have been sent to do something really wasteful." To which Olenick adds: "I would still fight for my country if I thought it was right. I'd probably fight even if it wasn't right." Olenick's my-country-right-or-wrong attitude may not jibe with the view of all club members, but few if any are prepared to demonstrate *against* their country, either.

"I have no desire to protest," says another ex-marine, Thomas Flaws, who considers the United States the aggressor in Vietnam. "If you have a protest, it gets out of hand and destroys property." Basically, members of the Veterans' Club, probably representative of a majority of students who have served in Vietnam, prefer to remain as noncommitted as possible on social issues—a position their critics say belies passive support of the establishment.

Symbolic of their conventional approach is that some of them would actually like to introduce Greek fraternity-style letters and perhaps even wear special jackets—social, seemingly nonpolitical gestures that still have deep political overtones if one views the entire fraternity system as fundamentally conservative. "We have people representing all views," says Janicki, one of the club's founders, but the real protesters gravitate toward Vietnam Veterans Against the War.

"Probably 80 percent of the Vietnam veterans don't want to join any kind of protest," says Al Hubbard, executive secretary of the VVAW's executive committee in New York. "They just want to forget about the war and go back to whatever they were doing. They figure they spent two or three years in one organization, the military, and they don't want to join another." The experience of the VVAW at the Circle bears out this thesis. The VVAW campus leader, Phil Rubin, who served as an infantryman northwest of Saigon, admits that only a handful of veterans have signified any real interest in joining the campus chapter.

Rubin, who studied engineering at the University of Michigan before he was drafted and now majors in philosophy, wants to do more than catch up. He is crusading for complete withdrawal of all American troops from Vietnam. His most persistent enemy is not any serious opposition to his viewpoint but rather the apathy of students who, like many other Americans, may not care if the United States maintains a presence in Indochina so long as the war is winding down.

Rubin, who has grown his hair in a ponytail since his discharge from the army two years ago, does not look with disdain or dislike on his less radical colleagues. Indeed, he is more likely to view with some contempt the noisy anti-war protests of students who have never served in Vietnam. "Maybe it's an age thing. I'm 24, three years older than the average kids in my class. Some of the younger ones seem so impetuous. They spout these socialist ideas, and that's great. Then they come up and tell us about Vietnam. I resent that. You can read all the books in the world, and it's not like being there."

As a matter of fact, Rubin may identify more easily with the drinkers at the Veterans' Club than with the protesters on campus. "It's common experience. You just relate to each other. You see a guy wearing a military patch you recognize, or just walking around in fatigue jacket and boots. Or maybe you hear a word common to GIs in Vietnam, like *beaucoup*, or 'numbah one,' or *di di* for 'go away.' Other students think we're all nuts. They're convinced we're nuts. All they have to do is sit around and listen to this language thing. They don't understand you." All of which may go to symbolize the alienation of the Vietnam veteran from his environment, in this case the academic community.

Midlothian, Illinois, October 1971

Those who regard college students, like blacks and drug addicts, as societal rejects, rebels at best, fall back on their own special form of rebuttal to social protest. Beyond the urban ghetto or the urban campus, they remind the critics of the war and American policy, lurks the vast expanse of the "real America," home of the fabled "silent majority," "middle America."

In quest of this silent majority of patriots and true believers, I drive 20 miles south of Chicago to this prototypical middle-class suburb named Midlothian, a name that catches my imagination as more mid-American than, say, such socially upscale communities as Highland Park or Wilmette.

The American flag flies 24 hours a day over Midlothian, whose elders, appropriately enough, have chosen to call it "the community of the lighted flag." The operator of the village's foremost hamburger stand was the first, as noted on a bronze plaque beside the food counter, "to call the nation's attention to the fact that the American flag, when illuminated, can be displayed at night." As a result of "the great public interest in flying the American flag by night," the plaque goes on, "the White House illuminated their [sic] flag August 21, 1970."

It seems almost unfair, in view of this effusion of patriotic spirit, that Midlothian's Vietnam veterans should display the same acute problems, the same sense of revolt in readjusting to this society as students at large universities or blacks in the ghetto.

"When I got home, I was really confused," says Ronald McSheffery, sitting at a smooth-paneled table several feet from the plaque, munching a hamburger. "I didn't know whether to like this place or hate it." Perhaps the most shocked and confused were McSheffery's father, James, a carpenter, and his mother, who had just moved into a neat two-story home from which one could see the American flag flapping away over a well-manicured high school several blocks away.

"I was just about 20 pounds underweight and looked like I had jaundice," explains Ronald, who was granted a general discharge "under honorable conditions" a year ago after rebelling completely against his commanders in Vietnam. "I'd been shooting heroin over there and began coming off it on the plane coming back. My mother was really scared just looking at me. First thing she did was make sure I got my weight back and got some sleep."

Ronald's parents had viewed him as the rebel of the family ever since he dropped out of high school after his junior year, but they stopped criticizing him after older brother Andy, 22, eldest of the eight McSheffery youngsters, dropped out of the navy last June 7. "I thought the war was a big joke, a waste of time," says Andy, whose commander in Vietnam once tried to have him court-martialed for flashing the V-for-peace sign instead of saluting. "He asked me what the sign meant, and I said, 'Peace, no fightin', like the whole thing's solved.' He said, 'What do you mean, peace?' and I said, 'Peace, man, what are you anyway, a warmonger?' Then he called me in his office and gave me a whole thing about respect."

Andy's case was so petty that the military court before which he was to appear refused to hear it, but he ran afoul of another commander in Hawaii after completing his Vietnam tour. "He saw me sitting around with my feet on the desk and said if I didn't watch it, I'd get demoted. I said I didn't want any demotion, I wanted my discharge. So I wrote a letter explaining how I felt about the war and the navy, and the bureau of personnel let me out."

The attitudes of the McSheffery brothers conflict not only with the established values of Midlothian but also with those of their own relatives: their father, a World War II veteran; an uncle, a retired chief petty officer in the navy; and another uncle, who once commanded a post of the Veterans of Foreign Wars. Like most Vietnam vets, the younger McShefferys would not consider a visit to the local VFW post, whose aging members concede they're concerned about the future of the VFW "after we're all gone."

Andy, consenting to accompany me on a visit to the bar at the VFW post, looks embarrassed and self-conscious as a couple of World War II veterans shake hands with him and tell him about their tours in Europe a generation ago. "Here's the most decorated man at the post," says a silver-haired railroad detective, pointing to a swarthy man behind the bar. "He was with the marines in the South Pacific in World War II."

Andy listens politely, then, during a break in the conversation, suggests, "It's time we get going." As we are walking out the door, he mutters unhappily about the men at the VFW bar. "What a waste, they're not even real."

If Ronald and Andy McSheffery typify disillusioned Vietnam vets in terms of attitude and outlook, they also illustrate the desperate search among ex-GIs for jobs, education, and new roots in a society that seems much more alien to them now than when they left home two or three years ago. "I'll do anything," says Ronald. "Wash dishes, sweep floors, anything. I need work. One time there I was filing ten applications a day. They all said, 'We'll call if we have anything.' I never heard."

Since returning home in August, Andy has been trying to find a job in construction. "I can't find nothin', so I've gone to bartender's school for a week. Maybe I'll get somethin' there." Alternatively, he may enroll in a community junior college and live on part-time employment and educational benefits from the Veterans Administration.

A depressing factor in the brothers' search for jobs is that more companies are laying off workers while more veterans return from Vietnam. More than 30,000 vets are looking for work in the Chicago area, and another 40,000 will return to the region in the next few months as the last American combat units withdraw from Vietnam. "We're sponsoring job fairs around the state," says a government employment service man, but Ronald reports that personnel representatives at one fair all informed him there were no openings. "They said they just wanted us to know about them in case the situation changed. It was a big waste of time."

Besides, many veterans are too restless to want to resign themselves to long stints with companies that might resemble nothing so much as the army. Both Ronald and Andy reflect a desire to get away from their home, to wander around the country, before settling down.

The cases of Ronald and Andy fit in with attitudes already noted among ex-GIs by Robert Jay Lifton, research professor of psychiatry at Yale, who has conducted extensive studies among veterans protesting the war. "All veterans are in some kind of profound conflict," says Lifton. "No man had a very clear sense of justification of what he did or why we were in Vietnam. They all feel betrayed by this war. Everybody, even those who think we should have fought harder and bombed Hanoi, feels there was something not quite right about this war."

It is partly for this reason that veterans often join clubs—not the VFW or American Legion but their own groups—and tend to hang around with each other. "They can only find with each other that authenticity they seek," Lifton reasons. "They may not seek political goals. It's all a question of psychological needs."

Unconsciously, the McSheffery brothers may bear out a thesis whose verbiage they don't pretend to understand. "I can't see leading a regular life," Ronald remarks disconsolately, without suggesting exactly what he'd like in its place. "This town is just dull and boring," echoes Andy. "Everybody watches television at night, and that's it."

Epilogue

Not all the returning veterans were forgotten. The exceptions, the ones who really aroused public interest and sympathy, were the prisoners of war. After the deaths and wounds and hardships suffered by so many thousands of Americans, and untold millions of Vietnamese, Cambodians, and Laotians, I was somewhat confused and surprised by the emphasis placed upon a handful of GIs in prison camps in North Vietnam or in Viet Cong jungle redoubts in the south. It was not that they personally did not deserve sympathy and support. It was just that their suffering was exaggerated out of all proportion to that of the many, many more who had died unknown and unmourned except by their immediate families and friends or else endured untold miseries in field hospitals.

Yet, beneath the level of overt concern for the POWs, there was the question of who, beyond their families, really cared about *their* fate either. For President Nixon, the existence of the POWs provided an easy rationalization for remaining in the war until conclusion of an agreement providing for their release. For those who opposed the war, visits to POW camps in North Vietnam resulted in facile anti-war propaganda, none of which gave any hint of the duress under which the POWs had to live.

Finally, the release of the POWs seemed to offer a great wet blanket with which the Nixon administration could save face and hide the defeat and failure inherent in the Paris Peace. The last surge of POW publicity was embarrassing—if not hypocritical and dishonest. While no efforts were spared to ensure the successful transition of POWs to civilian life, information officers barred reporters from talking to any of them, ostensibly for fear the journalists' questions might upset their psyches.

In reality, the White House was afraid that interviews might result in adverse publicity and criticism and mar the drummed-up spirit of "victory" surrounding "peace with honor." Another reason, perhaps, was that officials may have been afraid the POWs would report tales of torture—and thus jeopardize subsequent releases, spaced out at intervals over a 45-day period beginning on February 12, two weeks after the signing of the Paris Peace on January 27, 1973. Certainly many of the POWs, after the last releases in Hanoi on March 29, did not hesitate, this time at the urging of the Pentagon, to reveal the horrors to which they had been subjected in captivity.

Despite a sense of revulsion over the Nixon-serving, show-business aspect of the releases, one could not help but find them moving. I watched two of them, one of GIs and civilians held in the south, the other of pilots in Hanoi.

Tan Son Nhut, February 1973

The dusk of early evening was just turning to night when the row of helicopters, their red lights flashing, appeared in the distance over the fringes of the airbase. The helicopters had 27 passengers, prisoners from the shell-pocked airstrip of Loc Ninh, a district town captured by the Viet Cong and North Vietnamese at the beginning of the "Easter Offensive" of April and May 1972—the first district town to fall permanently to the communists.

It was the first day of the POW releases, and the Viet Cong had finally let them go after a twelve-hour delay during which they had insisted first on the arrival at Loc Ninh, aboard C130 transports, of some 150 of their own prisoners released by the South Vietnamese. As reporters watched from behind a cordon guarded by military policemen, the Americans, no longer POWs, jumped out of the helicopters, laughing and joking, and walked across the tarmac to the waiting C9 hospital plane, as if they were figures in a movie setting.

There they were, wearing blue-and-green Viet Cong pajamas with

American medical tags on them, waving at the row of journalists and photographers 100 feet away, then shaking hands with Ambassador Ellsworth Bunker and other officials before boarding the plane for the next lap in their homeward journey, the ride to Clark Air Force Base in the Philippines. It was the final moment of ecstasy after a day of agony and frustration that had seemed at moments to cast doubts on the entire prisoner release program—and the Paris Peace. If the ex-POWs were unhappy about the long wait, however, they did not indicate as much as they strolled toward the white-painted C9.

"They all said it's great to be back," said Bunker, who shook hands with each of them by the stairs leading into the rear of the plane. "And we said in return, 'It's great to have you home, it's a great day for all of us.' " By the time of the release, said the brigadier general who had negotiated for the United States in Loc Ninh, "the feeling of satisfaction erased all the bad memories of the long day of waiting."

Hanoi, March 1973

The atmosphere of the final prisoner release in Hanoi was, if anything, still more tense, partly because most of the reporters who flew in on the Royal Air Lao charter flight from Vientiane had never previously been here. Our hosts showed us the rubble of bombed-out factories and apartment buildings on the way to one of the camps, which the camp commander gave us to believe had provided an almost idyllic daily diet of volleyball, movies, reading, studying—good food, too.

North Vietnamese guards let us view the POWs, standing beside their bunks or in even rows in front of one of the camp buildings, but they forbade any questions. One of the POWs, however, did not seem to care what his captors thought of his remarks as we questioned him through the door of his five-man cell.

"It was bad," said Major William James Elander, wearing prison regulation two-tone maroon T-shirt and shorts. "I'll talk about it." It was so bad that Elander was more than a little annoyed with reporters and photographers for seeming to accept just the picture the prison guards wanted to give them of life in the Hanoi Hilton. "We object to these pictures because this is not the way it really is here," said the major, a veteran of two combat tours in Southeast Asia.

"No talk, no talk," the North Vietnamese guards kept telling us as we looked through the bars toward the prisoners standing beside their cots. "Please, it is enough time for you," a guard informed me before shutting the windows on several cells of POWs.

A few hours later, on the tarmac of Gia Lam airport, the prisoners stood in even rows, two abreast, unsmiling, as a North Vietnamese officer barked out their names, one by one, in a slightly guttural accent. "American prisoners, listen to your name called and step out," the officer ordered as Air Force Brigadier General Russell G. Ogan stood poised to welcome each one to the American side and point them toward the waiting C141 Starlifter for the flight to Clark.

"Marian, Anthony Marshall," the North Vietnamese officer shouted into the loudspeaker, and Captain Anthony Marshall Marian, first of the last group, walked briskly forward to freedom. Some of the prisoners swallowed slightly as they stood in line, at attention, but none showed any real emotion until saluting General Ogan. Finally, only one of them, Navy Lieutenant Commander Alfred Howard Agnew, was waiting, the last man in the last of four columns. North Vietnamese photographers and soldiers surged around him, forming a circle, smiling and yelling at each other to take souvenir pictures.

A North Vietnamese captain, in pith helmet and baggy fatigues, stood beside Agnew, grinning broadly. The young pilot, the last American captured in North Vietnam during the final phase of the "Christmas bombing" in December, grinned, swallowed, and grinned again as his name was called.

Then, he walked through what was now a gauntlet of North Vietnamese and American reporters and photographers and saluted General Ogan, standing beneath a green parachute under slightly overcast skies. "I'm real glad to see you," said Agnew. "You must be a dignitary with all that delay," said Ogan. The crowd of North Vietnamese, several thousand of them in front of the partially destroyed terminal building, broke through security guards and milled across the runway.

Agnew, now accompanied by American liaison officers, walked to the plane. "Let's hit it," he said as he reached the gaping rear entrance to the Starlifter, and one of the air force officers sent to Hanoi to expedite the release let out a short yell. The war—for the Americans—was over.

The next stage of the conflict—the struggle between Vietnamese and Vietnamese, all suitably equipped with weapons supplied by their respective benefactors—was beginning. Yet the pilots, who never saw the damage they were doing as they swung gracefully down on their targets, were as oblivious of the future as they were of the past—and the futility of the war they had waged or the suffering they had either inflicted on others or endured themselves. "We negotiated a satisfactory conclusion," one of them remarked later in a talk before a group of wide-eyed schoolchildren. "I am confident we achieved our aims. That's why we fought, and that's why I'm here."

The plot, as the GIs on the ground, grunts and REMFs alike, knew better than the pilots, would not fit such a neatly happy scenario. The outcome, as the GIs had always known, was predictable. That's what the marine had meant when he told me, five years earlier at Khe Sanh, "Tell it to the dead."

Glossary

These are some of the terms used by Americans, military or civilian, in Vietnam context. Many were special to the war; others were in common usage before then and remain so today.*

AAA. Anti-aircraft artillery. *See* triple A.

ACR. Armored Cavalry Regiment. *See* CAV.

adviser. U.S. military officer, civilian official advising South Vietnamese officer, bureaucrat, liaising with U.S. headquarters and, in case of officers in field, calling in U.S. artillery, air strikes for South Vietnamese forces. *See* counterpart.

AFVN. Armed Forces Vietnam Network, U.S. military radio and television service.

Agent Orange. Chemical defoliant used to strip wide regions of vegetation, depriving enemy of hideouts; revealed as carcinogen.

Air America. CIA-financed private airline, like Continental Air Services, that ferried troops and supplies, sometimes including drugs, in Laos and elsewhere throughout the war.

AK, a-k. Conversational abbreviation for AK47.

AK47. Rifle, originally designed and made in Soviet Union, made in China as basic infantry weapon for North Vietnamese and Viet Cong troops. (The AK47 is the same as the Kalashnikov, rifle made by Eastern bloc countries, but the term "Kalashnikov," often used in the Middle East, was not used in Vietnam.)

---

*Dale Andrade and Vincent Demma, with U.S. Army Center of Military History; Arthur Dommen, Chad Huntley, and Mike Morrow, journalists during the war; and Duong The Tu, my former assistant in Saigon, added to the list, otherwise derived from memory.

Amerasian. Person of American and Asian parentage, usually off-spring of American GI and Southeast Asian woman, especially Vietnamese or Filipino, seldom in reference to one of mixed American and Chinese, Japanese, or Korean blood. *Cf.* Eurasian.

Americal. U.S. army 23rd division, named for its origins in World War II in the American Caledonian islands; headquartered at Chu Lai on central South Vietnam coast; achieved notoriety in My Lai massacre; disbanded after war.

American Legion. Veterans' organization, spurned for years after Vietnam War by majority of Vietnam veterans.

ammo. Ammunition.

AO, a-o. U.S. military; area of operations.

ao dai. Vietnamese, pronounced *ao-zai*; Vietnamese women's national dress, flowing garment over silken trousers, usually white or black.

APC. Armored personnel carrier. *See* tracks.

arclight. Code name, air strike, bombing by B52s flying back-to-back in three-plane formation over a specific target. *See* tracks.

arty. Military abbreviation; artillery.

ARVN. Acronym; pronounced arvin, Army of the Republic of (South) Vietnam.

A-team. U.S. army special forces unit, operating from A-team camps, sometimes called A-camps, manned also by Vietnamese special forces and local Vietnamese, Chinese Nung, montagnards hired by special forces, mainly along Cambodian, Laotian borders. *See* CIDG.

AWOL. Acronym; pronounced a-wall, absent without leave.

bad guys, the. Enemy troops; term, from western movies, often used by American officers, others, in referring to hostile forces.

Ba Muoi Ba, 33. Vietnamese name for popular French beer, also 33 in French, brewed in Saigon; pronounced ba-mee-ba by Americans.

Bank of India. Slang; network of black-market money changers from India, mostly Madras, who operated in small bookstores, in offices in the Eden building, in Saigon, offering exchange rates for dollars many times higher than official rate of formal banks.

bao chi. Vietnamese; journalism, media. *See nha bao.*

BAR, b-a-r. Browning automatic rifle, infantry weapon

bar fine. Term mainly used in Philippines; sum paid by customer at hostess bars to check bargirl out of bar, in addition to hostess drinks, fees.

BDA. Bomb damage assessment, analysis of impact of air strike, conducted by aerial reconnaissance, on the ground, etc.

beaucoup. French; many, a lot of, much; frequently used by GIs, who got it from the Vietnamese, as in *"beaucoup* VC," *"beaucoup* money."

B40, B41. Chinese-made rockets used by North Vietnamese, Viet Cong. *See* RPG.

Big Red One. U.S. army first division.

bird. Helicopter, chopper; also abbreviation for "bird colonel," full colonel; Abbreviation derived from eagle insignia denoting colonel's rank.

bird dog. U.S. army 01, L19 observation plane. *See* FAC.

black berets. Elite South Vietnamese strike force with first ARVN division in Hue; also South Vietnamese force and their American advisers. *See* Black Panthers, Hoc Bao.

Black Liberation Front. Radical black group active in Vietnam; similar to Black Panthers.

Black Panthers. Radical black group; derived name, inspiration from Black Panther Party in United States, active among GIs in Vietnam; also elite South Vietnamese unit. *See* black berets, Hoc Bao.

body count. Actual eyewitness count, supposedly not estimate, of number of bodies of the dead, usually enemy, routinely used by American command as measure of military success. *See* kill ratio.

boldshow. Exclusively Philippine term; show featuring complete nudity.

bonze. Buddhist monk, usually Vietnamese; word derived from Chinese, Japanese.

boonies. Boondocks, often meaning the bush, the field, outlying regions, jungle; from Tagalog, *bundok,* mountain, incorporated into military slang in Spanish-American war, Philippine insurrection.

Bright Light. Code name for intelligence material concerning MIA or POW sightings during the war. *See* JCRC, JPRC.

Bronco. U.S. army OV10 observation plane. *See* FAC.

brother. Soul brother, black man, black GI, often used in address, as in "Brother Rap."

brown-water navy. U.S. navy vessels on operations in Mekong River delta, including support of riverine force, joint army-navy venture.

bush. Jungle, the field. *See* boonies.

butterfly. Flirt, unfaithful person, male or female, usually used in GI/bargirl banter. Example: "You too much butterfly."

buy the farm. To die, as in "he bought the farm," derived from idea of buying a site for a grave; often used by pilots.

BX. Base exchange; U.S. air force equivalent of PX. *See* PX.

café den. Thick Vietnamese style black coffee.

café française, café filtre. Strong black coffee brewed French-style, filtered over cup.

call in. Select targets and direct fire from in, near, or above the scene, as in "call in air strikes" or "call in artillery."

C and C, C&C. Command and control helicopter, usually a Huey, in which commander, usually a colonel, flew over area directing operations from the air; sometimes called a command ship.

Cao Dai. Religious sect derived from different faiths, philosophies, including Confucianism, Buddhism, Christianity, among others; headquartered in Tay Ninh, northwest of Saigon.

CAP. Acronym; combined action platoon, marine program for winning hearts and minds among civilians in "pacified" areas.

Cav, the. Usually first air cavalry division, also used to refer to armored cavalry regiments (e.g., eleventh armored cavalry).

CCC. Command Control Central, MACV-controlled unit headquartered in highlands; conducted secret operations into Laos, northeastern Cambodia. *See* MACVSOG.

CCN. Command Control North, MACV-controlled unit headquartered in northern South Vietnam; conducted secret operations into Laos, North Vietnam. *See* MACVSOG.

CCS. Command Control South, MACV-controlled unit headquartered in southern highlands; conducted secret operations into Laos and Cambodia. *See* MACVSOG.

Central Highlands. Mountainous region of central South Vietnam. *See* high country.

Charlie. From Victor Charles, radio lingo for Viet Cong; not a pejorative, sometimes used by American officers, rarely by enlisted men, who preferred pejoratives. *See* gooks, slopes, dinks.

cheap Charlie. A person too stingy to spend much money; often used by bargirls to Americans if reluctant to buy them drinks, as in "You cheap Charlie, numbah ten."

check it out. Term frequently used by GIs in everyday conversation, often derisively, in argument, complaint.

cherry girl. Virgin or one claiming to be one. *See* family girl.

CH47. Chinook helicopter. *See* shithook.

CH53. Sea Stallion, U.S. navy and marine helicopter.

Chicom. Acronym; U.S. bureaucratic, military slang for Chinese Communists; fell out of vogue after Vietnam war.

chieu hoi. Program under which the United States and South Vietnam accepted NLF and North Vietnamese defectors. *"Chieu hoi"* means "appeal for return (to arms)." One who accepted the appeal was called *"hoi chanh,"* meaning "returnee to just cause."

China Beach. In-country rest and recreation center near Danang.

Chinook. CH47, heavy-duty helicopter, large enough to carry platoon of troops; also carried supplies. *See* shithook.

chopper. Helicopter, bird, slick. Note: helo is navy slang.

Christmas bombing. The American bombing of targets in and around Hanoi before the signing of the Paris Peace.

CIDG. Civilian Irregular Defense Group, Chinese Nung, Vietnamese, or montagnards serving U.S. army special forces mainly near Laotian and Cambodian borders. *See* A-team, mercenaries, Nung.

CINCPAC. Acronym; pronounced sink-pak, commander-in-chief, Pacific, U.S. navy admiral, headquartered in Hawaii.

citadel, the. Hue citadel, built by last Vietnamese dynasty in the nineteenth century; scene of four-week battle in Tet offensive. Note: there is also a less-famous citadel in Quang Tri.

CKC. Czech-made semiautomatic rifle. *See* SKS.

claymore. U.S. military; claymore mine, small explosive, easily transported, hidden by hand, set off by direct contact or trip wire. *See plastique.*

cluster-fuck. GI slang; group of soldiers bunched too close together, making easy target. Usually used as noun, sometimes verb form (e.g., sergeant to troops on patrol, "No cluster-fucking."); term derived from "cluster bomb."

CO, c-o. U.S. military; commanding officer.

Cobra. Two-seat attack helicopter. *See* snakes.

COMUSMACV. Acronym; pronounced co-mus-mac-vee, commander U.S. Military Assistance Command, Vietnam.

Continental Air Services. CIA-financed private airline, like Air America, that ferried troops and supplies, sometimes including drugs, in Laos, elsewhere throughout the war.

CONARC. Acronym; pronounced co-nark, Continental Army Comman (in U.S.).

CONUS. Acronym; pronounced co-nus, U.S. military term, continental United States; also CONARC, co-nark, continental army command.

CONUS boxes. Crates, used to ship military supplies from U.S., often converted into hootches by Vietnamese.

CORDS. Acronym; Civil Operations and Revolutionary Development Support, U.S. "pacification" organization headquartered in Saigon, umbrella for USAID, CIA, USIS activities.

COSVN. Acronym; pronounced koz-vin, Central Office for South Vietnam, Hanoi's elusive headquarters for all operations in South Vietnam.

counterinsurgency. Overall effort to defeat communist revolt, pacify the countryside. A favorite term of American strategic planners, civilian officials, think-tank experts, it connoted range of activities, including economic reform, clandestine terrorism, military and paramilitary training. *See* pacification.

counterpart. American adviser parallel to South Vietnamese civilian official or military officer and vice versa. Each South Vietnamese military unit down to battalion, sometimes company level, had American officer adviser, "counterpart" to unit CO. (American was usually one rank below, never outranked Vietnamese "counterpart.")

cowboy. Motorcycle hoodlum, usually young Vietnamese.

C-rations, C-rats. GI field rations.

cyclo. Slang; three-wheeled bicycle taxi or pedicab in which driver pedalled behind passenger seat; standard conveyance in Vietnamese cities; from French term *cyclo-pousse*.

DA, d-a. District adviser, adviser to district chief, head of U.S. district team under CORDS in each district, governing unit below province level; also (little used in Vietnam), Department of the Army.

dac san. Vietnamese; specialty dishes, special restaurant, especially in Hanoi.

daiui. Vietnamese word for captain, pronounced die-wee by Americans, who often used the term in addressing South Vietnamese army captains. (Americans did not seem ordinarily to grasp Vietnamese words for other military ranks.)

Dai Viet. Great Vietnam party, formed in 1940 as splinter off VNQDD; later split into several factions for nationalist, noncommunist, sometimes anti-communist struggle.

DAP. Acronym; fist-on-fist greeting among black GIs, derived from "Dignity for Afro Peoples."

delta, the. Mekong River delta, Vietnam.

Delta Tango. From radio lingo, defensive target; also Dak To, a firebase north of Kontum, scene of fierce battles in 1967 and 1972.

di, di di. Pronounced dee, Vietnamese word for "go," second *di* often added for emphasis; commonly used by American GIs.

di di mau. Vietnamese; go away fast; widely used GI phrase.

dien cai dau. Vietnamese; crazy in the head; "dinkydow" in GI slang. Example: GI to bargirl, "You dinkydow." Bargirl to GI: "You numbah ten."

dinks. Less pejorative than gooks, also used by GIs for enemy troops, sometimes for ARVN troops, too, but not usually for Vietnamese in general; from dinky, small, inconsequential.

dinkydow. GI slang; crazy, crazy in the head. *See dien cai dau.*

Dixie Station. Location in South China Sea from which carrier-based U.S. Navy planes flew missions over South Vietnam. *See* Yankee Station.

DMZ. Demilitarized Zone, on either side of Ben Hai River along 17th parallel between North and South Vietnam; also DMZ that still divides Korea approximately around 38th parallel.

doc. Slang; enlisted military medical worker equipped to administer first aid to troops in the field. *See* medic.

DOD, d-o-d. Department of Defense, the Pentagon.

dogtag. Aluminum tag giving name, rank, and serial number, worn on chain around the neck of every GI, stuck between front teeth of bodies on battlefield for identification purposes.

doi moi. Renovation, Hanoi's term for overhauling economy with emphasis on free enterprise.

domino theory. View, first expressed by President Eisenhower, that Asian nations would fall like "a row of dominoes" to communism if communist forces took over Vietnam, Cambodia, and Laos.

dong. Vietnamese currency, also called piastres, piasters. South Vietnam used same word as North for basic unit of currency—though currency and exchange rates were different. *See* P.

dove. Anti-war advocate, opponent of U.S. policy, conduct of war in Vietnam; opposite of hawk; adjective, dovish.

Dragonfly. A37 jet aircraft, used by U.S. air force and VNAF.

DRV. Democratic Republic of Vietnam, North Vietnam; renamed Socialist Republic of Vietnam, including all Vietnam, north and south, after reunification in 1975. *See* SRV.

dustoff. Medical evacuation by helicopter. *See* medevac.

Easter Offensive. North Vietnamese offensive of spring 1972.

elephant gun. M79 grenade launcher; also called blooper.

extreme prejudice. By execution, as in "terminated with extreme prejudice" (i.e., executed). *See* terminate with extreme prejudice.

Eye Corps. I Corps, northernmost of four regions into which South Vietnam was divided for military administrative purposes.

FAC. Acronym; forward air controller, usually small propeller-driven plane, O1, L19, O2, OV10, OH6, OH58, seeking signs of enemy activity, spotting targets for artillery, air strikes.

family girl. Proper young lady, living with family, awaiting marriage to proper young man. *See* cherry girl.

farang. Thai; foreigner, term applied to foreigners from western countries, ranging from GIs on r and r to long-term residents; derived from "France," whose people were among first foreign visitors.

Fatherland Front. Above-ground, largely ceremonial organization of different groupings sponsored by Hanoi government.

firebase. Battalion-level base of operations from which artillery was fired while troops patrolled surrounding areas. *See* LZ.

First Air Cav. U.S. army first air cavalry division. *See* the Cav.

fishhook. Portion of Cambodia north of the parrot's beak that appears to form a fishhook on map of border with Vietnam.

five o'clock follies. Briefing given correspondents at 5 P.M. each day by JUSPAO and MACV officials. Briefing was given for first few years of the war at JUSPAO in the Rex Hotel, later switched to South Vietnamese briefing center on Lam Son Square near the corner of Le Loi and Tu Do streets when South Vietnamese officers participated. Term "five o'clock follies" fell into disuse in latter period when briefing usually began at 5:30 P.M.

Flaming Dart. U.S. military; code name, retaliatory air strike.

FO, f-o. Forward observer.

follies, the. *See* Five o'clock follies.

frag. Verb, to frag; GI term meaning to assassinate or attempt to assassinate with fragmentation or hand grenade, in context of killing unpopular officer, not enemy; also, to issue special order for air strike, as in "frag a mission," or to order helicopter, "frag a chopper"; from formal term fragmentation operations order.

Freedom Fighter. F5, jet fighter given Third World and client countries including South Vietnam, Taiwan.

freedom bird. Commercial passenger plane chartered to carry GIs home to United States at end of tour in Vietnam.

free fire zone. Area declared totally open by U.S. forces to bombing, artillery fire. *See* H and I.

friendlies. Friendly forces, troops on same side in conflict; opposite of hostile forces.

friendly fire. Shooting, shelling, bombing by friendly forces—American, South Vietnamese, or other Allied troops. Example: "killed by friendly fire" (i.e., killed accidentally by friendlies).

FTA. Fuck the Army, painted on rocks, etched into barracks walls, scrawled in rest rooms and other likely places by GIs in Vietnam.

FUNK. Acronym; Front Uni National du Kampuchea, United National Front of Kampuchea, pro-Sihanouk front formed after his overthrow in March 1970.

gedunk. U.S. navy slang; small snack or snack stand, usually on navy ship, also on shore.

GI. Government issue, World War II term for American soldier, still commonly used during and after Vietnam war.

Giai Phong. Liberation, referring in particular to Hanoi's final victory of April 30, 1975.

gook. Pejorative term of contempt used by GIs for enemy troops, sometimes applied to Vietnamese in general; probably originated in U.S. military offensives against Filipino forces after defeat of Spanish in 1898; originally from Tagalog, *gugu*, liquid derived from type of tree bark, used as shampoo or herbal medicine; note "goo-goo" used by marines in Nicaragua in 1920s; also possibly from Tagalog slang *ugok,* crazy or stupid; note "gook" used by marines in Haiti after 1915; term "gook" not widely used in World War II in reference to Japanese, more often called "Japs" or "Nips," but widely used during Korean war, hence sometimes said to have derived from *guk*, Korean for nation, as in Hankuk, Korean name for Korea; also may derive partly from English "gook," slimy substance.

gourd. GI slang; head. Example: "Got him in the gourd."

Green Berets. U.S. army special forces. Term rarely used by Green Berets themselves. Included A-team at forward sites, B-team and C-team for administrative purposes. *See* SF.

GRUNC, sometimes **GRUNK.** Acronym; Gouvernement Royal d'Union Nationale du Cambodge, Sihanouk front government set up in Beijing after his overthrow; never governed the country.

grunt. Slang; American infantryman. *See* legs.

gunboat. U.S. navy; armed vessel operated by navy, also manned by army troops in joint army-navy riverine force; included heavily armed Monitors, Swift boats, PBRs.

gunner. Marine warrant officer.

gunny. Marine gunnery sergeant.

gunship. Helicopter, fixed-wing aircraft, or navy vessel. Often applied in Vietnam to Huey helicopter, deployed specifically for firing on enemy rather than carrying cargo and troops; also applied to fixed-wing propeller-driven plane (e.g., C119 or C130) if equipped solely for massive rapid fire on enemy; did not apply to jet aircraft. Less often in Vietnam context, gunship may refer to navy vessel equipped with big guns for firing on targets on shore.

GVN. Government of (South) Vietnam, common term in American bureaucratese for Saigon government; regularly used in briefings, formal statements, press releases.

H and I, H & I. Harassment and interdiction, as in "H and I fire," in which artillery was fired to harass and interdict the enemy on roads, trails, canals, etc. where enemy forces were believed to move men and supplies, also sometimes on free fire zones.

Hanoi Hilton. Prison compound in Hanoi for American POWs.

hard times. Marijuana seeds and stems.

hawk. Pro-war advocate, supporter of U.S. policy, prosecution of war in Vietnam, often in favor of escalation of war to neighboring countries, including Laos, Cambodia, even China, opposite of dove; adjective, hawkish.

hearts and minds, winning. Gaining the loyalty of the people by appealing to both emotions and reason rather than through military force. Term often used in connection with pacification, counterinsurgency efforts.

helo. Helicopter, U.S. navy slang; not applied to army choppers.

Hercules. C130, four-propeller-engine transport plane. The word, however, was not ordinarily used in Vietnam except in press releases, news stories. C130s were called C130s.

HES. Acronym; hamlet evaluation survey, computerized system set up by USAID for regularly evaluating security, status of every hamlet in South Vietnam, placing each in one of several categories, ranging from totally secure to VC-controlled.

HH3. U.S. air force rescue helicopter. *See* jolly green giant.

high country, the. Highlands, mountain country in central Vietnam; *see* Central Highlands.

higher higher. U.S. military slang; headquarters above next highest headquarters in chain of command; also headquarters at or near the top of the chain.

Hoa Hao. Militant anti-communist reform Buddhist movement in the Mekong River delta region of Vietnam.

Hoc Bao. Elite South Vietnamese army strike force. *See* black berets, black panthers.

Ho Chi Minh sandals. Sandals, made from used-tire rubber, worn by North Vietnamese and Viet Cong troops.

Ho Chi Minh Trail. Road and trail network over which the North Vietnamese shipped men and supplies from North to South Vietnam via southern Laos and eastern Cambodia.

Honda, honda. Name of Japanese motorcycle widely used in Vietnam. Also became generic term for any motorcycle, motor scooter.

hooch, hootch. Vietnamese house, hut, sometimes also in reference to small thatched or wooden buildings housing U.S. troops.

hot LZ. Landing zone under hostile fire.

Huey. UH1B helicopter, army workhorse of the war, also produced in C, D, E, F, G, and H models. UH1B and UH1C often used as gunships.

hump, humping. GI slang; carrying a heavy load, as in "humping ammo," patrolling jungle on foot, as in "humping the boonies," etc.

ICC. International Control Commission, set up under Geneva agreement of 1954 that divided Vietnam at the 17th parallel, also monitored Geneva agreement of 1962 on Laos; included Canadian, Indian, and Polish members.

ICCS. International Commission for Control and Supervision, including Polish, Hungarian, Indonesian, and Canadian delegations, set up to supervise the Paris Peace "ceasefire." (Skeptics disparaged the initials as meaning "I Can't Control Shit.")

I Corps, II Corps, III Corps, IV Corps. U.S. military nomenclature for areas into which South Vietnam was divided, from north to south, for purposes of U.S., South Vietnamese administration. I Corps included five northernmost provinces below DMZ; II Corps, the Central Highlands and central coast; III Corps, from fishhook, parrot's beak to coast, including greater Saigon and Long Binh complex; IV Corps, the entire Mekong delta region, including southern coast. Note: I Corps pronounced "eye corps"; others, "two," "three," and "four corps."

MACV in midwar reverted to French nomenclature, dividing South Vietnam into "military regions," MR I, MR II, MR III, MR IV.

IG. i-g. U.S. military; inspector-general.

in-country. In Vietnam, as in "in-country r and r."

incoming. Artillery shell, rocket, or other projectile coming in on your position; often shouted as warning to jump into bunker, as in, "incoming, incoming!" *Cf.* outgoing.

Indian country. U.S. military slang, from army's 19th-century wars against Native Americans, for areas infested with hostile forces, as in, for emphasis, "That's real Indian country out there."

Indochina. This term, for Vietnam, Laos, Cambodia, was widely used when France ruled all three, known as *L'Indochine*; originally acronym for India and China, may be broadened to include Myanmar (Burma), Thailand, and Malaysia.

insurgent, insurgency. Words often used by American bureaucrats, strategic planners and pacification experts for communist rebel, revolt, revolution. *See* counterinsurgency, pacification.

Iron Triangle. Area northwest of Saigon, Ho Bo Woods in the northwest, Ben Cat on northeast, Cu Chi at the southern point. VC stronghold with extensive tunnel complex. *See* War Zones C and D.

IVS. International Voluntary Service, U.S. volunteer group involved in agricultural, economic projects throughout South Vietnam; withdrew in protest against U.S. policy in 1967.

JCRC. Joint Casualty Resolution Center, U.S. military team in charge of analyzing reports on MIAs and POWs in Vietnam.

JMC. Four-party Joint Military Commission formed under the Paris Peace, with representatives from all warring parties, including North Vietnam, PRG, South Vietnam, and the United States.

jolly green giant. HH3, U.S. air force rescue helicopter.

Jonesed, Jonesing. Slang; forms of verb denoting excruciatingly painful withdrawal from hard drugs. Noun: the Jones, Joneses.

JPRC. Joint Personnel Recovery Center, predecessor to JCRC, under MACVSOG, set up to locate POWs, MIAs during war.

juicer. Slang; alcoholic, one who preferred alcohol to drugs.

JUSMAAG. Acronym; pronounced jus-mag, Joint U.S. Military Assistance and Advisory Group, U.S. military team in countries receiving U.S. military aid, including Thailand and South Vietnam before MACV. *See* MAAG.

JUSPAO. Acronym; pronounced jus-pao, Joint U.S. Public Affairs

Office, U.S. government media organization, both civilian and military, headquartered during war in Rex Hotel, Saigon.

KIA, k-i-a. Killed in action.

kill ratio. The ratio of enemy deaths to those of Americans or Americans and South Vietnamese—another index often used by American commanders to show success in the war. *See* body count.

KKK. Khmer Kampuchea Krom, Cambodians from Mekong River delta region of Vietnam, trained by U.S. army special forces.

Khmer Rouge. Red Khmers, Cambodian Reds or communists, responsible for deaths of hundred of thousands of Khmer or Cambodians in 1970s, still engaged in revolution, smuggling.

Lam Son. Mountain stronghold of Vietnamese national hero Le Loi, who drove out the Chinese in the 15th century. Name of small square with large statue of South Vietnamese soldier in downtown Saigon in front of opera house; also name for series of South Vietnamese military operations, notably Lamson 719 into Laos in 1971.

land of the big PX. Sardonic reference to the United States.

land reform, land-to-the-tiller. Program pushed by American bureaucrats for dividing vast holdings of rich landlords among those who actually farmed them.

Lao Dong. Workers' Party, ruling party of the Democratic Republic of Vietnam, North Vietnam, called Socialist Republic of Vietnam since 1975.

LBJ. Long Binh Jail, not Lyndon Baines Johnson. LBJ was U.S. military stockade at Long Binh, large U.S. base north of Saigon.

legs. Infantrymen, foot soldiers, grunts.

Liberation. *See Giai Phong.*

Lien So. Vietnamese; Soviet Union. Note: often used after the war as Soviet bureaucrats appeared; seldom heard during the war.

lifer. GI slang; career military person.

light colonel. Military slang; lieutenant colonel.

little people, the. Condescending GI term for South Vietnamese troops fighting with Americans; connoted big-brother attitude, not used in reference to hostile forces. Cf. "little brown brothers," from entry of American forces into Philippines.

LLDB. Luc Luong Dac Biet. South Vietnamese special forces. (Initials sometimes derisively said by Americans to stand for "lousy little dirty bug-out," "look long, duck back.")

LOH. Acronym; pronounced loach (rhymes with roach), light observation helicopter. *See* OH6, OH58.

LT, l-t. U.S. military slang; lieutenant, without the name, as in "the LT says . . ."

LURP. Acronym; U.S. army; long-range reconnaissance patrol.

LZ. Landing zone, sometimes used for firebase, battalion-level outpost from which helicopters landed and took off, but LZ had a broader meaning: anywhere a chopper landed was also an LZ.

MAAG. Military Assistance and Advisory Group.

MACCORDS. Military Assitance Command, Civil Operations and Revolutionary Development Support. *See* CORDS, MACV.

MACV. Acronym; pronounced mac-vee, Military Assistance Command Vietnam, headquarters of all U.S. military forces in Vietnam, near Tan Son Nhut air base.

MACVSOG. Acronym; pronounced mac-vee-sog, Military Assistance Command Studies and Observations Group, originally MACV Special Operations Group, in charge of top secret operations in North Vietnam, Laos, Cambodia. *See* SOG, CCN, CCC, CCS.

mamasan. Woman in charge of girls in bar, massage place, brothel. This term, from Japanese English, used by GIs throughout Asia.

medevac. Medical evacuation, usually by helicopter. *See* dustoff.

medic. Enlisted medical aid worker, technician, both in field and in field hospitals, etc. *See* doc.

mercenaries. Pejorative word routinely used by Western journalists, etc., for Chinese Nung, Vietnamese, montagnards, etc., hired by U.S. special forces as local troops. *See* A-team, CIDG, Nung.

merks, the. U.S. military slang; the mercenaries.

M41, M48. American tanks. Americans used the M48, ARVN mainly the M41.

MIA, m-i-a. Missing in action.

Monitor. Heavily armed navy boat named for Civil War ironclad the *Monitor*, with turret in front, low in water, in brown-water navy.

montagnards. French word, pronounced mon-tan-yards by Americans, for mountain tribal people (e.g., Bru, Meo, Yao, Hmong). *See* yards.

MOS, m-o-s. Military occupational specialty (e.g., 11B, infantry).

MP. U.S. Military police.

MPC. Military payment certificate, dollar-denominated currency printed by U.S. military for use at military facilities, including post exchanges and base exchanges, officers' clubs, etc.

MR I, MR II, MR III, MR IV. The "military regions" into which South Vietnam was divided, from northern to southern provinces. *See* I Corps, II Corps, III Corps, IV Corps.

M79. Grenade launcher, U.S. *See* elephant gun, blooper, bloop-gun.

M16. American-made rifle, basic infantry weapon of American, South Vietnamese forces.

M60. Machine gun, U.S.

mule. Small motorized springless vehicle used for carrying troops, ammunition short distances; also one who loaded, unloaded supplies for CIA-financed airlines, mainly in Laos.

'Nam. Vietnam. Note: " 'Nam," often used in the States, in movies, articles, etc., was much less used by Americans in Vietnam, Asia.

napalm. Gasoline jelly compound, dropped in canisters from airplanes, exploding in fireball, incinerating all it touched.

Neo Lao Hak Sat. Lao Patriotic Front, communist side in Laos. *See* PL, Pathet Lao.

NCO. U.S. military; noncommissioned officer, sergeant or above. *See* noncom.

NDP. Night defensive position.

never happen, never happened, nevah hoppen. Meaning impossible, no way. Example: GI to bargirl: you do (whatever); bargirl to GI, "nevah hoppen." Also used in numerous other contexts. (Note: term "no way" did not come into widespread use until after the war.)

nha bao. Vietnamese; journalist, reporter, newsman.

night logger position. Circle or oval formed by armored vehicles for defensive purposes at night. *Cf.*, "circling the wagons."

NLF. National Liberation Front, the Viet Cong, southern Vietnamese communist organization.

no *biet*. Mispronounced "no bich" in GI slang, meaning "do not understand." (*Biet* or *bik* rarely used by GIs for "understand.")

no money no honey. Term used by bargirls, especially in Saigon and such GI r and r centers as Bangkok and Manila, to customers reluctant to buy drinks, pay hostess fees, etc.

noncom. Noncommissioned officer, enlisted grades E5 and above, below commissioned officer, warrant officer. *See* NCO.

numbah one. GI/Vietnamese slang; the best.

numbah ten. GI/Vietnamese slang; the worst.

nuoc mam. Fermented fish sauce or dip, staple of Vietnamese diet.

Nung. Chinese group in highlands, delta, whose members were hired by U.S. army special forces. *See* mercenaries.

NVA. North Vietnamese Army, initials used by American bureaucrats, diplomats, CIA officials, military officers, briefers. *See* PAVN.

NVN. U.S. bureaucratese term, North Vietnam. *See* DRV.

OCS, o-c-s. U.S. military; officer candidates' school.

ODP. Orderly Departure Program, U.S. program under which Vietnamese who had worked for Americans, had relatives in the United States, had suffered through reeducation camps for service in South Vietnamese forces, could leave legally to live in the United States.

OH6, OH58. Observation helicopters. *See* LOH.

old man, the. GI slang for CO, as in "the old man says . . . "

outgoing. Artillery shell, rocket, or other projectile fired from your position. Example, GI to civilian visitor startled by sound of nearby explosion: "Relax, it's outgoing." *Cf.* incoming.

outstanding. Self-congratulatory word often used by American military officers to describe their successes in the field, high quality of their troops, their Vietnamese counterparts, etc. Also, slang; great, wonderful; added emphasis, out-*fucking*-standing.

P, piastres, piasters (not pence, pennies, or pesos). French term for *dong*, Vietnamese unit of currency. Americans called them "P," in singular, as in negotiation with taxi driver, "I give you 50 p." *See dong*.

pacification, pacification program. American effort aimed at "pacifying the countryside" (i.e., stopping insurgency). Included CIA, para-military efforts, not main-force military activities.

papasan. GI slang; elderly Vietnamese man, often cyclo driver or gateguard. (Note: not exactly the male counterpart of "mamasan," woman in charge of bargirls, bar, etc.)

Paris Peace. The accords signed by Henry Kissinger and Le Duc Tho in Paris on January 27, 1973.

parrot's beak. Portion of Cambodia that juts into Vietnam in the form of a parrot's beak south of route one frontier crossing.

PAVN. Acronym; pronounced pa-vin, People's Army of Vietnam, translation of formal name for army of DRV. *See* NVA.

PBR. Patrol boat river, U.S. navy patrol boats used in riverine force, brown-water navy, made of fiberglass, armed with machine guns.

PDJ. Plaine des Jarres, in Laos.

PF. Popular Forces (South Vietnamese), local forces operating in their own villages, under provincial or district chiefs. *See* Ruff Puff.

Phantom. F4, basic American fighter-bomber of Vietnam war period.

PHILCAG. Philippine Civic Action Group, Philippine army civil affairs unit, engaged in engineering, medical projects in Tay Ninh; Philippines' lone contribution to allied effort.

Phoenix program. CIA-run program of assassination of undesirables, usually NLF agents. Named for the mythological bird that rises from its own ashes; operated under umbrella of CORDS, set up by William Colby, top CIA official and CORDS chief.

pig man, hog man. Army slang; soldier in squad operating M60 machine gun.

pink team. U.S. army slang; team including LOH and Cobra helicopters, sometimes a C and C ship, deployed for drawing fire, then attacking the source of the fire.

PL. *Pathet Lao*, communist forces in Laos, literally "Land of the Lao"; formal name *Neo Lao Hak Sat*, Lao Patriotic Front.

PLAF. People's Liberation Armed Forces, translation of formal name for VC forces. *See* VC.

plastique. An explosive molded in different shapes, as in C4 in claymore mine, from the French, who developed the technology.

pot. Marijuana.

POW, p-o-w. Prisoner of war.

PRG. Provisional Revolutionary Government, front government of the Viet Cong's National Liberation Front.

PRU. Provincial reconnaissance unit, commando unit under Phoenix program charged with assassinations, kidnapping, and terrorism.

PSA. Province senior adviser, top U.S. official in charge of "province team" of American advisers, under CORDS, in each South Vietnamese province. PSA was adviser to Vietnamese province chief.

PSDF. People's Self-Defense Force, under local GVN control.

PUFF. Acronym; People's Union to Fight Fascism, radical organization active among black GIs in Vietnam.

Puff the Magic Dragon. C47, equivalent of twin-propeller-engine DC3 Dakota, equipped as gunship. *See* Spooky.

punji stick. Bamboo spike, smeared with poison, usually excrement, hidden where patrolling GI might step, impaling foot.

puppet. As in "puppet army" and "puppet government," terms used in Hanoi lexicon for U.S.-backed South Vietnamese forces, regime. Also found frequently in Chinese, North Korean propaganda.

PX. Army; post exchange, supermarket for American military and civilians with MACV passes, including accredited journalists.

RA, r-a. U.S. military; regular army.

r and r, r & r. Rest and recreation, rest and relaxation. Every GI got one "r and r" in Pacific region outside Vietnam, ranging from Australia to Taiwan, during one-year Vietnam tour. There was also "in-country r and r" (e.g., at China Beach near Danang).

RD. Revolutionary Development Program, U.S. scheme for "revolutionizing" Vietnamese rural society through land reform, other pacification efforts; also know as "rural development."

recon by fire. Fire into the bush to flush out enemy soldiers.

redball. Main highway, open to military traffic.

red berets. Members of South Vietnamese army airborne division.

REMF. Acronym; pronounced remf, rear-echelon mother fucker, everyday GI term for those serving in rear areas.

reunification. Uniting of North and South Vietnam into one country. *See Giai Phong*, liberation.

RF. Regional forces (South Vietnamese), organized into companies under control of regional commander. *See Ruff Puff*.

RIF. Acronym; U.S. military; pronounced rif, reconnaissance in force; also, reduction in force, especially, cut-back in number of officers.

riverine force. Joint U.S. army-navy force formed to patrol upper Mekong River delta. *See* gunboat, Monitor, PBR.

RLG. Royal Lao Government.

rocket belt. Rings around major cities, especially Saigon, Danang, from which North Vietnamese, VC fired rockets into the city.

rocket city. Danang, often hit by rockets.

Rome plow. Large U.S. military vehicle for plowing up large strips of earth. Also used as verb, as in, "rome-plowed."

ROTC. Acronym; pronounced rot-see, or initials, R-O-T-C, U.S. military, reserve officers' training corps, at colleges in U.S.

round-eye. Western woman, non-Asian woman, usually applied to white woman. Also, round-eye alert, spreading of word that young Western woman has entered bar, club, etc.

RPG. Chinese, Eastern bloc rocket-propelled grenade. *See* B40, B41.

rubberlegs. GI slang; radio operator, usually on company level, responsible for carrying and operating field radio.

rubber road, the. Route 13 north of Saigon as it passed through rubber plantations up to the Cambodian border.

Ruff Puff. Acronym; slang, U.S. military; civilian, for RF/PF, Regional Forces and Popular Forces.

RVN. Republic of Vietnam, South Vietnam. *See* SVN.

RVNAF. Acronym; pronounced ar-ve-naf, for Republic of (South) Vietnam armed forces.

Saigon cowboy. Vietnamese hoodlum, often draft dodger, running wild on streets of Saigon. *See* cowboy.

Saigon tea. Nonalcoholic drink that bargirls drank when customers were buying the drinks for them at inflated prices. *See* tea.

Saigon warrior. U.S. soldier or civilian official who fought the war from a desk or other comfortable post in Saigon.

SAM missiles. Surface-to-air missiles. *See* SA2, SA3, SA6.

same-same. GI slang for "same," often used in talk with Vietnamese.

SA7. Soviet-made heat-seeking hand-held missile. *See* Strela.

SA2, SA3, SA6. Soviet-made SAM missiles deployed in anti-aircraft defense of North Vietnam, especially in and around Hanoi.

Screaming Eagles. U.S. army 101st airborne division.

SEAL. Acronym; U.S. navy; sea, air, land; frogman, specialist in underwater demolition, other special missions. *See* UDT.

search and destroy. U.S. military, seek out enemy troops, supplies, annihilate them; adjective, as in "search-and-destroy mission."

SEATO. Southeast Asian Treaty Organization, ineffective bloc of nations headquartered in Bangkok, modeled after NATO, under which the United States sought to win Allied support for the war effort.

SF. Special forces. Green Berets referred to themselves as SF, not Green Berets. *See* Green Berets.

Shadow. C130 equipped with high-powered spotlights, 105mm howitzer, other weapons for firing into target caught in beam.

shithook. GI slang; Chinook helicopter, heavy-duty carrier of troops and supplies; much larger, stronger than a Huey, UH1B.

short. GI slang; as in "getting short," "I'm short," nearing the end of tour in Vietnam, not in reference to physical height, size.

short round. An artillery or mortar round that fell far short of target, sometimes killing friendly forces or civilians.

skag. Heroin.

SKS. Soviet-made semiautomatic rifle, sometimes called Kilo Sierra in U.S. military radio lingo. Also CKC, Czech version.

Skyraider. Propeller-driven A1 plane, U.S. air force, VNAF.

slick. Troop-carrying Huey helicopter.

slopes. GI slang; pejorative, used less frequently than gooks, for enemy troops, often for Vietnamese, Asians, in general. Racist term related to "slant eyes," Western view of Asian facial appearance.

smack. Heroin.

snakes. Cobra attack helicopters.

SOG. Acronym; Studies and Observations Group, originally Special

Operations Group, in charge of top secret operations in North Vietnam, Laos, Cambodia. *See* MACVSOG, CCN, CCC, CCS.

Soul Alley. Street of bars near Tan Son Nhut favored by black GIs.

Spec 5. Specialist fifth class, U.S. army, equivalent of sergeant, E5 on enlisted pay, rank scale.

Spec 4. Specialist fourth class, U.S. army, equivalent of corporal, E4 on enlisted pay, rank scale.

Spectre. C130 gunship equipped with range of high-powered weapons.

spook. Slang; undercover intelligence operative, usually CIA.

Spooky. C47 gunship. *See* Puff the Magic Dragon.

SRV. Socialist Republic of Vietnam. *See* DRV.

Starlifter. C141, U.S. air force jet transport plane.

station chief. Head of CIA country team, usually based at American embassy as "special assistant" to the ambassador.

steam and cream. Steambath and massage, massage place, brothel.

Stinger. Twin-propeller-engine C119 aircraft with weapons for pouring intense rapid fire over wide area. Also U.S. hand-held anti-aircraft missile, not used in Vietnam.

stockade. Military jail, prison for GIs, not POWS. *See* LBJ.

strategic hamlets. Heavily fortified hamlets established as strong points against Viet Minh guerrillas under the strategic hamlet program of South Vietnam President Ngo Dinh Diem. Program was abandoned after Diem's assassination in 1963.

Street Without Joy. Road near Route One between Hue and Quang Tri, immortalized in book of same name by Bernard Fall.

Strela. SA7, Soviet-made hand-held, heat-seeking missile.

SVN. U.S. bureaucratese; South Vietnam. *See* RVN.

Sweep. U.S. military; sweep or scour area in pursuit of enemy, also noun, as in "conducting a sweep," "infantry sweep."

Swift boat. Fast, armed navy boat used as gunboat, troop carrier.

tac air, tacair. Tactical aircraft, fighter planes.

TAOR, t-a-o-r. U.S. army; tactical area of responsibility.

TDY, t-d-y. Temporary duty.

tea. Soft drink, sometimes actually tea, purchased for bargirl at inflated price. Commonly used term, as in, bargirl to GI, "You buy me tea." *See* Saigon tea.

terminate with extreme prejudice. Kill, execute, carry out death sentence, often in secret. Term used by SF, CIA operatives.

Tet. Vietnamese lunar New Year, end of January, early February, sometimes referring to the communists' 1968 Tet offensive.

there it is. Term frequently used by GIs in daily conversation, expression of resignation, futility, cynicism, anger. Example: First GI: "This war sucks." Second GI: "There it is."

third force. Neutral noncommunist South Vietnamese political grouping, loyal to neither the United States nor the communist side. General Duong Van "Big" Minh, South Vietnam's final leader, advocated this concept, which never went beyond talking stage.

Three MAF, III MAF. Acronym; third marine amphibious force, including all U.S. marines in Vietnam; often used to refer to "Three MAF" headquarters in Danang. (MAF rarely used separately.)

tiger cages. Notorious prison built by French on Cón Són island off the southern coast where political prisoners were held in cells resembling tiger cages.

Tiger division. One of two South Korean divisions in South Vietnam, both reputed for strength, cruelty in battle. *See* White Horse division.

titi. Pronounced "tee-tee," GI slang; from Vietnamese pronunciation of French *petit,* meaning "little."

TO&E. U.S. military; table of organization and equipment, every unit has one.

top. GI slang; first sergeant, highest-ranking enlisted man in U.S. Army company-level unit. Often used as informal term of address, as in "Mornin', top."

tracks. Military vehicles that run on tracks or treads, more often in reference to armored personnel carriers than tanks.

triple A. U.S. military slang; anti-aircraft artillery. *See* AAA.

T34, T54. Soviet tanks used by North Vietnamese.

tunnel rats. GIs assigned, on basis of small size, great strength, and daring, to enter and search enemy tunnel complexes.

UDT. Underwater demolition team, often if not usually including navy frogmen. *See* SEAL.

up-country. Far from the capital, up north; geographical term often used by foreigners in Thailand, not Vietnam.

USAID. Acronym; pronounced u-sayed, U.S. Agency for International Development.

USARV. Acronym; pronounced u-sar-vee, U.S. Army Vietnam.

USG. U.S. bureaucratese;U.S. government.

USIS. Acronym; pronounced u-sis, U.S. Information Service.

USOM. Acronym; u-som, U.S. Operations Mission, cover organization for CIA activities in Thailand.

VA. Veterans Administration.

VC. Viet Cong, Vietnamese Communists, southern communist forces, technically under NLF, PRG.

VFW. Veterans of Foreign Wars.

Viet Minh. Vietnam Alliance, communist front formed by Ho Chi Minh in 1930, center of anti-French struggle, disbanded after government of Democratic Republic of Vietnam installed in Hanoi in 1954.

Vietnamization program. Plan for transferring responsibility, authority, to South Vietnamese after signing of Paris Peace.

Vietnamize. U.S. bureaucratic, sometimes official, term to transfer responsibility, authority, especially for military security, to South Vietnamese government after Paris Peace.

ville, the. GI slang; village, hamlet, cluster of houses.

VNAF. Acronym; pronounced vee-naf, for (South) Vietnamese air force.

VNQDD. Vietnam Quoc Dan Dang, Vietnam People's National Party, nationalist, anti-communist, anti-French party formed in Hanoi in 1926, defeated by Viet Minh in 1940s, '50s.

VPL. Visible panty line, often noticeable and noted through trousers of silken *ao dai* worn by Vietnamese women.

V sign. Formed by index and middle fingers, for peace, not victory.

VVAW, v-v-a-w. Vietnam Veterans Against the War.

war of attrition. War based on cutting down, wiping out enemy's manpower, supplies, forcing settlement, rather than achieving clear-cut victory, surrender, territorial conquest. Term often used to explain U.S. policy. *See* body count, kill ratio.

War Zones C and D. Historic NLF nomenclature for jungle areas north, northwest of Saigon, guerrilla strongholds from the French colonial era. Terms sometimes used by Americans. *See* Iron Triangle.

White Horse division. One of two South Korean divisions in South Vietnam, both reputed for strength, cruelty in battle. See Tiger division.

white mice. Local Saigon police, named for their white shirts, white gloves, and grey trousers—and weakness in upholding law and order.

WIA, w-i-a. Wounded in action.

wider war. Conflict extending beyond Vietnam to neighboring Cambodia and Laos, possibly Thailand. President Nixon used this term in May 1970, saying U.S. did not seek "a wider war" while ordering American troops into Cambodia from Vietnam.

winning hearts and minds. *See* hearts and minds, winning.

world, the. GI slang for home or the United States, as in "back in the world" or "world food"—food from home.

Yankee Station. Location in South China Sea from which carrier-based U.S. Navy planes flew missions over North Vietnam. *See* Dixie Station.

yards. Slang for mountain tribal people. *See* montagnards.

Z, the. GI term for DMZ, which divided Vietnam.

Index

The author atop Marble Mountain, south of Danang, 1988. Photo by Vu Binh.

Donald Kirk arrived in Vietnam soon after the Big Red One, the first infantry division, in 1965 and covered the war through the release of the last captured pilots in Hanoi nearly eight years later. He reported for American newspapers and magazines, including *The Washington Star* and the *Chicago Tribune*, and received George Polk, Overseas Press Club, and Edward Scott Beck awards for his articles for the *Tribune*. Author of two books on the war, *Tell It to the Dead* and *Wider War*, he was Edward R. Murrow fellow at the Council of Foreign Relations in 1974–75, writing and joining seminars there and at Princeton. He has also reported on contretemps from the 1973 Mideast War to the Gulf War, from Baghdad during the American bombing, to the U.S.-Japan trade wars, to the Korean nuclear crisis, from Seoul and Pyongyang, and is the author of *Korean Dynasty: Hyundai and Chung Ju Yung*. He lives in Washington, D.C.

DATE DUE

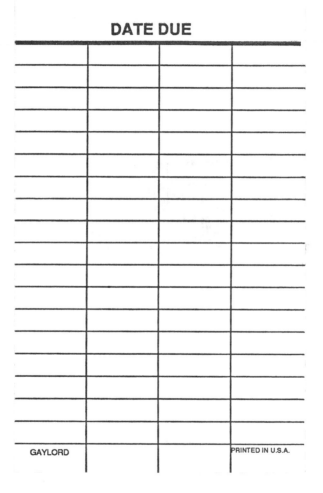